Scholastic Success With

KINDERGARTEN WORKBOOK

SCHOLASTIC
Teaching Resources

NEW YORK • TORONTO • LONDON • AUCKLAND • SYDNEY
MEXICO CITY • NEW DELHI • HONG KONG • BUENOS AIRES

Cover design by Anna Christian
Interior illustrations by Carol Tiernon, Kathy Marlin, Janet Armbrust, Sherry Neidigh, and Rusty Fletcher
Interior design by Quack & Company

ISBN 0-439-69528-7

9 10 11 12 13 08 16 15 14 13 12

Table of Contents

THE ALPHABET

NUMBERS AND COUNTING

HANDWRITING

BASIC CONCEPTS

PHONICS

ITTY-BITTY WORD BOOKS

"Nothing succeeds like success."

Alexandre Dumas the Elder, 1854

Dear Parent,

Congratulations on choosing this excellent educational resource for your child. Scholastic has long been a leader in educational publishing—creating quality educational materials for use in school and at home for nearly a century.

As a partner in your child's academic success, you'll want to get the most out of the learning experience offered in this book. To help your child learn at home, try following these helpful hints:

- Provide a comfortable place to work.
- Have frequent work sessions, but keep them short.
- Praise your child's successes and encourage his or her efforts. Offer positive help when your child makes a mistake.
- Display your child's work and share his or her progress with family and friends.

In this workbook you'll find hundreds of practice pages that keep kids challenged and excited as they strengthen their skills across the classroom curriculum.

The workbook is divided into six sections: The Alphabet; Numbers and Counting; Handwriting; Basic Concepts; Phonics; and Itty-Bitty Word Books. You and your child should feel free to move through the pages in any way you wish. The table of contents lists the activities and the skills practiced.

Take the lead and help your child succeed with the *Scholastic Success With Kindergarten* workbook!

The activities in this workbook reinforce age-appropriate skills and will help your child meet the following standards established as goals by leading educators.

Mathematics

- Understands that numerals are symbols used to represent quantities or attributes of real-world objects
- Counts whole numbers
- Understands symbolic, concrete, and pictorial representations of numbers
- Understands basic whole number relationships
- Understands basic properties of and similarities and differences between simple geometric shapes
- Understands the common language of spatial sense
- Understands that geometric shapes are useful for representing and describing real-world situations
- Extends simple patterns

Writing

- Uses conventions of print in writing (e.g., forms letters in print, uses upper- and lowercase letters of the alphabet, writes from left-to-right and top-to-bottom)

Reading

- Understands that print conveys meaning
- Uses basic elements of phonetic analysis (e.g., common letter/sound relationships, beginning and ending consonants, vowel sounds, blends, word patterns) to decode unknown words
- Uses a picture dictionary to determine word meaning
- Understands level-appropriate sight words and vocabulary
- Uses reading skills and strategies to understand a variety of informational texts

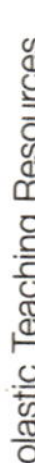

Scholastic Success With

THE ALPHABET

Name ______________________________

A Work of Art

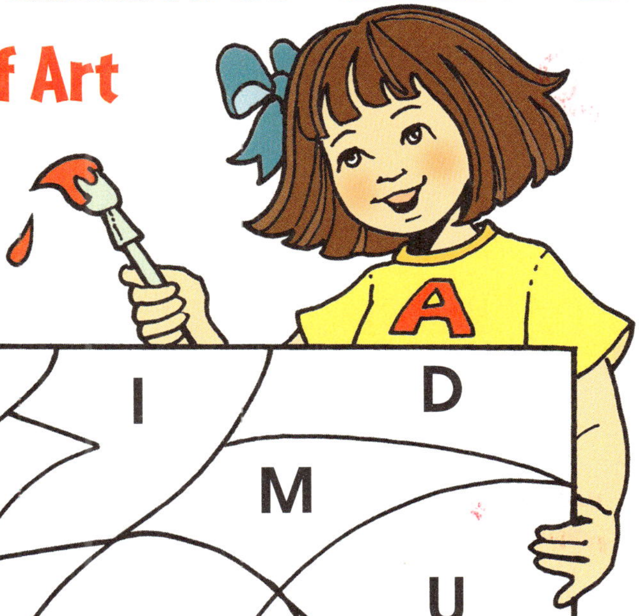

Color each space with the letter **A** red.

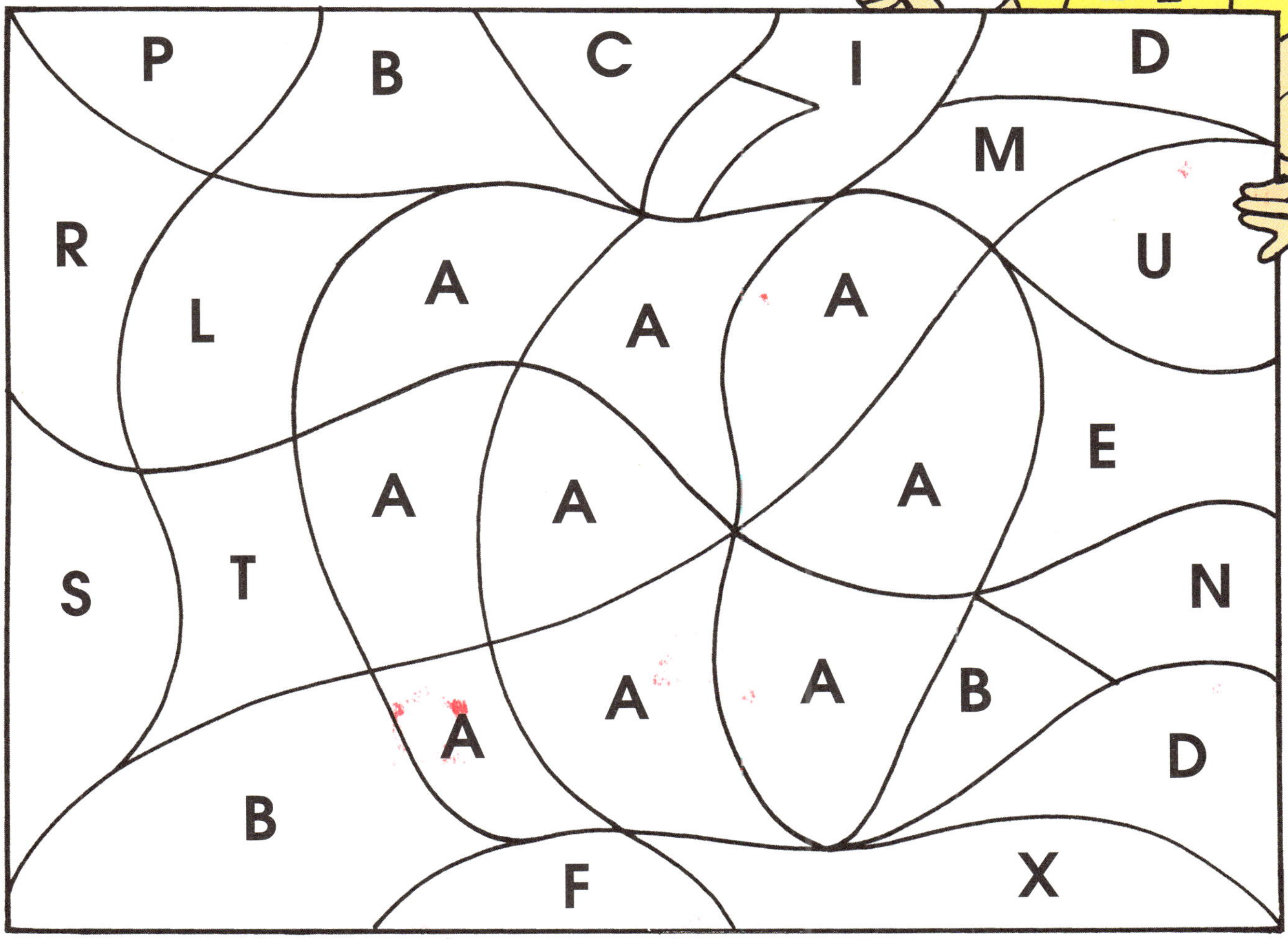

P B C I D
M
R U
L A A A
E
A A A
S T N
A A A B
D
B
F X

Trace and write.

Find an A in the newspaper.

Name ______________________________

Trace the A and a's.

Alligator paints an apple.

Now write the A and a's.

_lligator paints _n _pple.

Add a's and then read the words.

_pple	_lligator	_rm	Now draw and write your own **Aa** word.

Name ______________________________

Big Birthday Bash!

Find and circle each letter **B**.

A B C A B C

B B P B B P

B D B D B

B D P A

B D B P B B

Trace and write.

Bb

On another sheet of paper, draw a picture of your favorite birthday present.

Name ______________________

Trace the B's and b's.

Bubble Bear blows bubbles.

Now write the B's and b's.

_ubble _ear _lows _ubbles.

Add b's and then read the words.

_ed	_ag	_ird	Now draw and write your own **Bb** word.

Name ______________________________________ 

The King's Castle

Follow the letter **C**. Color the path that leads to the castle.

Start

Trace and write.

C c

Cat begins with the letter C. On another sheet of paper, draw a cat.

Name ____________________

- Trace the C and c's.

Cleo carries cocoa.

- Now write the C and c's.

_leo _arries _ocoa.

- Add c's and then read the words.

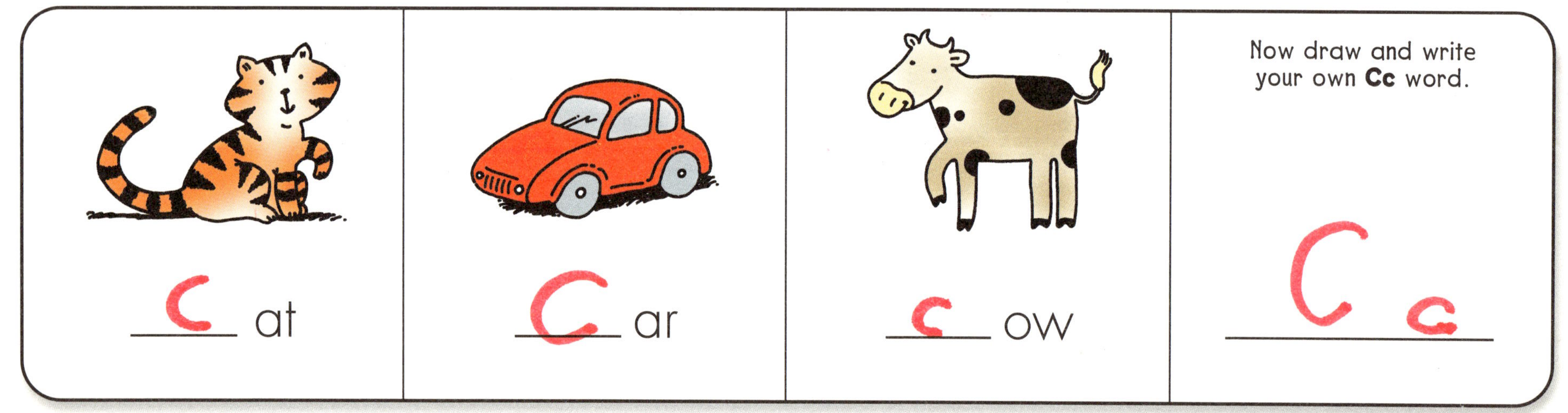

___ at

___ ar

___ ow

Now draw and write your own **Cc** word.

Name ______________________________

Dandy Duck

Color each duck track with the letter **D** orange.

D D D C F
A B D D
B P D B
D D D
D B P D R D
D O
G
D B B
P D D D

Trace and write.

D d

On another sheet of paper, draw three different ducks.

Name ______________________________

Trace the D's and d.

Detective Dog likes doughnuts.

Now write the D's and d.

__etective __og likes __oughnuts.

Add d's and then read the words.

Name ______________________________ 

Eggs Everywhere!

Find and color each egg with the letter **E**.

E E C E F A E F E E

Trace and write.

E e

On another sheet of paper, draw and color two decorated eggs.

Name ______________________

Trace the E's.

Elvin the Elephant makes an e.

Now write the E's and e.

___lvin the ___lephant makes an ___.

Add e's and then read the words.

___ lbow	___ ye	___ gg	Now draw and write your own **Ee** word. ______

Name ____ 

In Full Bloom

Color each space with the letter **F** yellow.
Color all the other spaces blue.

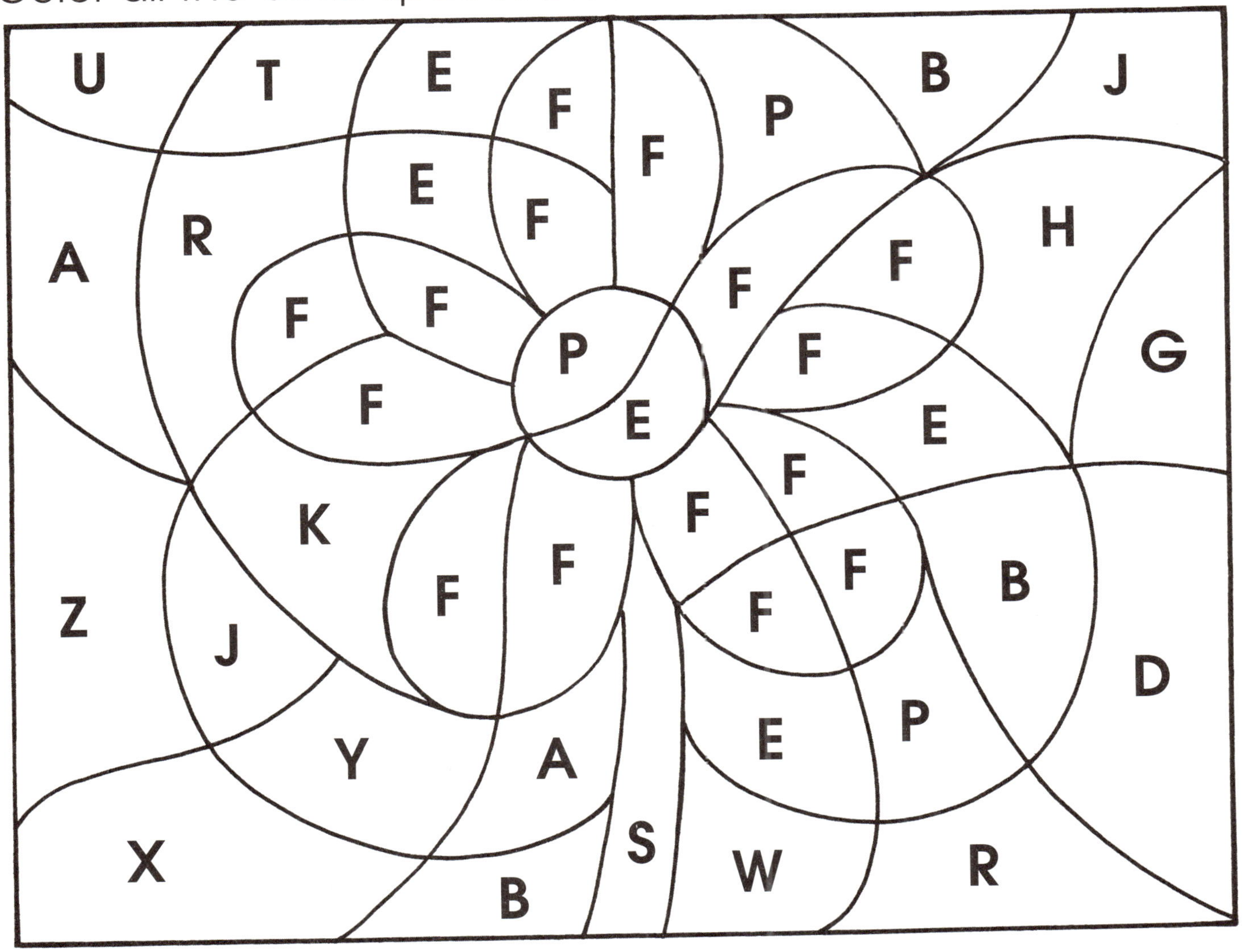

U T E F F P B J
A R E F F H
F F F F F G
P F E E
F F K F F B
F F Z J D
P E Y A
S X R W B

Trace and write.

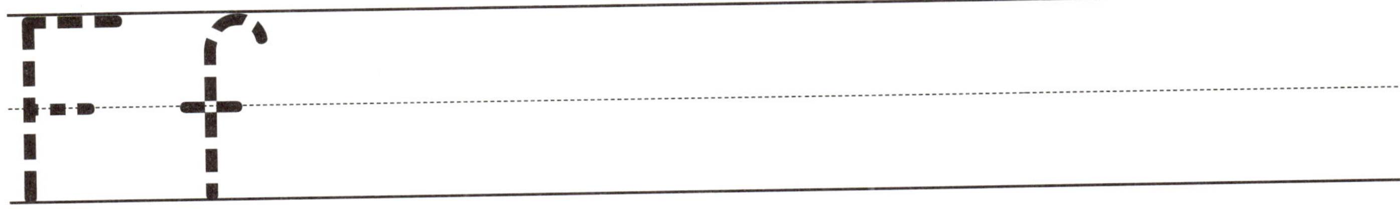

Flower begins with the letter F. On another sheet of paper, draw a red flower.

Name ______________________

Trace the F's and f.

Fifi the Ferret plays the flute.

Now write the F's and f.

__ifi the __erret plays the __lute.

Add f's and then read the words.

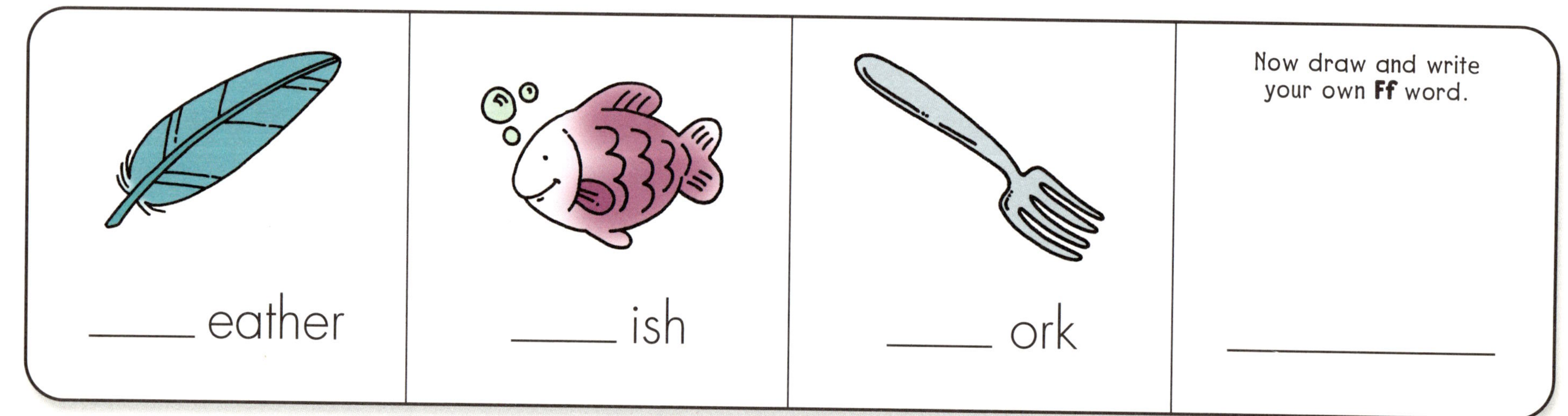

____ eather	____ ish	____ ork	Now draw and write your own **Ff** word. ______

Name ____________________

A Grape-Eating Gorilla

Follow the letter **G**. Color the path that leads to the grapes.

G G G G G G G G F G G G G G G B G G G G G B G G G G G G G G O G G D O G G G G G G G G G G

Start

Trace and write.

Name ______________________

Trace the G and g's.

Gorilla gobbles gooseberries.

Now write the G and g's.

___orilla ___obbles ___ooseberries.

Add g's and then read the words.

____ame	____uitar	____ate	Now draw and write your own **Gg** word. ____________

Hippo's Hats

Color each hat with the letter **H**.

H H R I H N A H H B H

Trace and write.

H h

On another sheet of paper, draw a picture of a word that rhymes with hat.

Name ______________________

Trace the H and h.

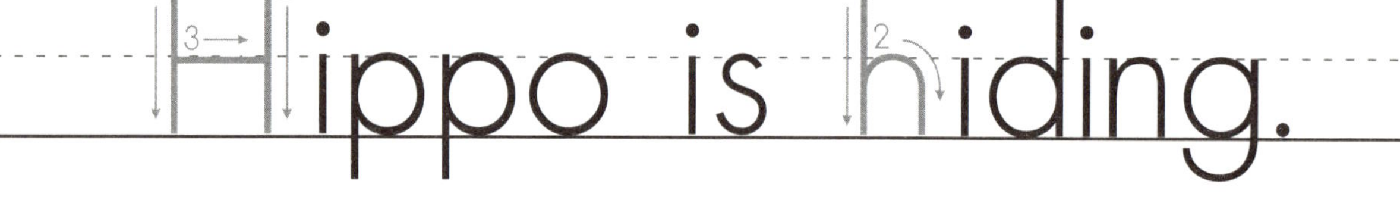

Now write the H and h.

___ippo is ___iding.

Add h's and then read the words.

Name ______________________________ 

Icky Insects

Color each insect with the letter **I**.

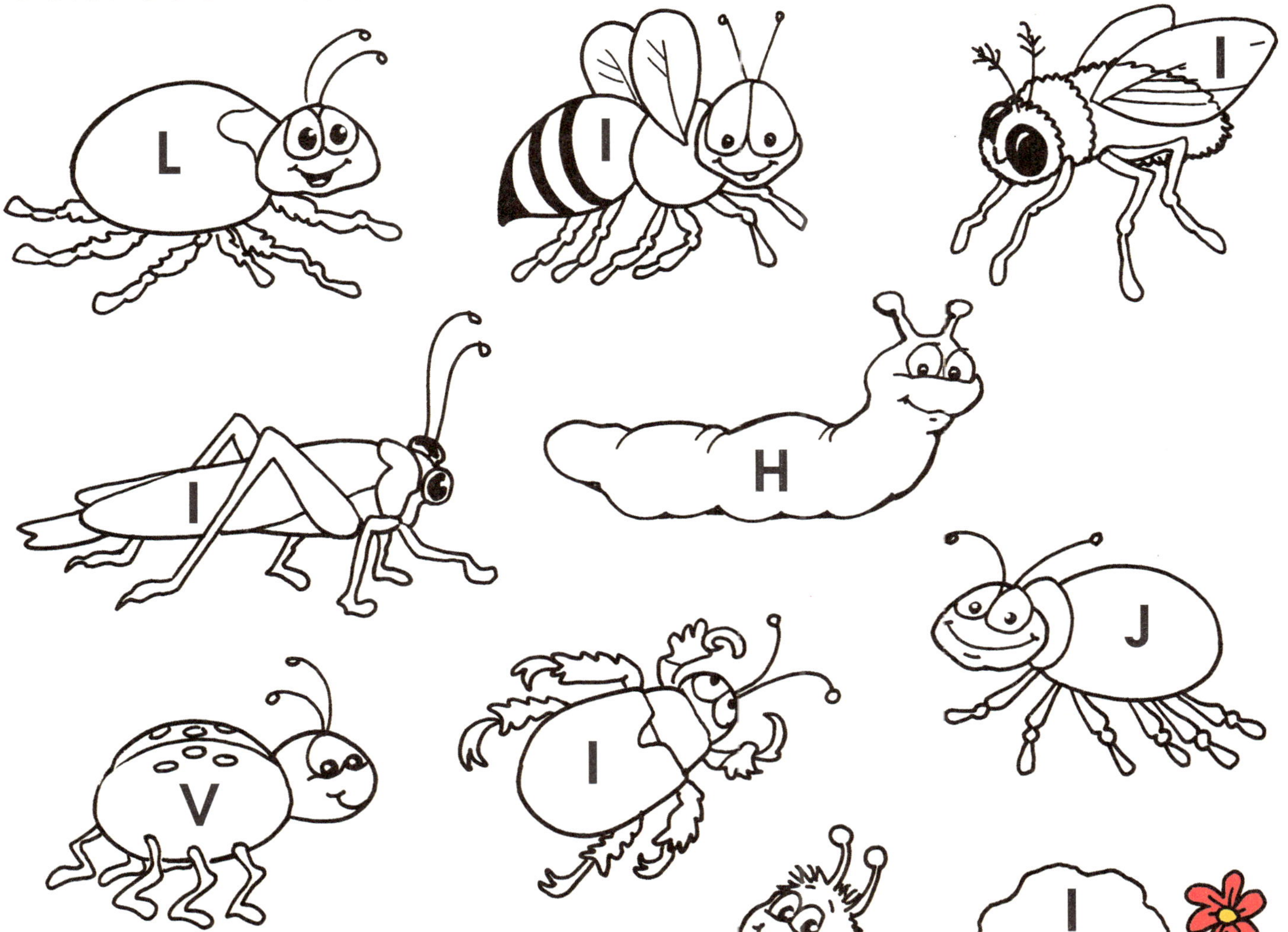

L I I

I H

J

V I

I

Trace and write.

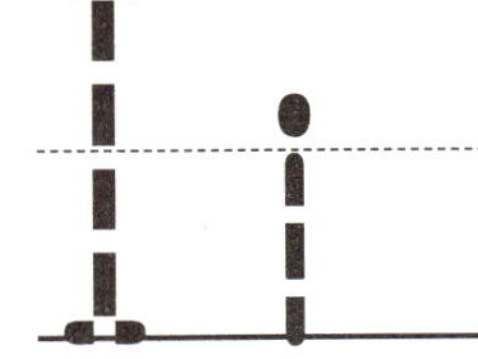

On another sheet of paper, draw a picture of something you think is icky.

Name ____________________

Trace the I and i's.

Iguana is on an iceberg.

Now write the I and i's.

_guana _s on an _ceberg.

Add i's and then read the words.

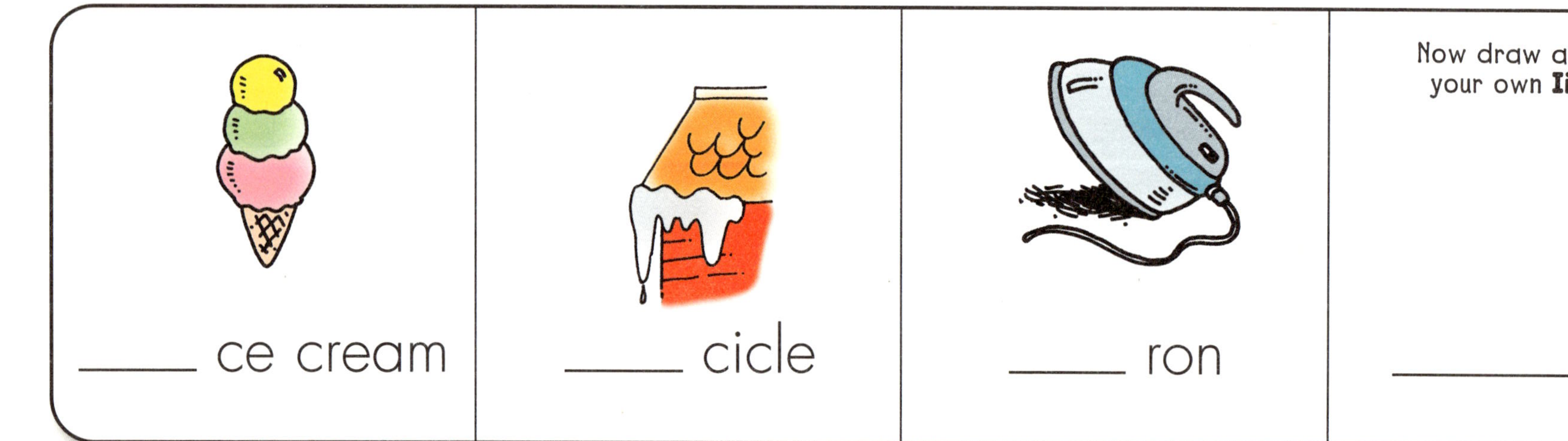

____ ce cream	____ cicle	____ ron	Now draw and write your own **Ii** word. ____________

Name ______________________________ 

Jelly Beans

Color each jelly bean with the letter **J**.

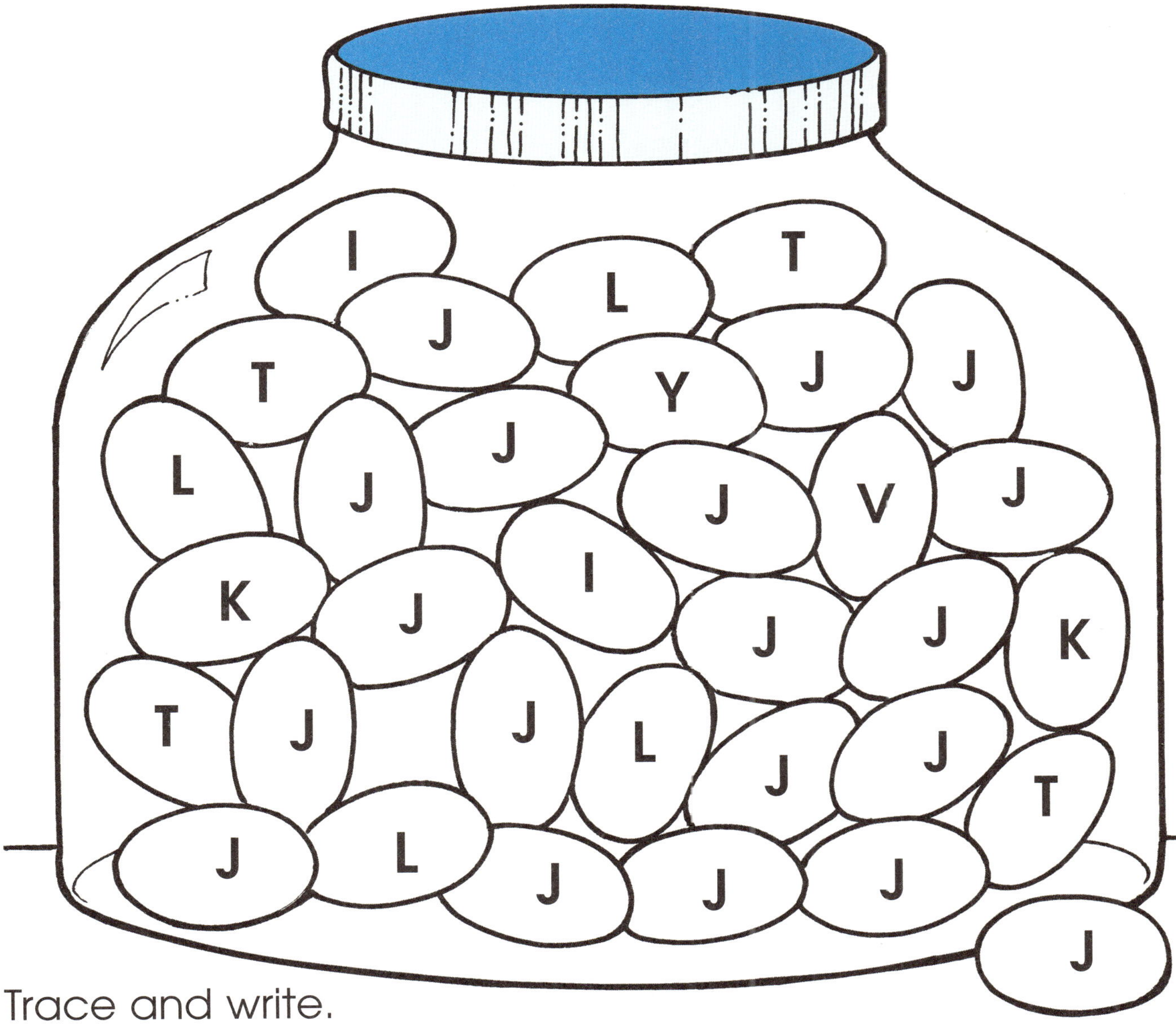

Trace and write.

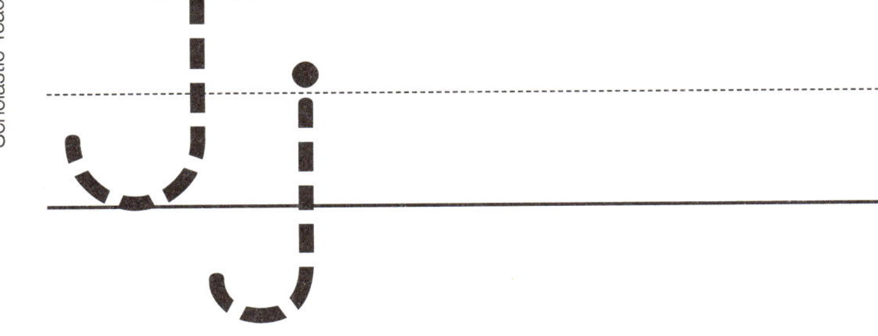

Name ____________________

Trace the J and j.

Jaguar loves jam.

Now write the J and j.

_aguar loves _am.

Add j's and then read the words.

____ ar	____ ump	____ eans	Now draw and write your own **Jj** word. ____________

Name ______________________________ 

Colorful Kites

Draw a line from each kite with the letter **K** to the boy. Color each kite with the letter **K**.

I K L K J K K

Trace and write.

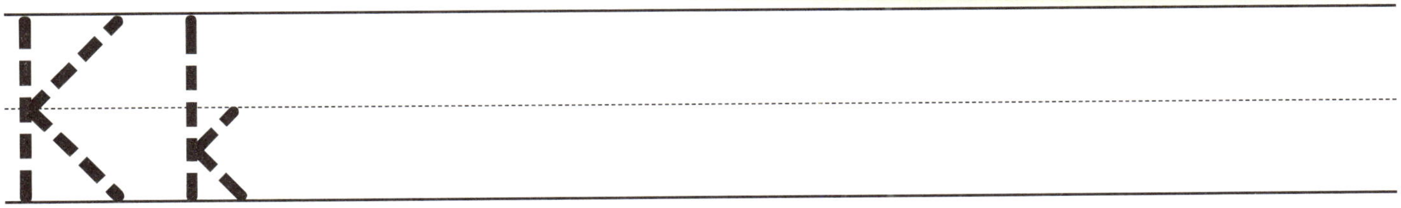

K k

 **On another sheet of paper, draw a picture of a beautiful kite.**

Name ______________________

Trace the K and k.

Kangaroo plays kazoo.

Now write the K and k.

__angaroo plays __azoo.

Add k's and then read the words.

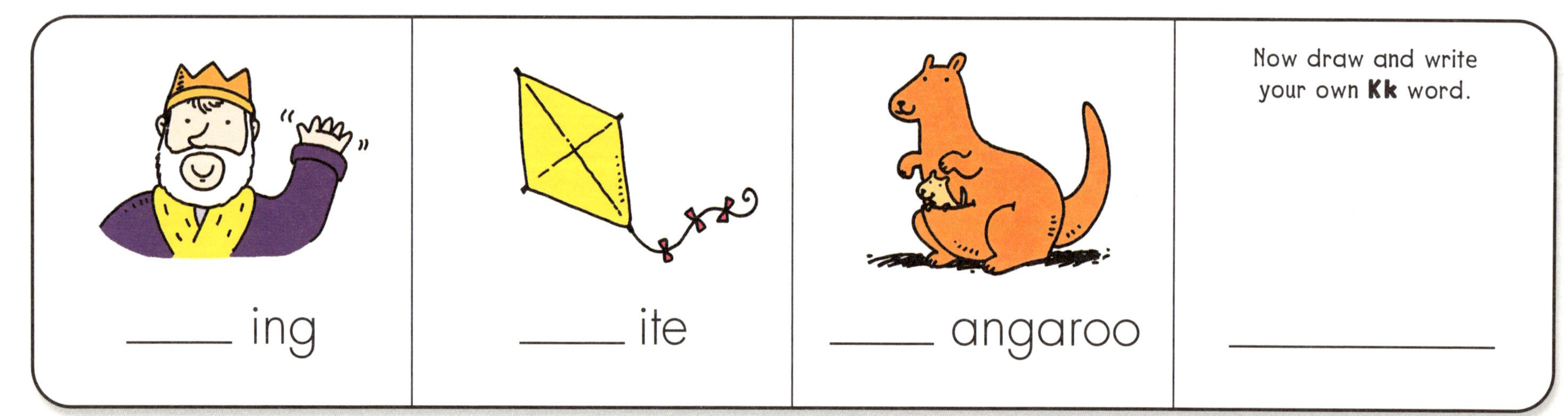

____ ing	____ ite	____ angaroo	Now draw and write your own **Kk** word. ____________

Name ______________________________________ 

Check It Out!

Find and circle each letter **L** hidden in the library.

Trace and write.

L L

Check out a book from the library.

Name ____________________

Trace the L and l's.

Lamb loves to laugh.

Now write the L and l's.

_amb _oves to _augh.

Add l's and then read the words.

___ emon	___ eaf	___ ion	Now draw and write your own **Ll** word. ______

Name ________________________________

Musical Mouse

Follow the letter **M**. Color the path that leads the mouse to the mandolin.

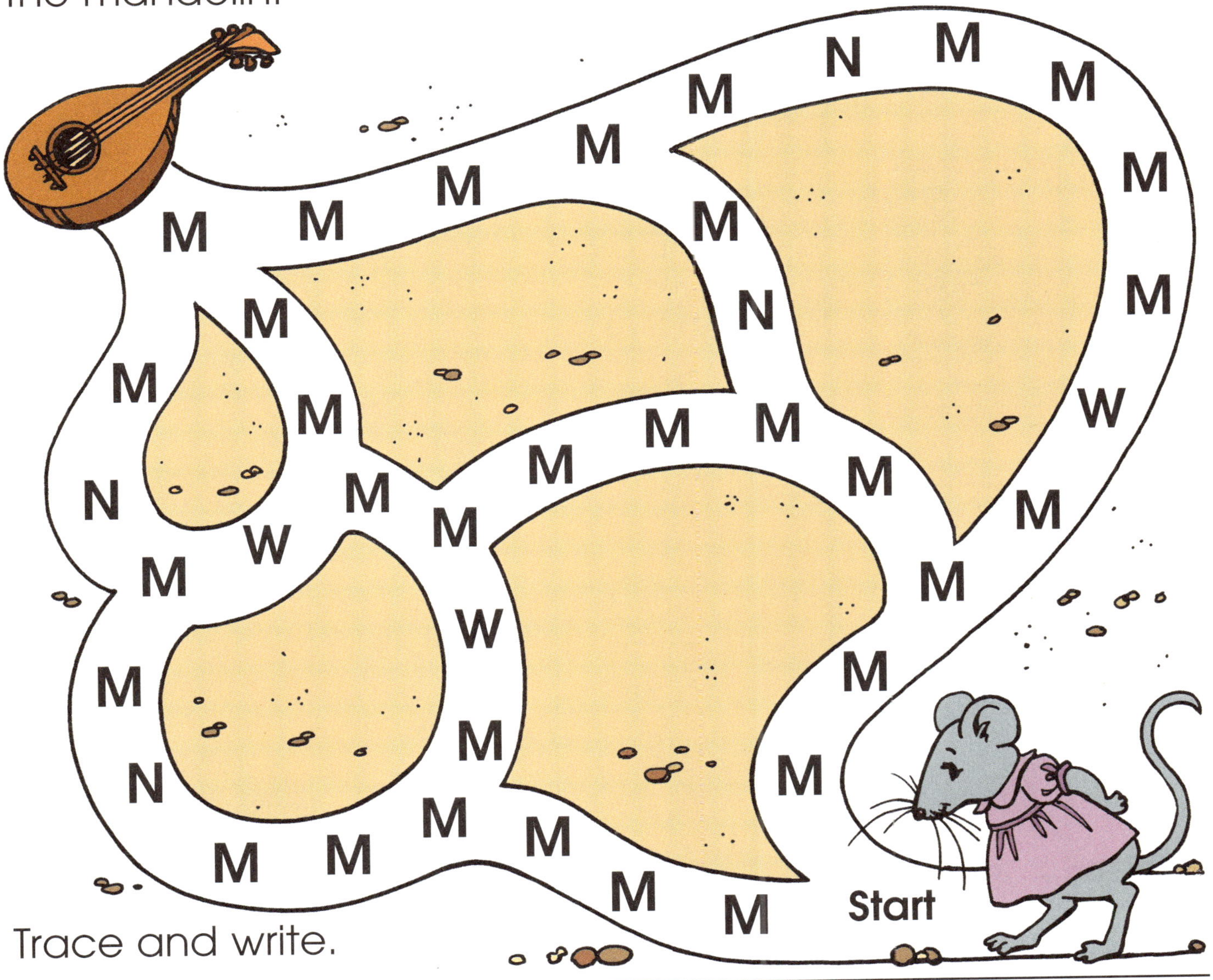

Trace and write.

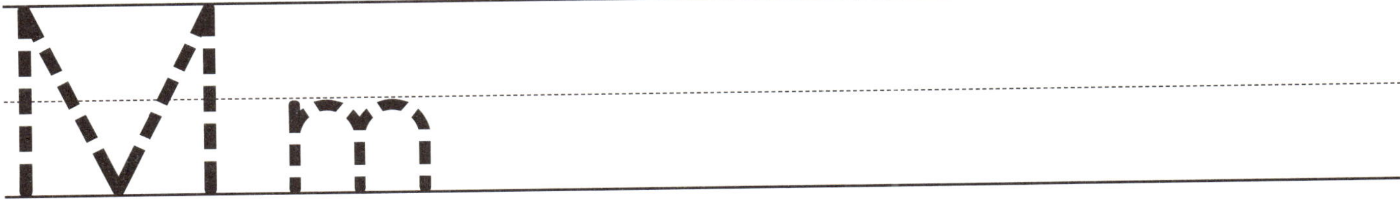

On another sheet of paper, draw a picture of a mouse house.

Name ______________________

Trace the M and m's.

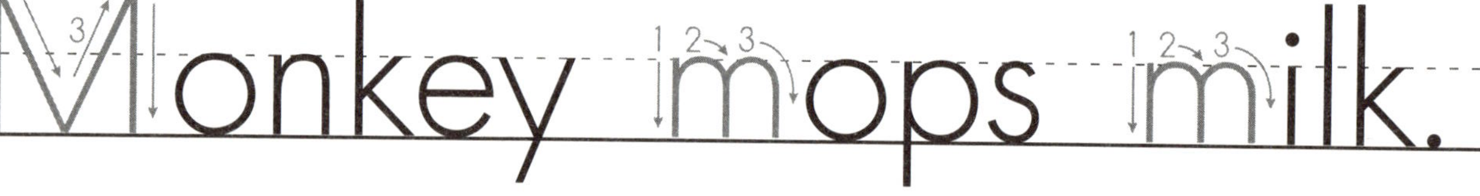

Now write the M and m's.

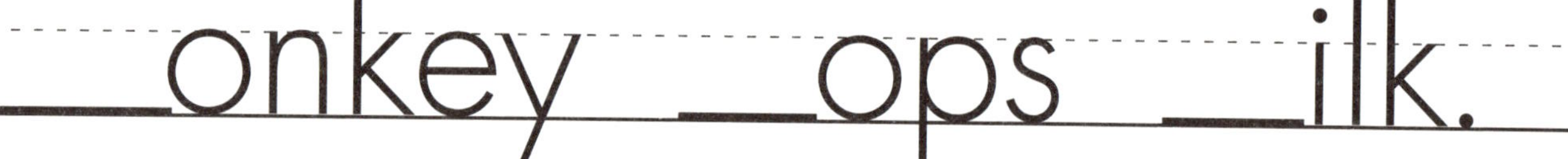

Add m's and then read the words.

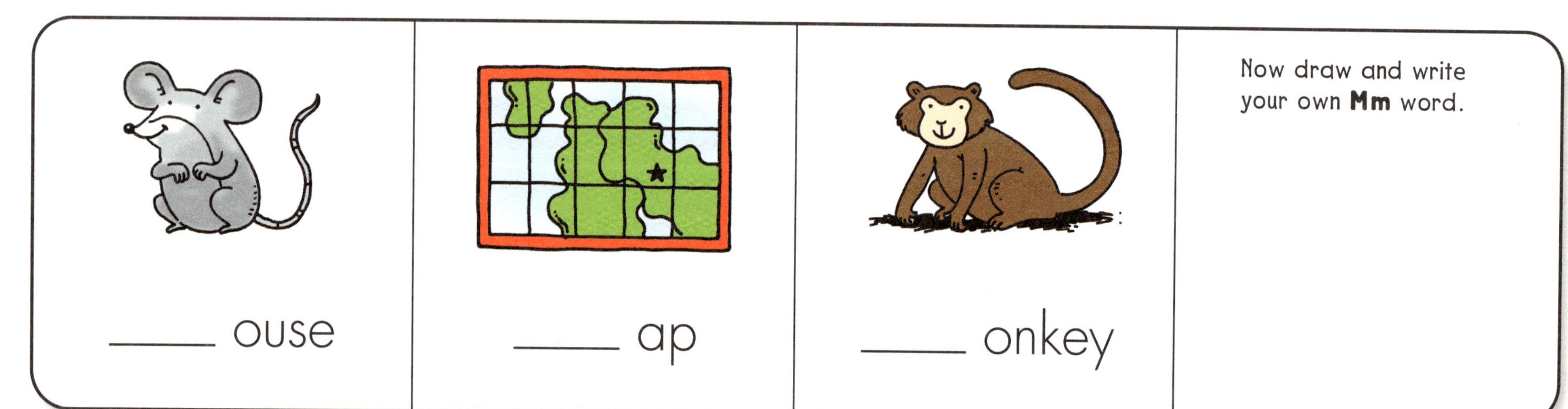

Name ___________________________

Noodle Doodle Soup

Circle each **N** in the bowl of soup.

Trace and write.

N n

Name ____________________

Trace the N's and n.

Nate the Newt has a nickel.

Now write the N's and n.

___ate the ___ewt has a ___ickel.

Add n's and then read the words.

___ est	___ ewspaper	___ ut	Now draw and write your own **Nn** word. ___

What Is Ollie?

Color each space with the letter **O** purple. Color all the other spaces blue.

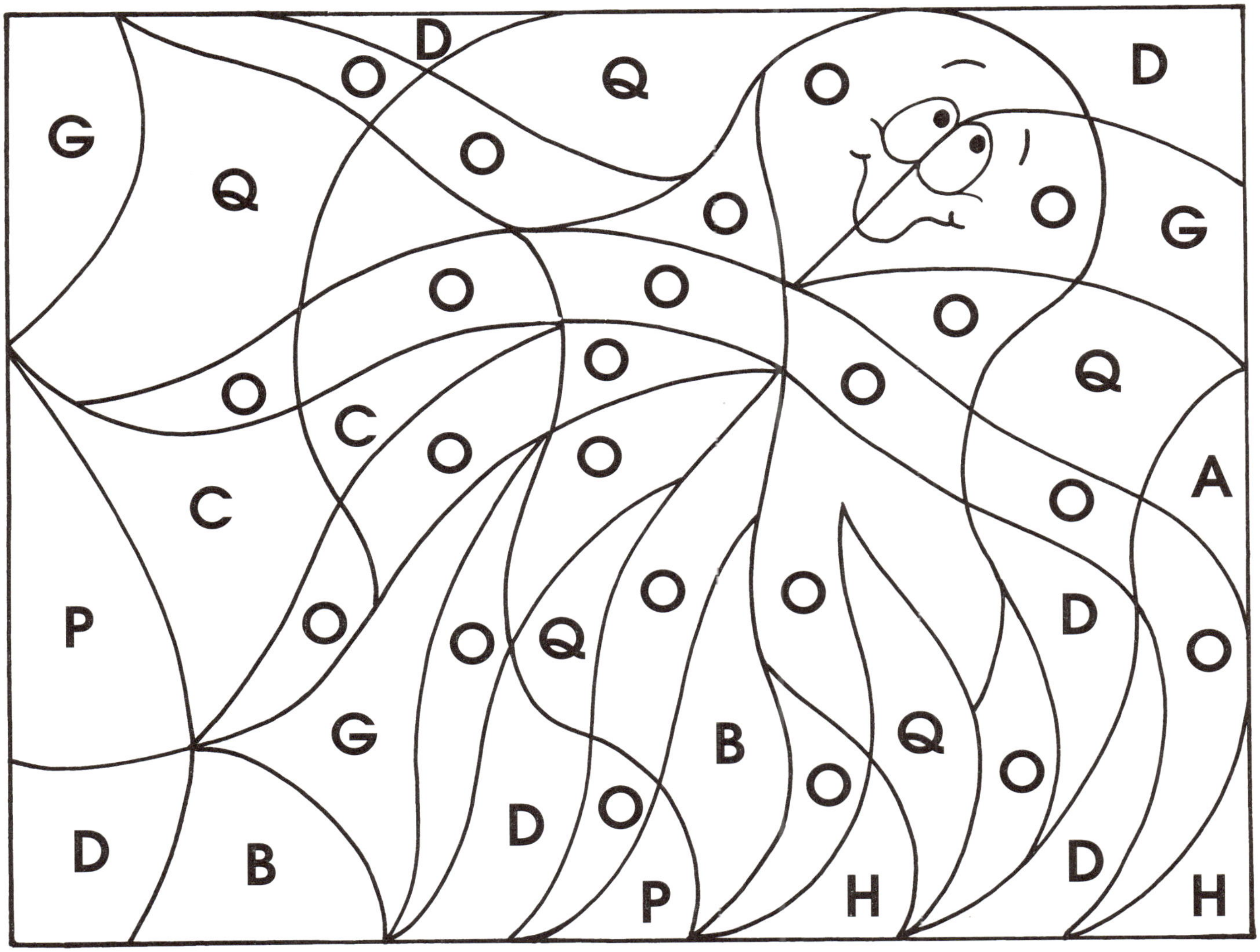

Trace and write.

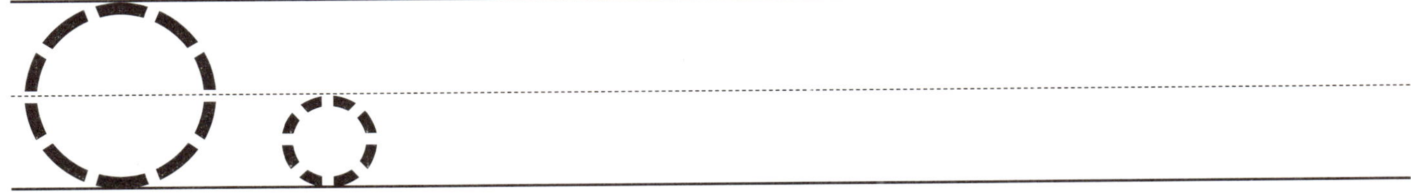

Orange begins with the letter O. On another sheet of paper, draw an orange.

Name ______________________

Trace the O and o's.

Olive the octopus loves onions.

Now write the O and o's.

__live the __ctopus loves __nions.

Add o's and then read the words.

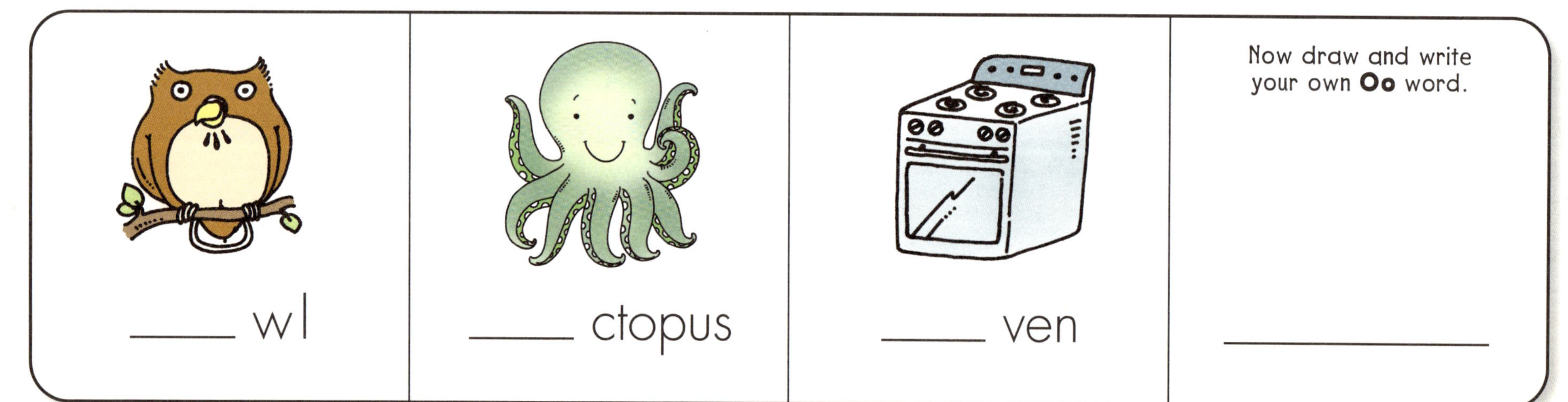

____ wl	____ ctopus	____ ven	Now draw and write your own **Oo** word. ____________

Name ______________________

Plenty of Popcorn

Help Pete find his popcorn. Color each piece of popcorn with the letter **P**.

Start

Trace and write.

P p

Name ____________________

Trace the p's.

The pigs planned a picnic.

Now write the p's.

The __igs __lanned a __icnic.

Add p's and then read the words.

Name ______________________________

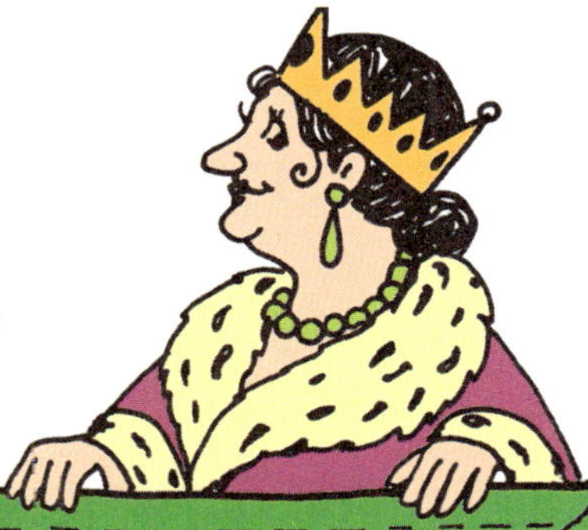

The Queen's Quilt

Color each space with the letter **Q** yellow.
Color all the other spaces green.

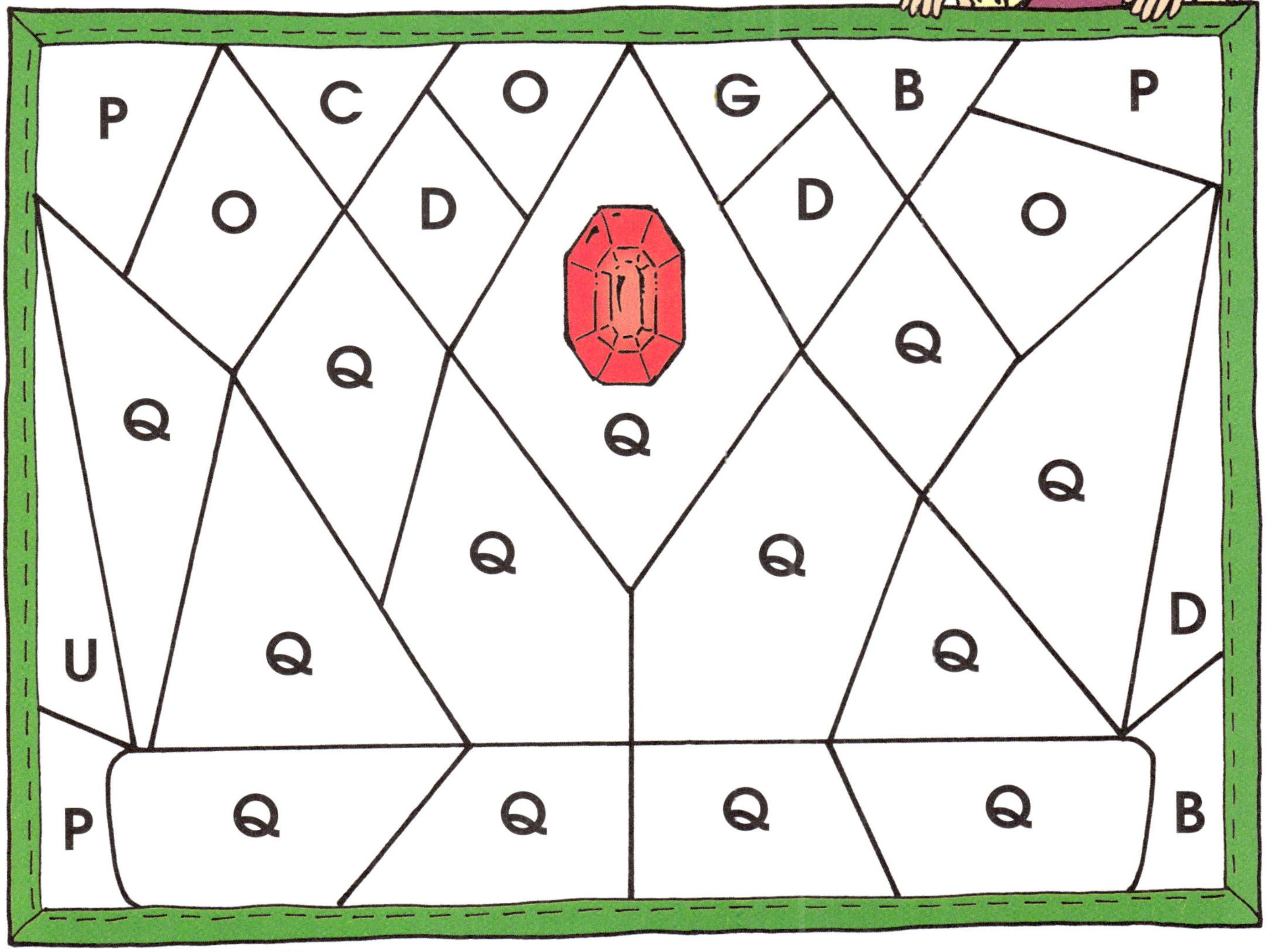

P C O G B P
O D D O
Q Q Q Q
Q Q
U Q Q D
P Q Q Q Q B

Trace and write.

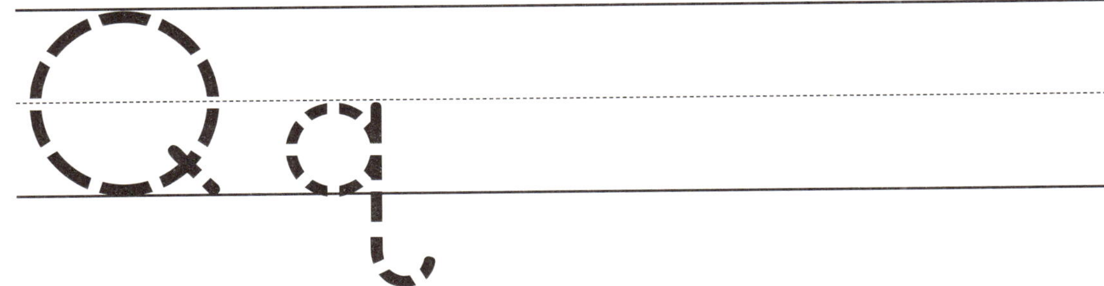

Name ______________________

Trace the Q's and q.

Quincy Quail likes quiet.

Now write the Q's and q.

___uincy ___uail likes ___uiet.

Add q's and then read the words.

____ ueen	____ uilt	____ u iet	Now draw and write your own **Qq** word. ____

Raindrops

Find and circle each letter **R** on the umbrella. Color each raindrop with the letter **R** blue.

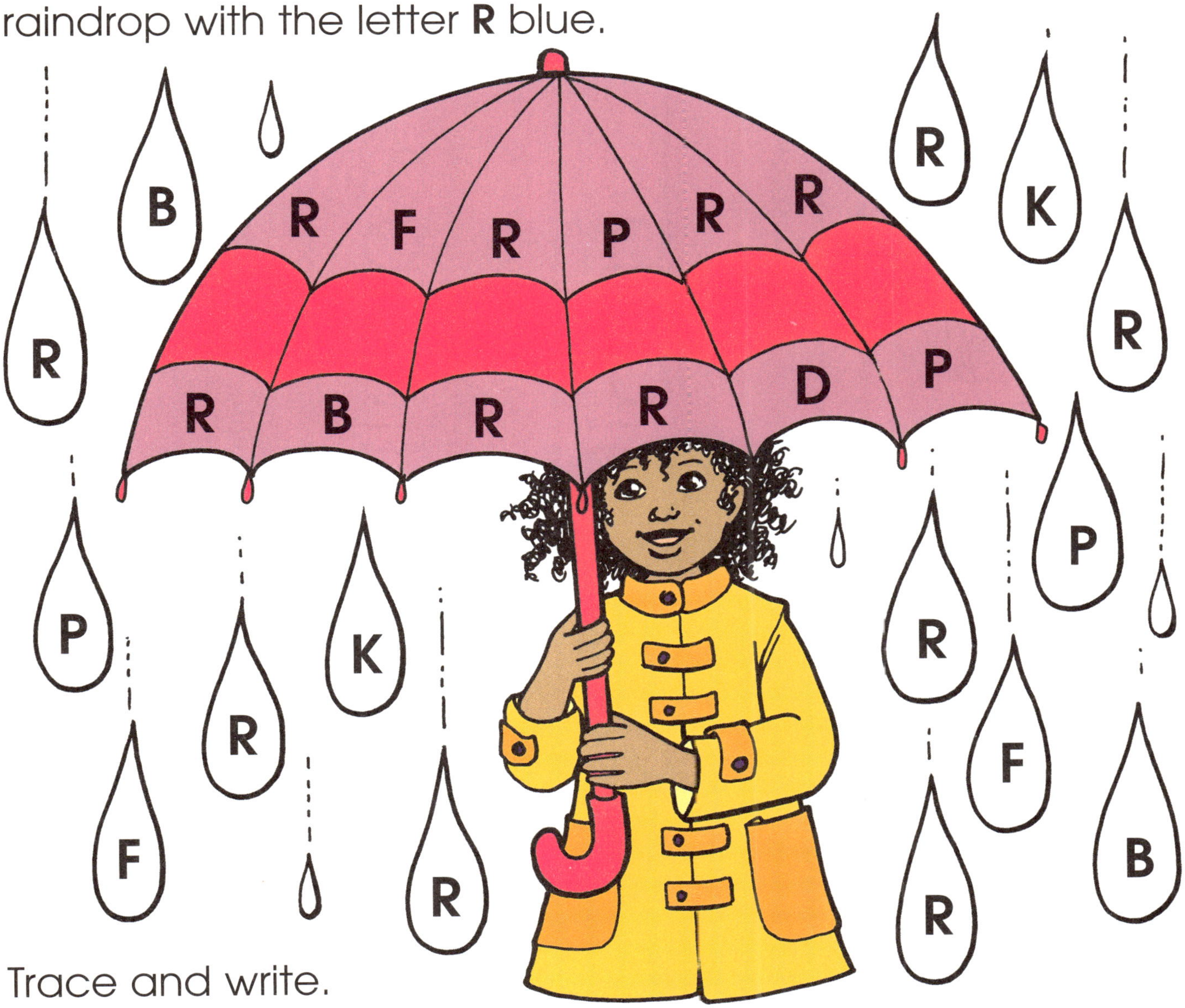

Trace and write.

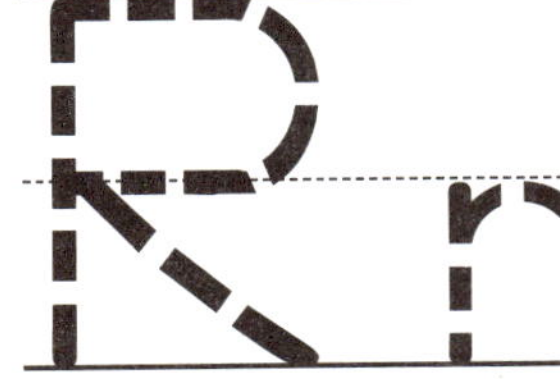

Rainbow begins with the letter R. On another sheet of paper, draw a rainbow.

Name ______________________

Trace the R's and r's.

Rosie Rabbit rakes rocks.

Now write the R's and r's.

_osie _abbit _akes _ocks.

Add r's and then read the words.

Name ______________________________________

Building a Sand Castle

Find and circle each letter **S**.

Trace and write.

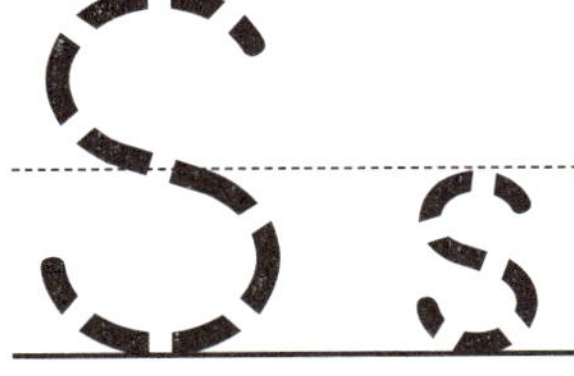

Sandwich begins with the letter S. On another sheet of paper, draw a picture of your favorite sandwich.

Name ______________________

Trace the S and s.

Seal makes a sandwich.

Now write the S and s.

_eal makes a _andwich.

Add s's and then read the words.

___ andwich	___ ock	___ oap	Now draw and write your own **Ss** word. ______

Name ______________________________

Fast Track

Follow the letter **T**. Color the path that leads Tommy Train to the station.

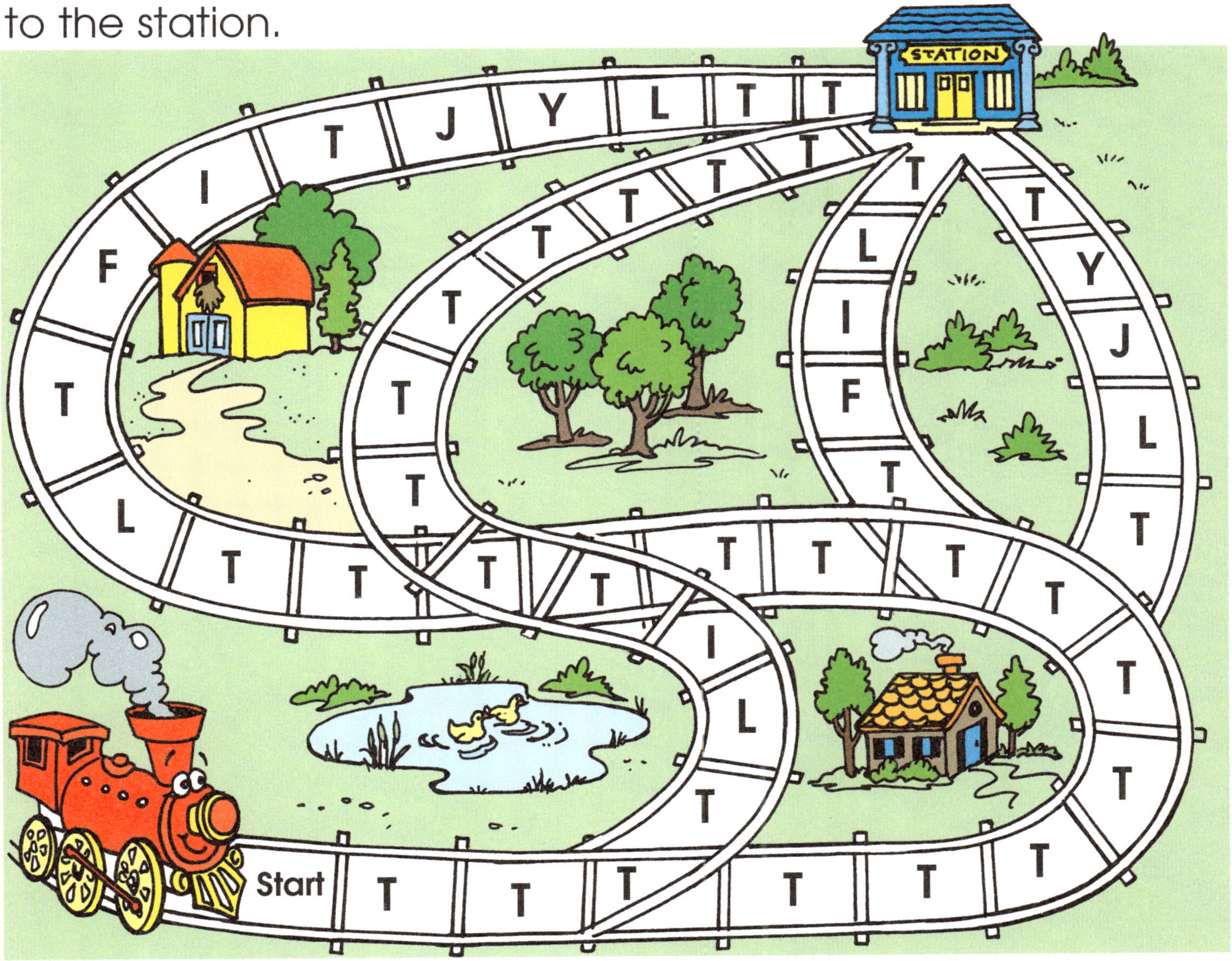

Trace and write.

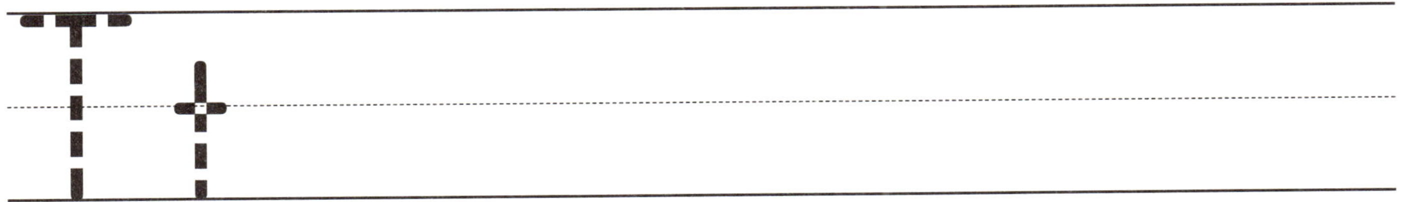

Turtle begins with the letter T. On another sheet of paper, draw a picture of a turtle.

Name ____________________

Trace the T's and t's.

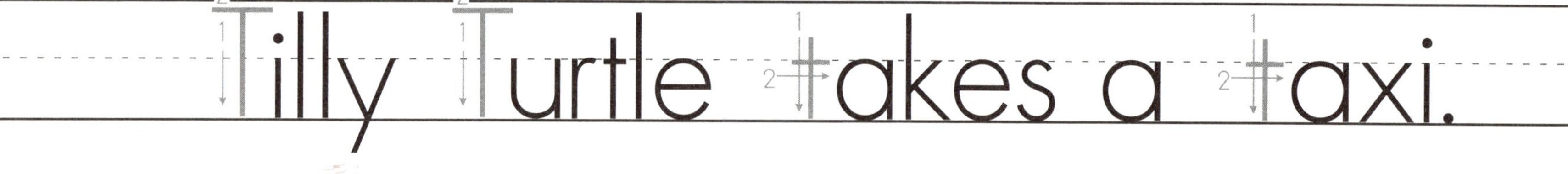

Now write the T's and t's.

Add t's and then read the words.

Name ______________________________

Under the Umbrella

Circle each letter **U**.

Trace and write.

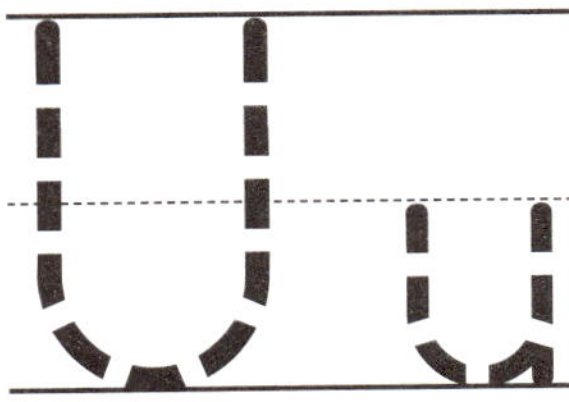

U u

Under begins with the letter U. On another sheet of paper, draw a picture of something hiding under a shell.

Name ______________________

Trace the U and u.

Umbrellabird rides a unicycle.

Now write the U and u.

__mbrellabird rides a __nicycle.

Add u's and then read the words.

___ mbrella	___ nicorn	___ p	Now draw and write your own **Uu** word. ______

Name ______________________________________ 

Voting for Veggies

Color each veggie green that has the letter **V** hidden on it.

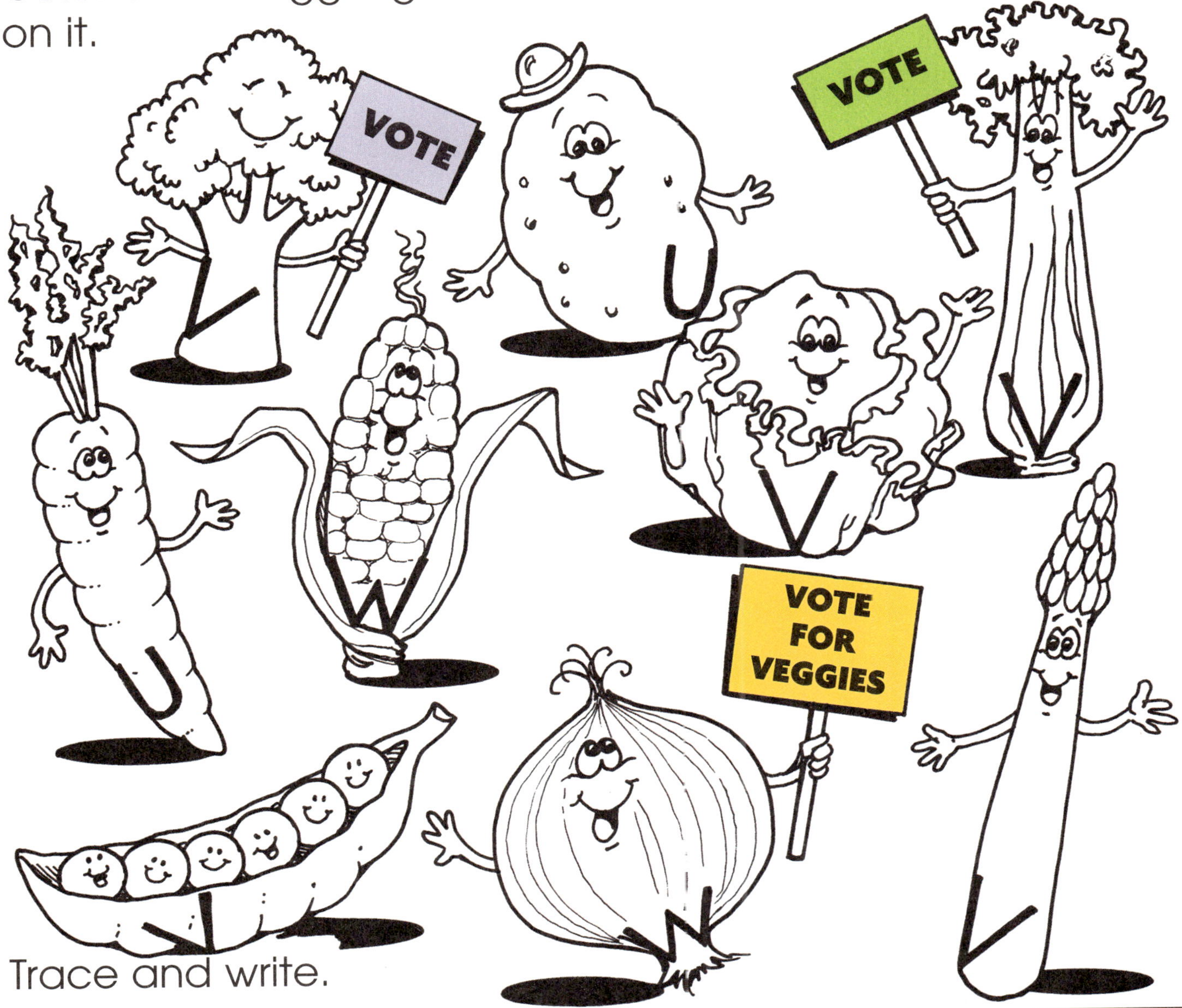

Trace and write.

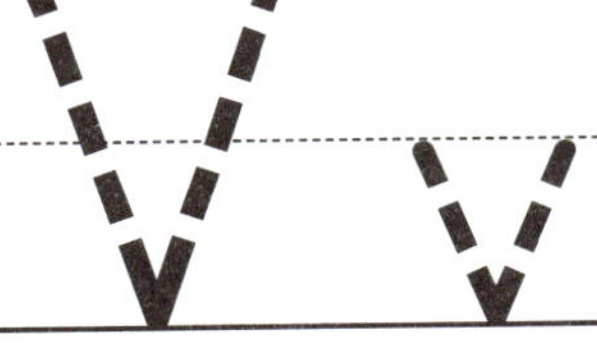

Veggie begins with the letter V. On another sheet of paper, draw your two favorite veggies.

Name ______________________

Trace the V's and v.

Vera Viper has a valentine.

Now write the V's and v.

_era _iper has a _alentine.

Add v's and then read the words.

Name ________________________________ 

Guess Who?

Color each space with the letter **W** green. Color all the other spaces brown.

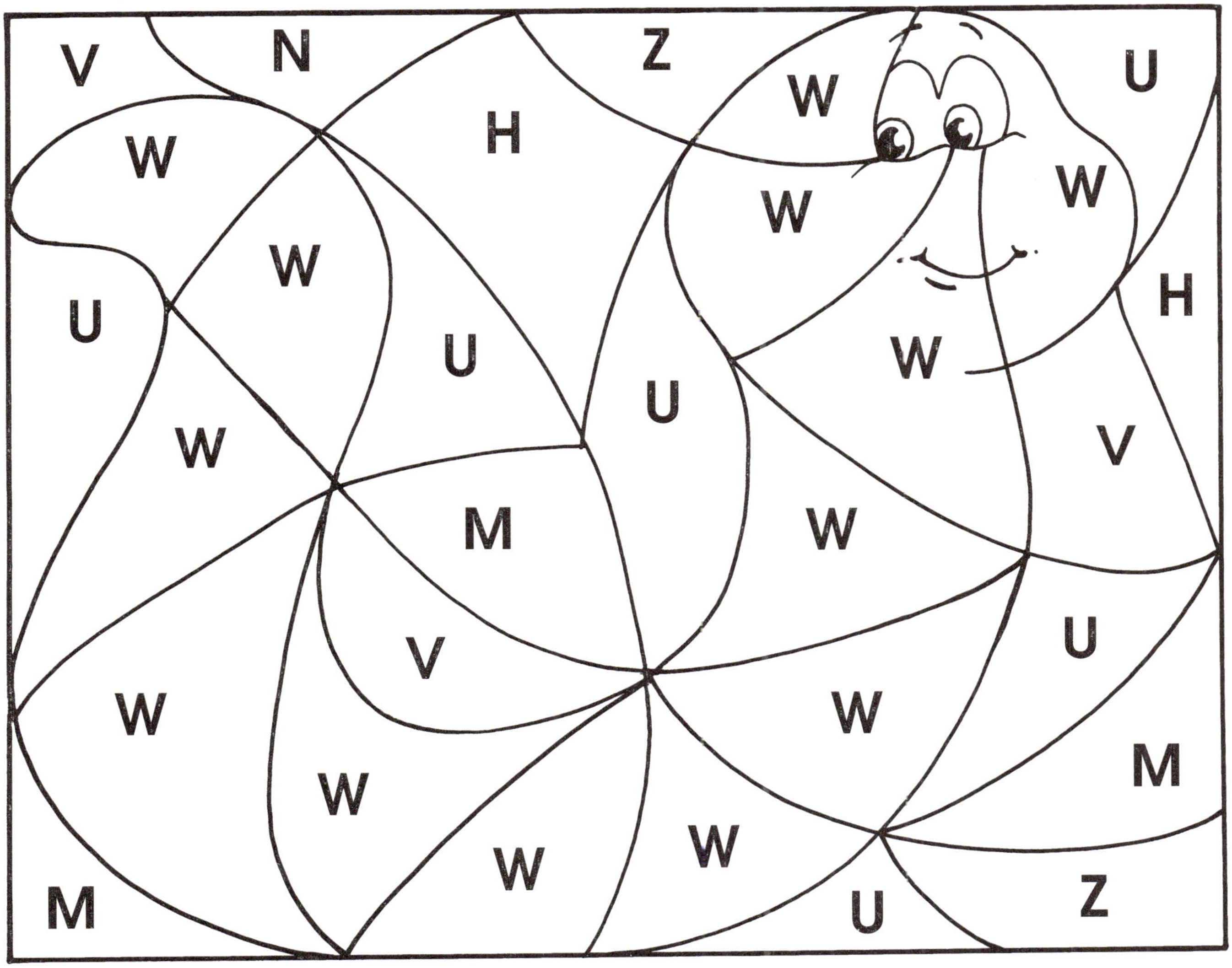

V N Z W U W H W W W U W H U W U V W M W V U W U W W W M W M Z

Trace and write.

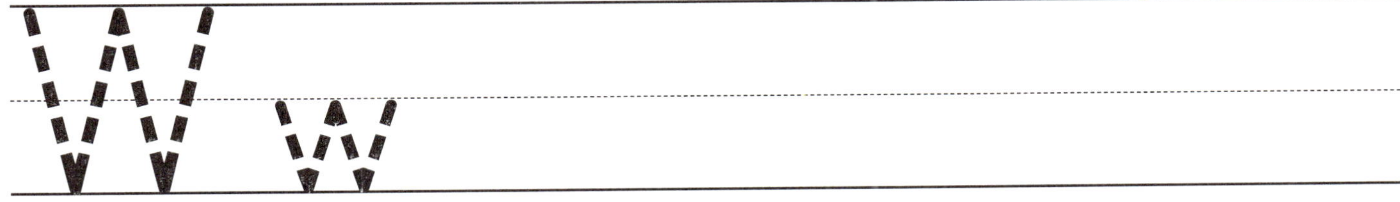

Whale begins with the letter W. On another sheet of paper, draw a big whale.

Name ____________________

Trace the W and w.

Worm had a wagon.

Now write the W and w.

___orm had a _agon.

Add w's and then read the words.

____ eb

____ orm

____ indow

Now draw and write your own **Ww** word.

____

Name ______________________________

X Marks the Spot!

Follow the letter **X**. Help the girl find her way to the treasure chest.

Start

Trace and write.

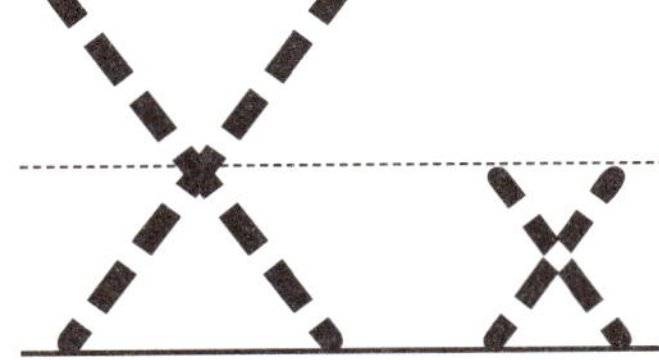

Draw five X's in a row.

Name ____________________

Trace the X and x.

X-Ray fish plays xylophone.

Now write the X and x.

__-Ray fish plays _ylophone.

Add x's and then read the words.

Name ______________________________

Yummy Yogurt

Color each space with the letter **Y** yellow. Color all the other spaces green.

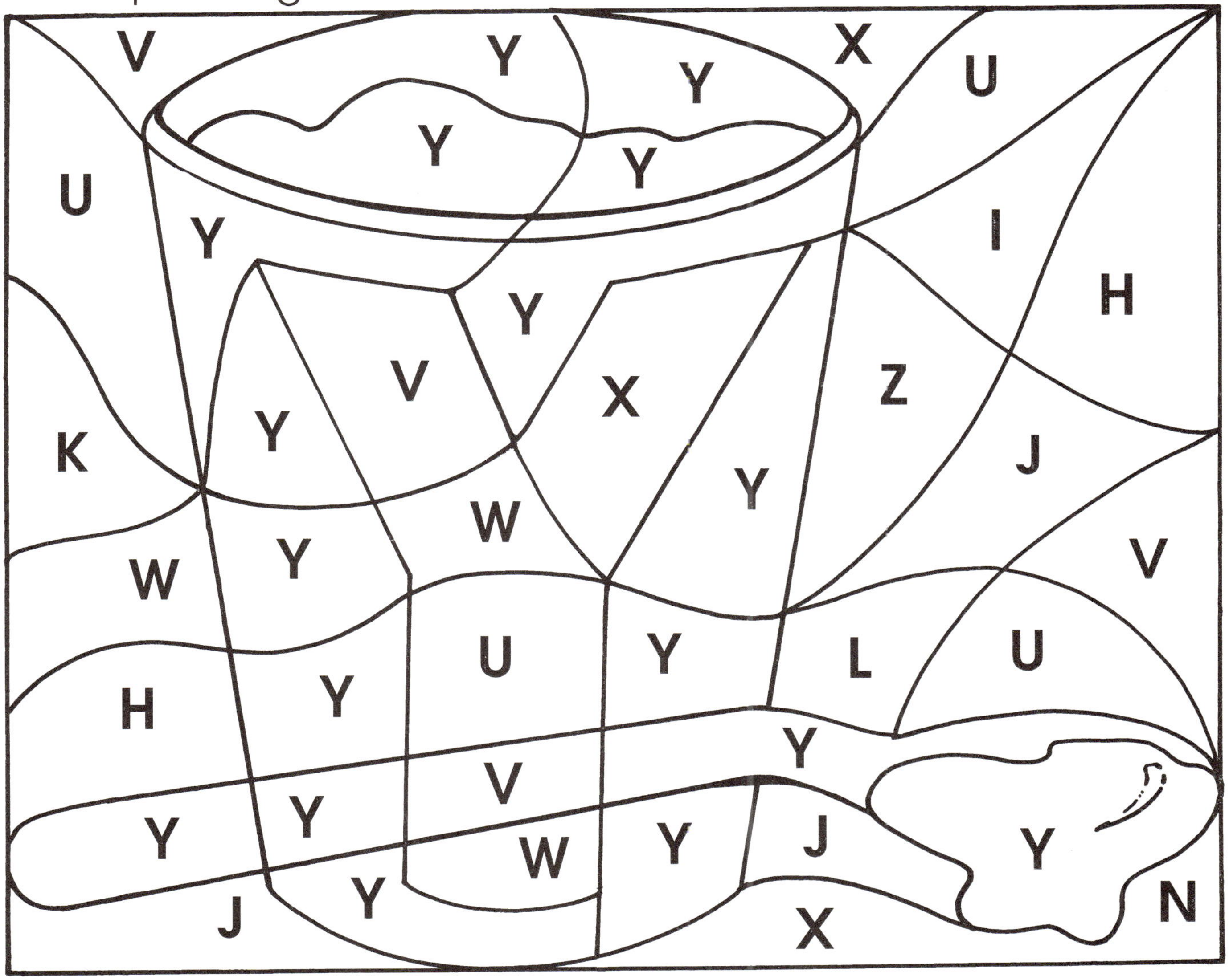

Trace and write.

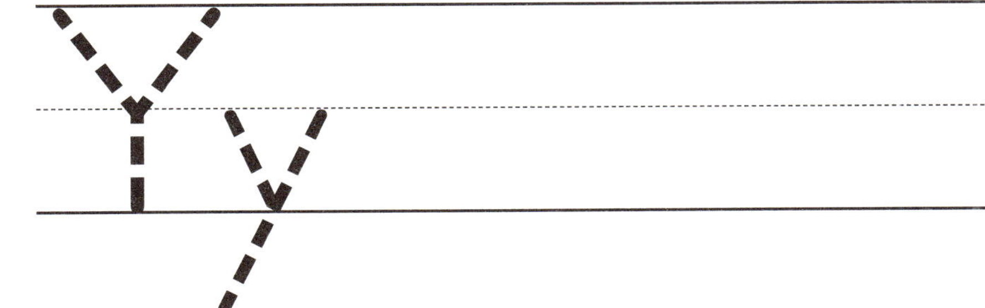

Name

Trace the y's.

The yak ate yogurt.

Now write the y's.

The _ak ate _ogurt.

Add y's and then read the words.

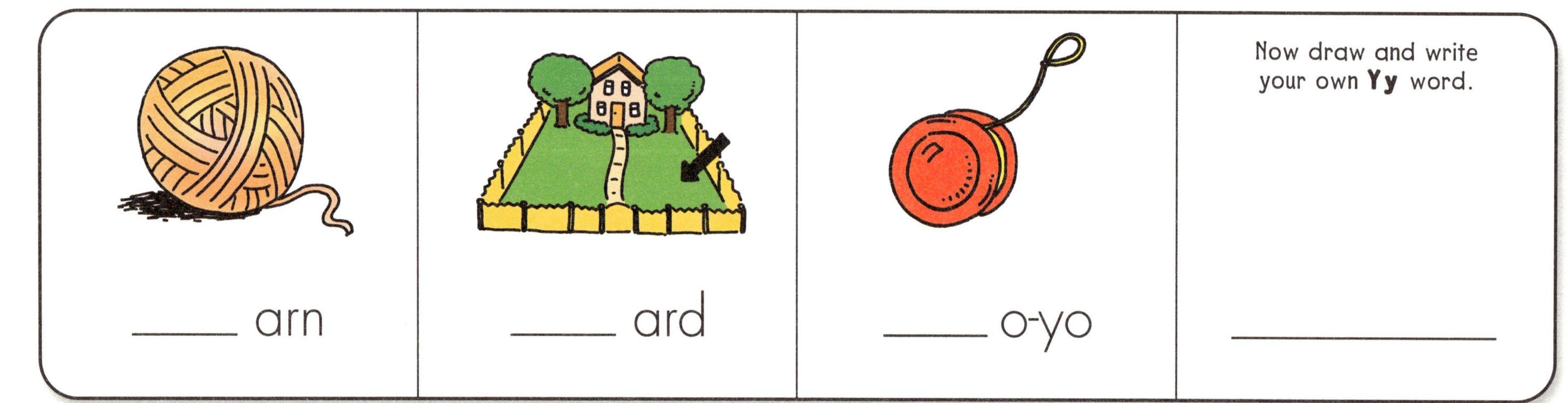

____ arn	____ ard	____ o-yo	Now draw and write your own **Yy** word. ____________

Name ______________________________ 

Zany Zookeeper

The zookeeper lost the zebra. Find and circle each letter **Z**.

Trace and write.

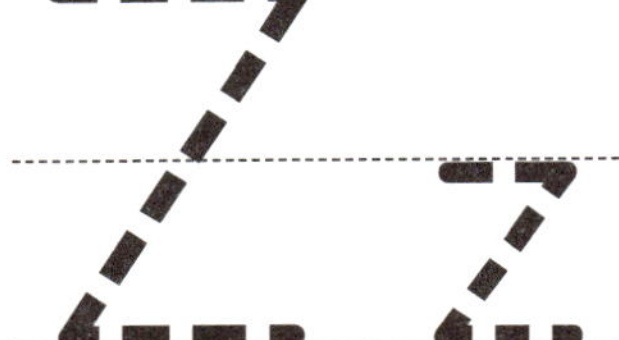

Zero begins with the letter Z. Draw five zeros in a row.

Name ____________________

Trace the Z and z.

The Zebra lives at the zoo.

Now write the Z and z.

The __ebra lives at the __oo.

Add z's and then read the words.

____ ebra	____ ero	____ ipper	Now draw and write your own **Zz** word. ____________

Band of Ants

Color each drum with the letter **a** red.
Color each drum with the letter **b** blue.
Color each drum with the letter **c** green.

Trace and write.

a b c

On a sheet of lined paper, write Aa, Bb, Cc.

Name ____________________ 

Dinosaur Dig

Follow the letters **d**, **e**, **f** in order. Color the path that leads to the dinosaur bones.

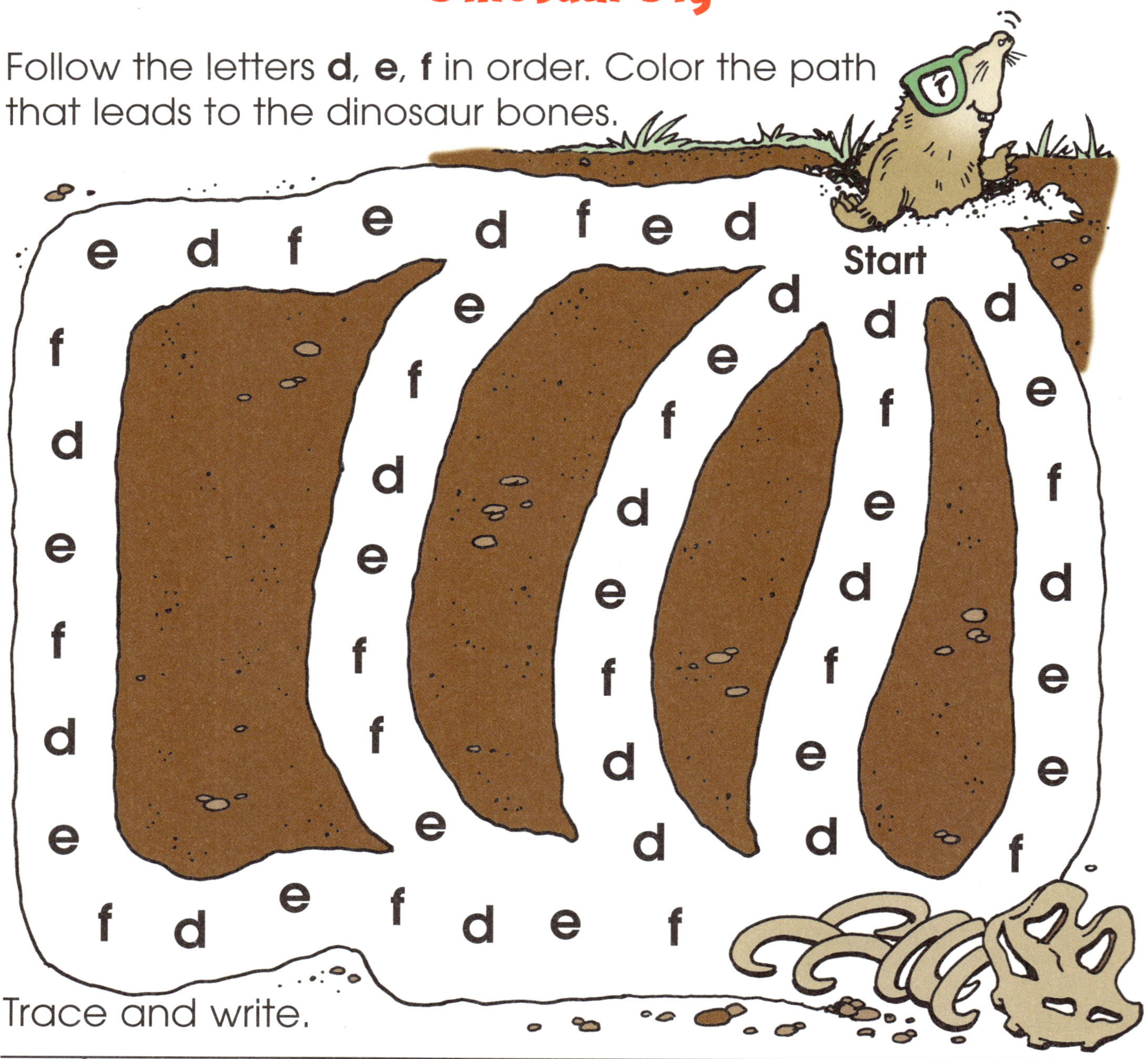

Start

e d f e d f e d d d d e e e f f f f d d e e d e d d f f e f f f e e e d d d d e e f f d e e d f d e f d e f

Trace and write.

d e f

Look in the newspaper to find the letters d, e, and f.

Name ______________________________________

Inch by Inch

To find out what insect moves about an inch at a time, color each space with the letter **g** orange. Color each space with the letter **h** yellow. Color each space with the letter **i** black.

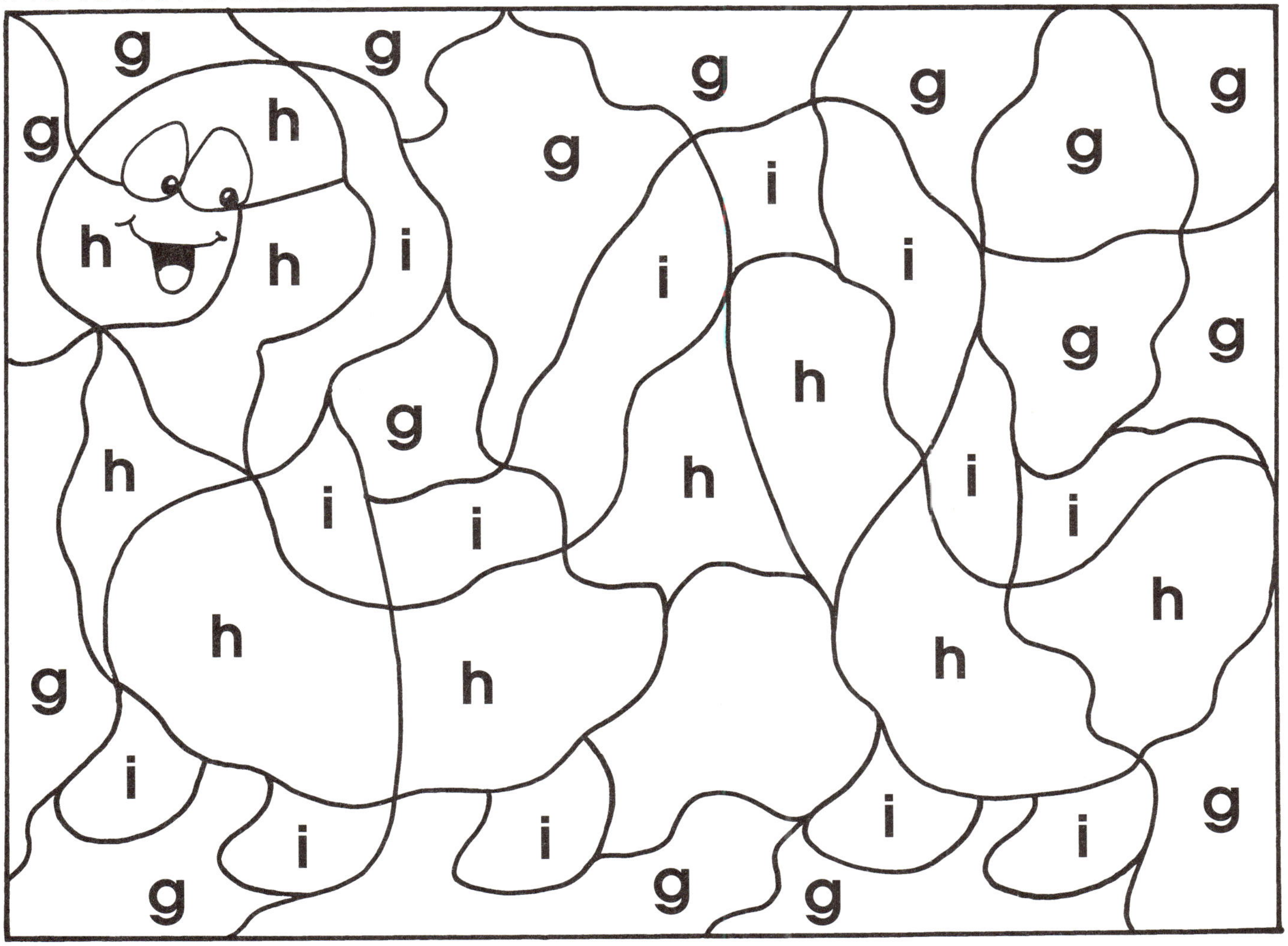

Trace and write.

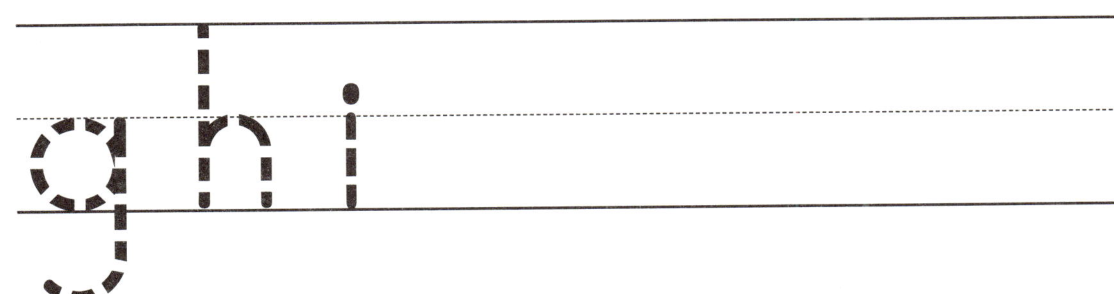

Name ______________________________ 

Kicking Kangaroos

Draw a line from each kangaroo to the soccer balls with the same letter.

k j l j l

j k l

j k l j k

Trace and write.

j k l

Name ____________________

Ocean of Letters

Find and circle the letters **m**, **n**, and **o** in the picture.

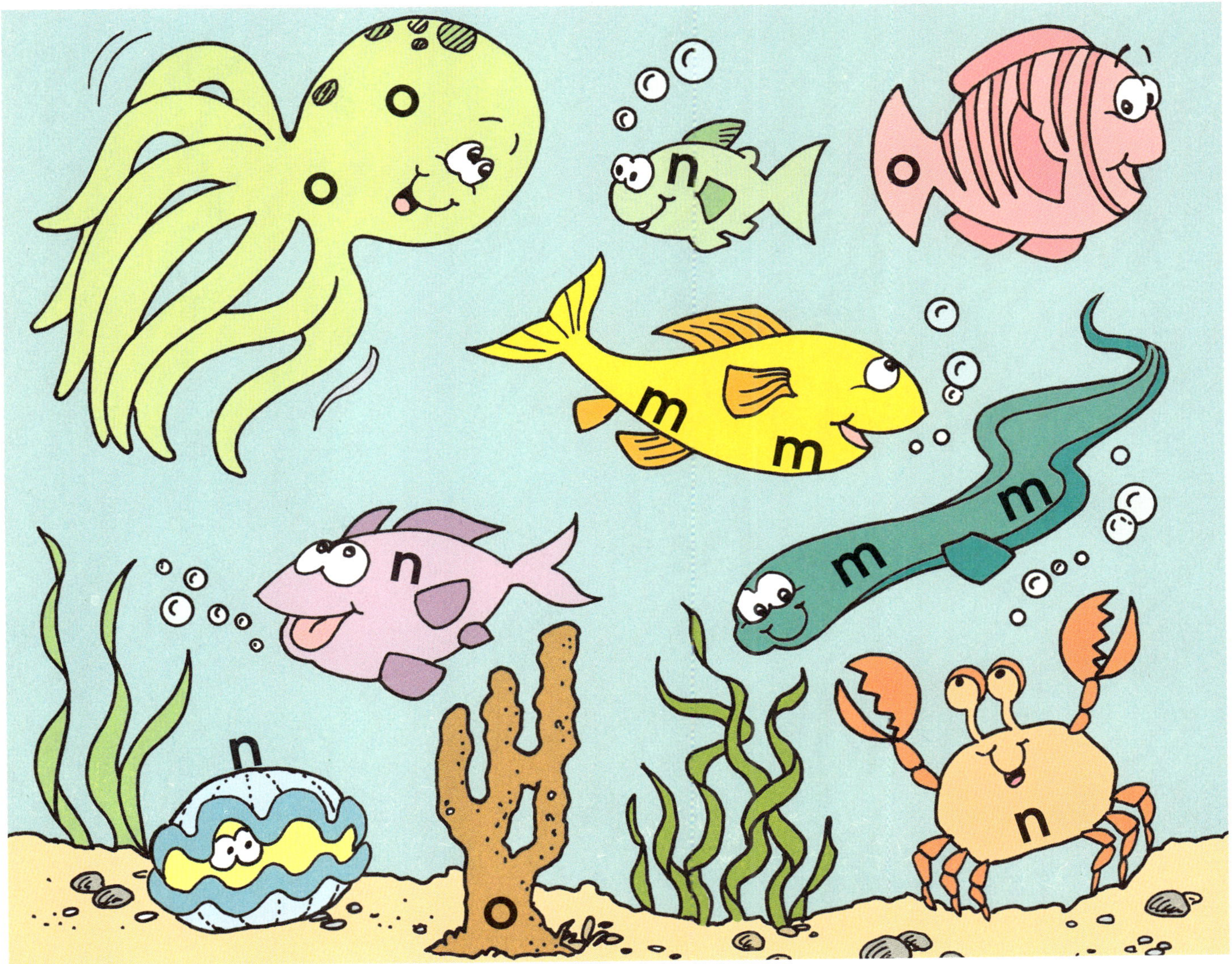

Trace and write.

On a sheet of lined paper, write the letters m, n, and o with their matching capital letters.

Name ________________________________

Plenty of Penguins

Circle each penguin with the letter **p**. Mark an *X* on each penguin with the letter **q**. Underline each penguin with the letter **r**.

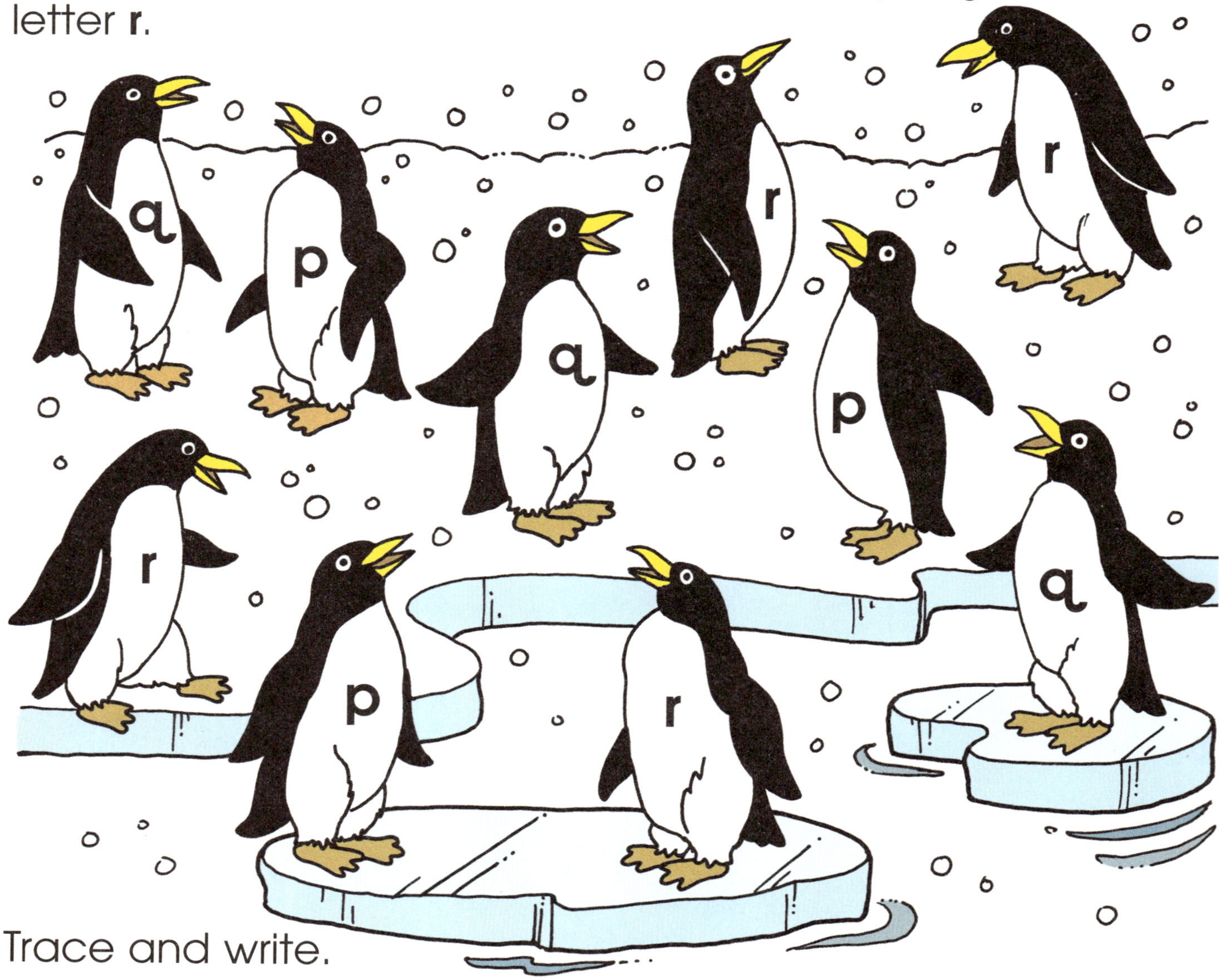

Trace and write.

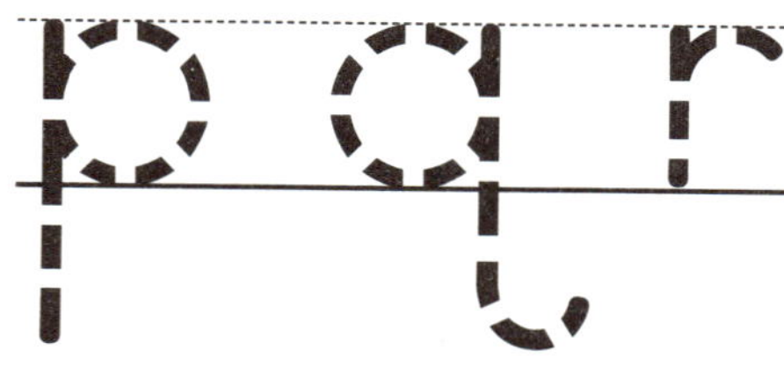

Name ______________________________

Spotted Turtle

Color each space with the letters **s**, **t**, or **u** to find a hidden letter.

s	u	u	w
t	f	c	m
u	s	s	a
f	w	t	w
t	s	u	f

Trace and write.

s t u

Circle the hidden letter. s t u

Name ______________________________

Watermelon Fun

Color each seed with the letters **v**, **w**, or **x** black.

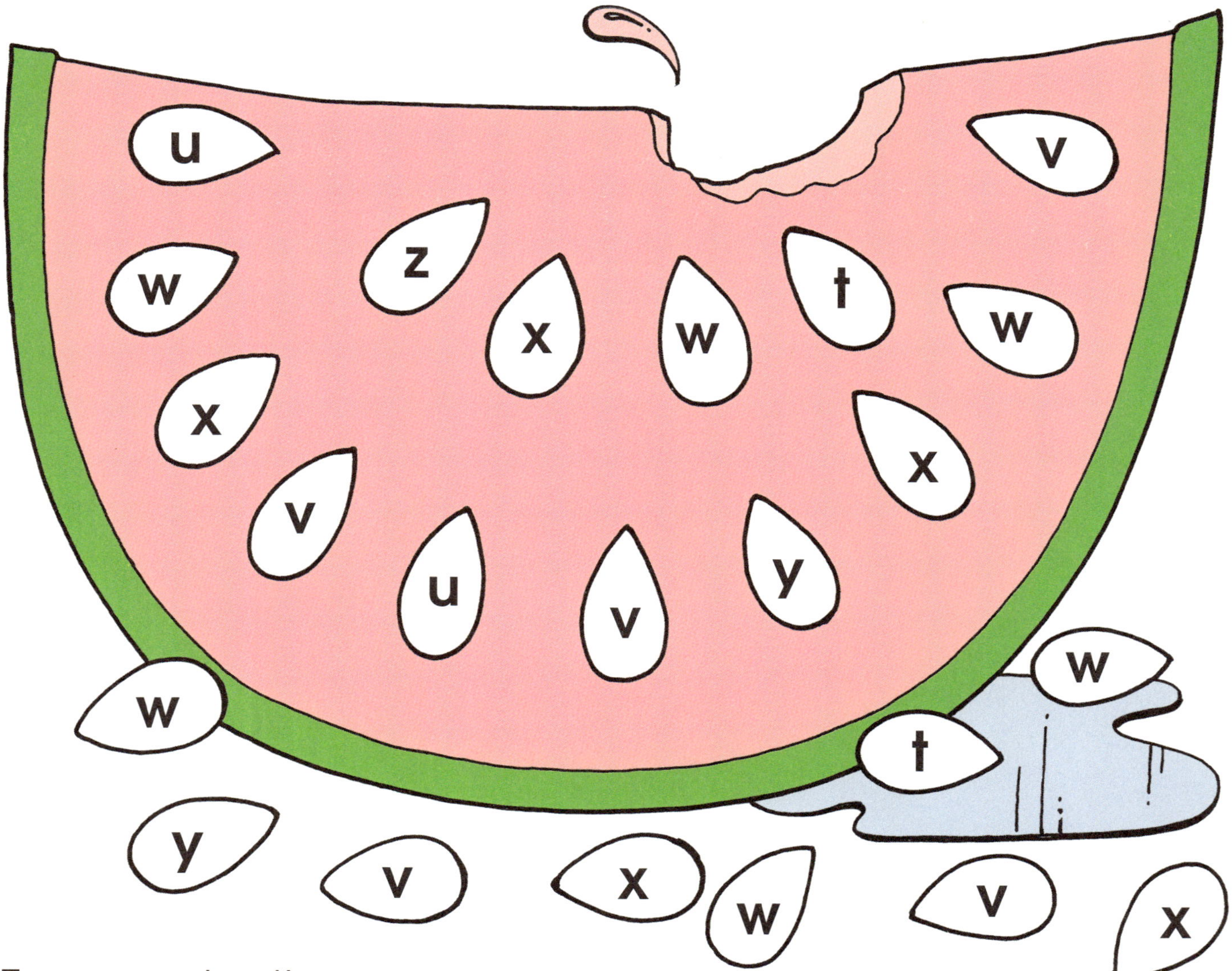

Trace and write.

On another sheet of paper, draw a picture of your favorite fruit.

Name ___________________________________

Follow the Yellow Brick Road

Follow the letters **y** and **z**. Color the road that leads to the zoo.

Trace and write.

y z

Name ____

Careers From A to Z

Finish the alphabet.

A G

M

P

Z

On another sheet of paper, draw a picture of what you would like to be when you grow up.

Name ____

Blast Off!

Color the stars in alphabetical order that lead to the moon.

Start

A B C D E F G H I J K L M N O P Q R S T U V W X Y Z

On another sheet of paper, draw a picture of a rocket flying into outer space.

Lost and Found

Find and circle each uppercase letter of the alphabet in the picture.

A	B	C	D	E	F	G	H	I	J	K	L	M
N	O	P	Q	R	S	T	U	V	W	X	Y	Z

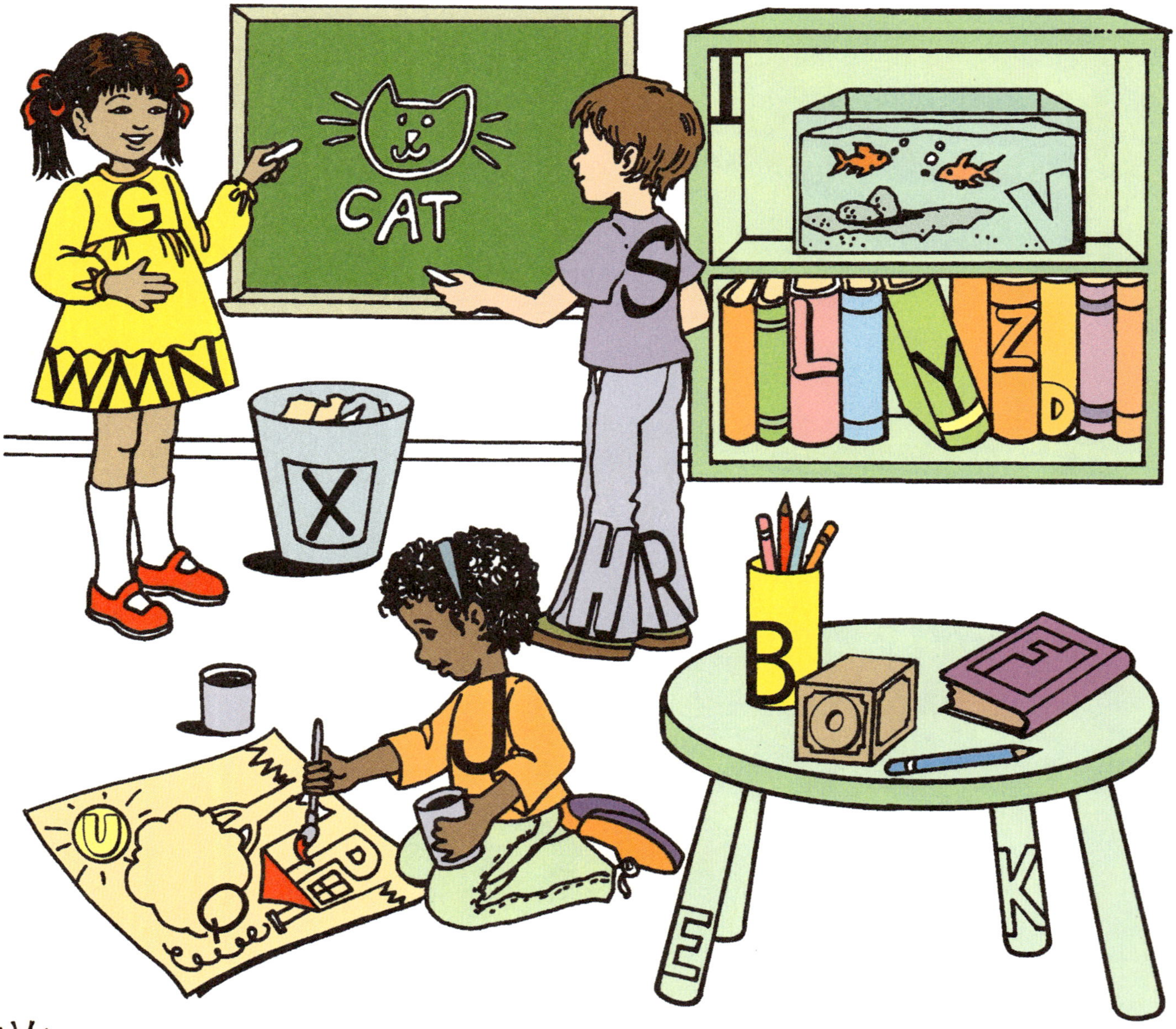

Circle the letter your first name begins with in the letter box above.

Name ___________________________

ABC Picture

Connect the dots in ABC order to find the hidden picture. Tell a story about the picture.

A B C D E F G H I J K L M N O P Q R S T U V W X Y Z

Name ________________________________

Write It Right!

Write the missing lowercase letters.

		a		c
d				h
				m
n				
				w
	y			

Name ______________________________

Playing in the Park

Find and circle each lowercase letter of the alphabet in the picture. Say the letters as you find them.

a b c d e f g h i j k l m
n o p q r s t u v w x y z

Name ____

Letters on Parade

Connect the dots from **a** to **z**.

y x z v w u t b s r a q p c o d m e h n f l g i j k

Name ____

Be a Better Builder

Write the lowercase letter.

A___

D___ G___ J___

L___ N___ P___

S___ U___ W___

Y___ K___ Q___

O___ B___ R___

On a sheet of lined paper, write the first and last letters of your name.

Name ____

Match and Learn

Draw a line from each uppercase letter to the matching lowercase letter.

A	c	O	t
B	d	P	u
C	a	Q	s
D	b	R	q
E	g	S	o
F	f	T	p
G	e	U	r

H	k	V	z
I	l	W	x
J	h	X	v
K	m	Y	w
L	j	Z	y
M	n		
N	i		

Ask the people in your home what uppercase letters begin their names.

Stack It Up!

Connect the dots from **a** to **z**. Then write the uppercase letters in order on the blocks.

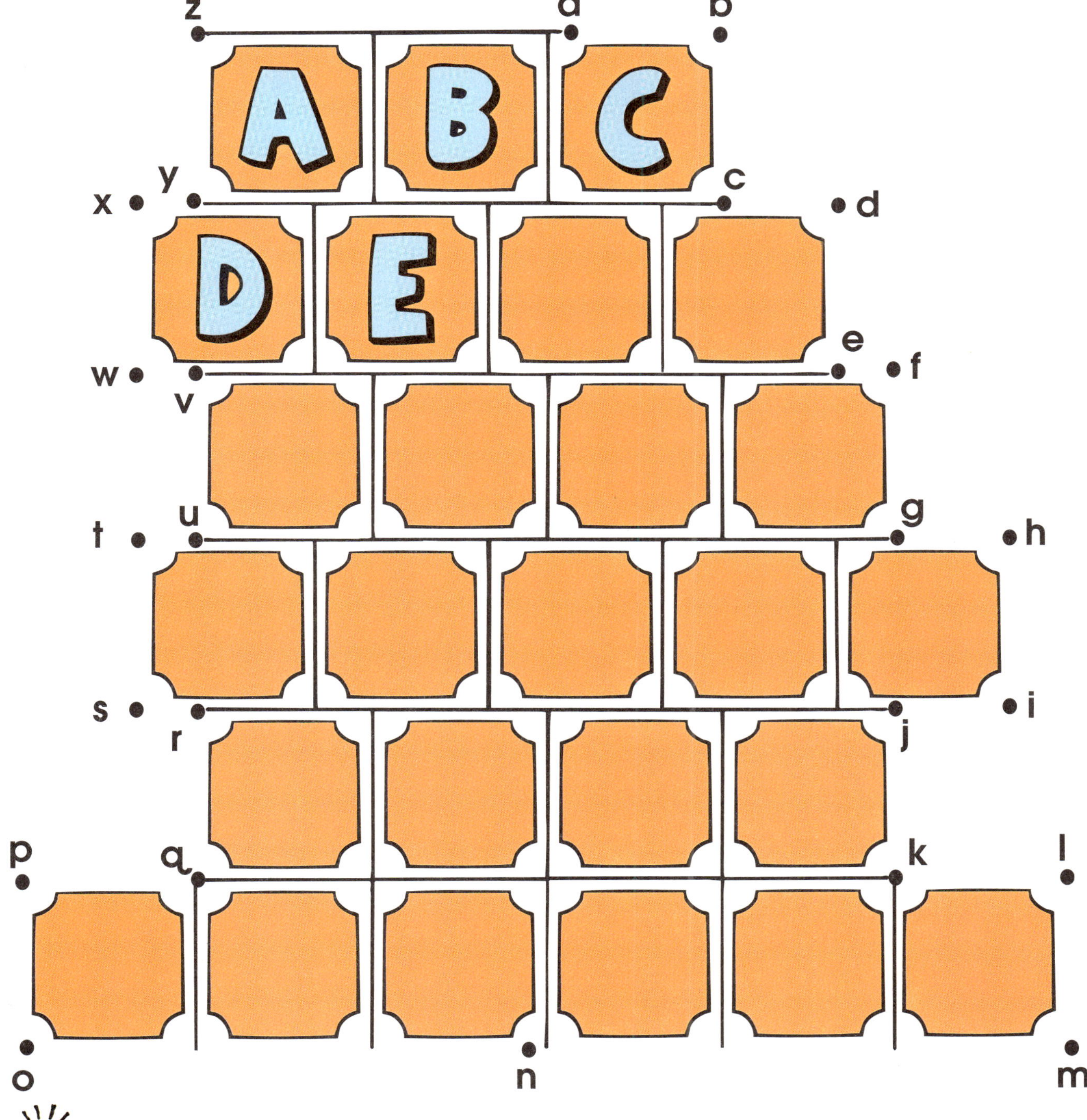

Color the blocks with the letters in your first name red.

Name ___________________________________

Clowning Around

Match the letter on each clown to its lowercase letter.

Oh, no! There they go!

Picking Letters

mini-book

I have Q, R, S, and T.

I have E, F, G, and H.

I have A, B, C, and D.

I have U, V, W, and X, Y, Z.

I have I, J, K, and L.

I have M, N, O, and P.

Scholastic Success With

NUMBERS AND COUNTING

Name ____________________

Zero at the Zoo

Trace and write.

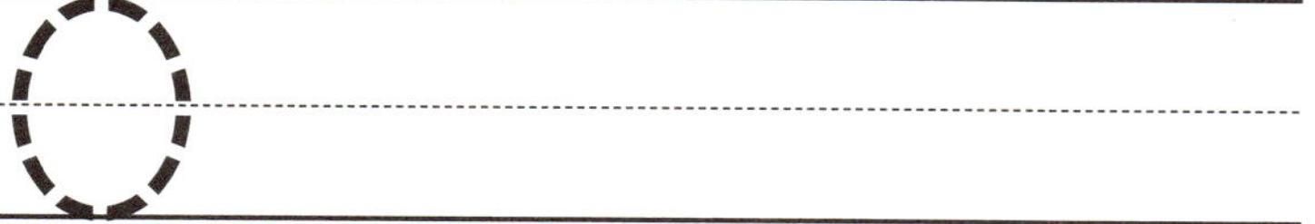

Zero is the number word for 0. Zero means none.
Circle the number that tells how many.

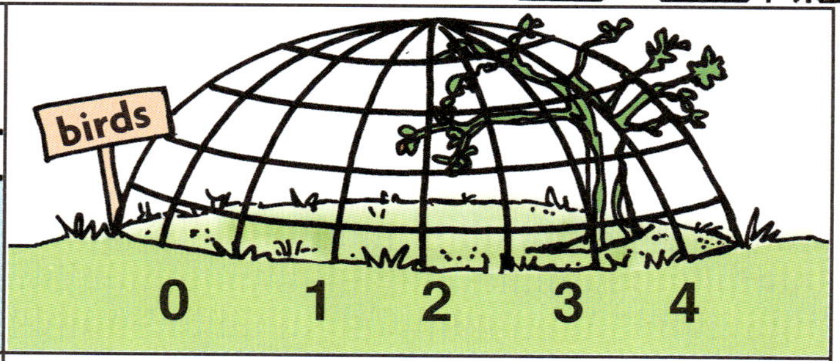

bears 0 1 2 3 4	birds 0 1 2 3 4
penguins 0 1 2 3 4	lions 0 1 2 3 4
camels 0 1 2 3 4	ducks 0 1 2 3 4
monkeys 0 1 2 3 4	seals 0 1 2 3 4

Name ______________________________

One Old Octopus

Trace and write.

1

Color each shape with 1 fish.

An Underwater Home

Count each group of things found in the sea. Color one of each.

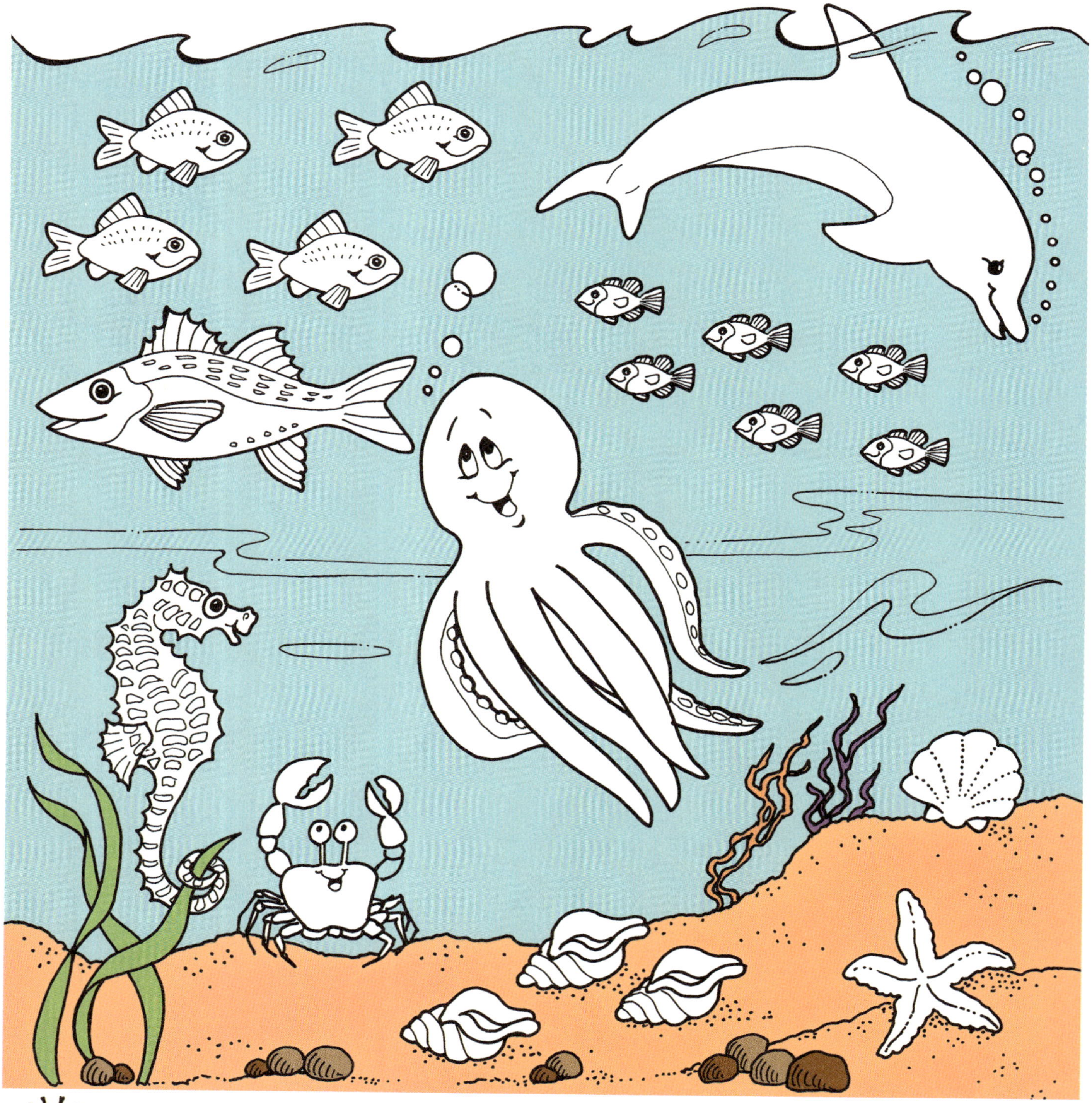

How many objects did you color?

Name ______________________________

Two Talking Turtles

Trace and write.

2

Color each circle with 2 dots.

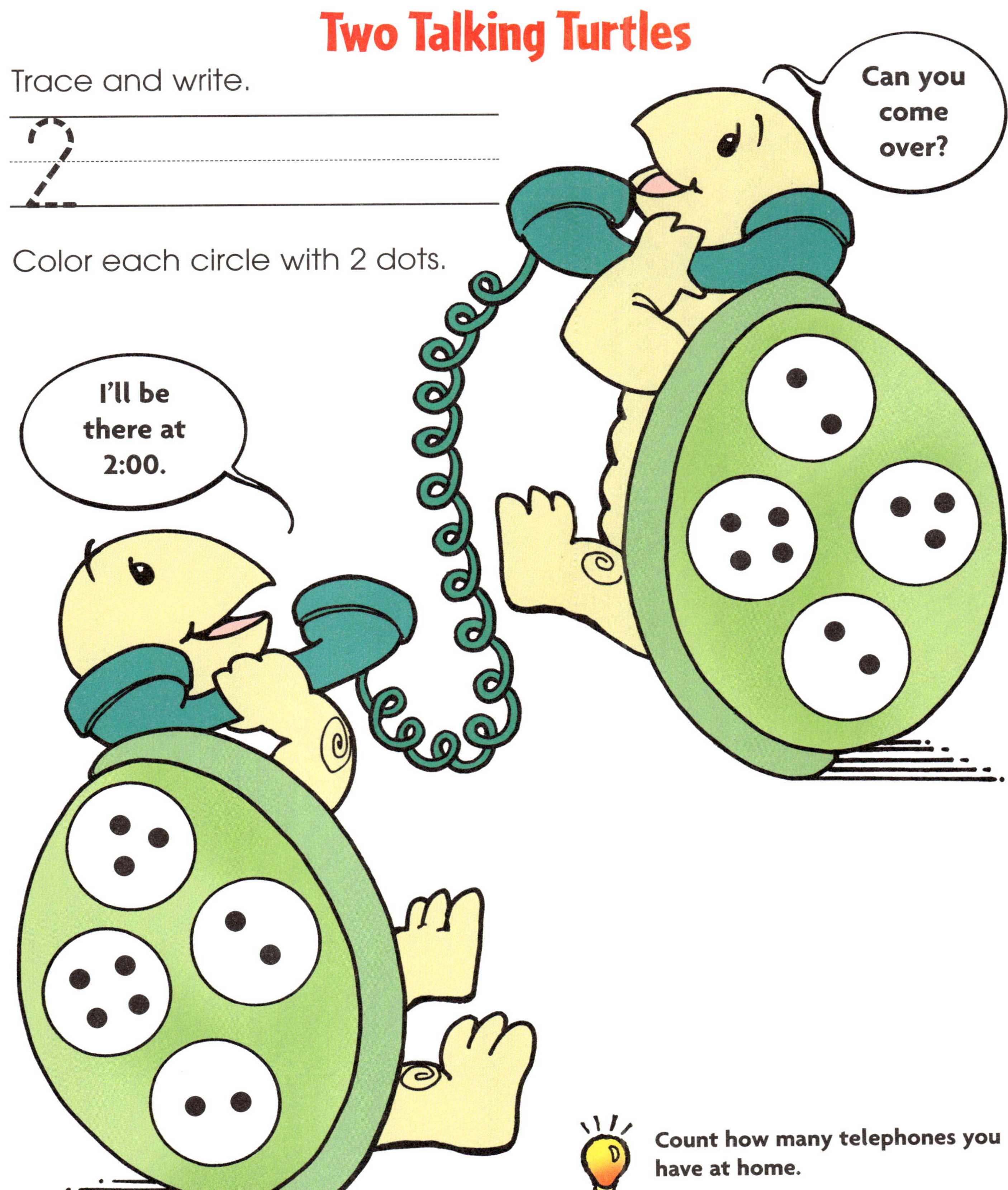

Count how many telephones you have at home.

Name ______________________________

Mrs. Tacky Turtle

Circle the number that tells how many.

ring	1	2
glasses	1	2
feather	1	2
shoe	1	2
purse	1	2
flower	1	2
bracelet	1	2

What else could Mrs. Turtle wear? Draw 2 of them.

Name ______________________________

Three Tiny Tugboats

Trace and write.

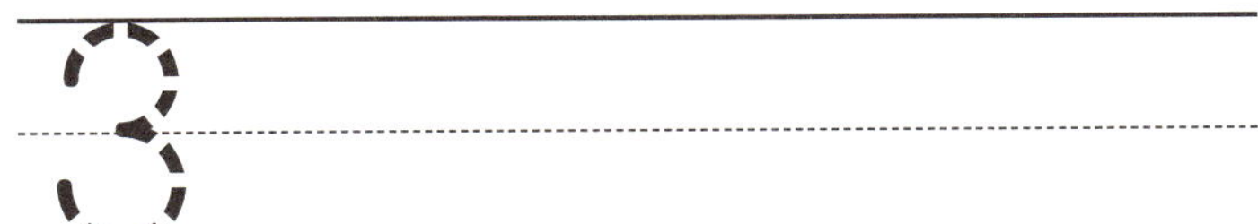

Color each barge with 3 objects.

Draw 3 logs on each barge.

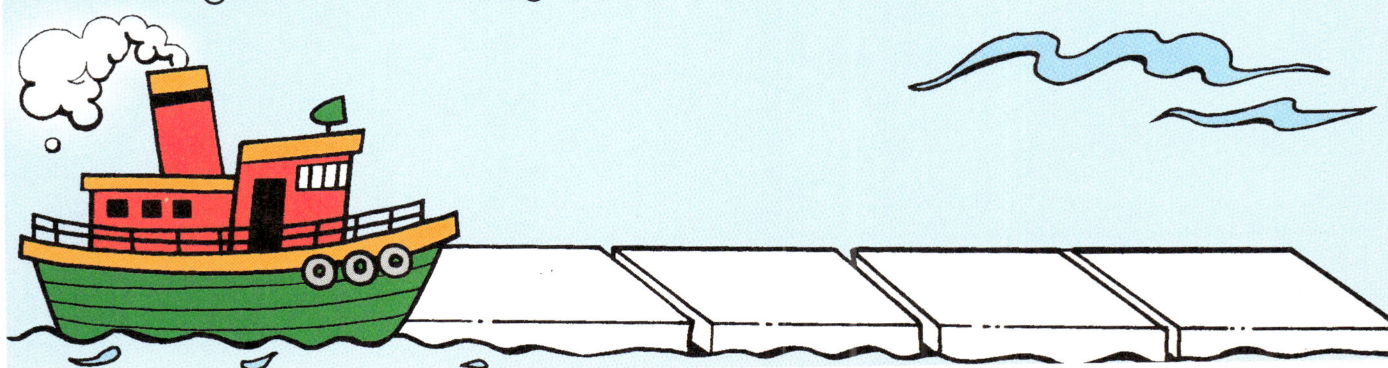

Name ______________________________________ 

Tugboat Tow

Use the code to color the picture.

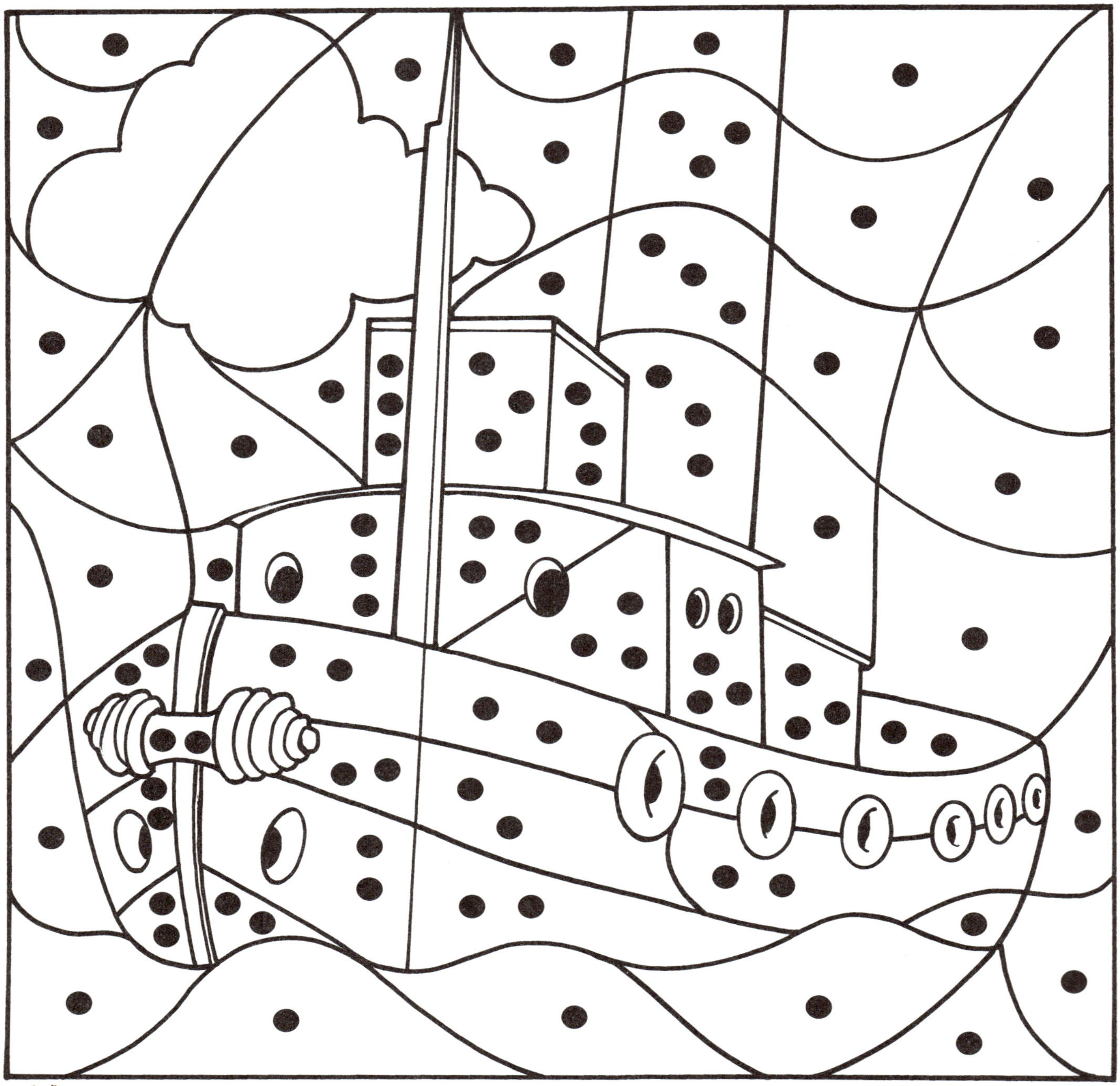

● 1 blue ● ● 2 

● ● ● 3 

Which color did you use to color the most spaces?

Name ______________________________

Four Fine Firefighters

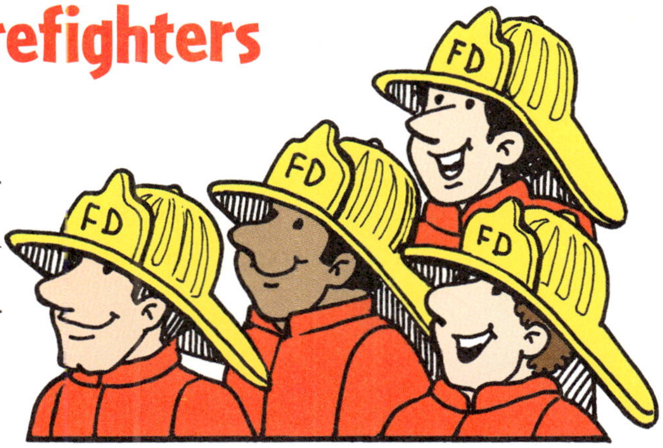

Trace and write.

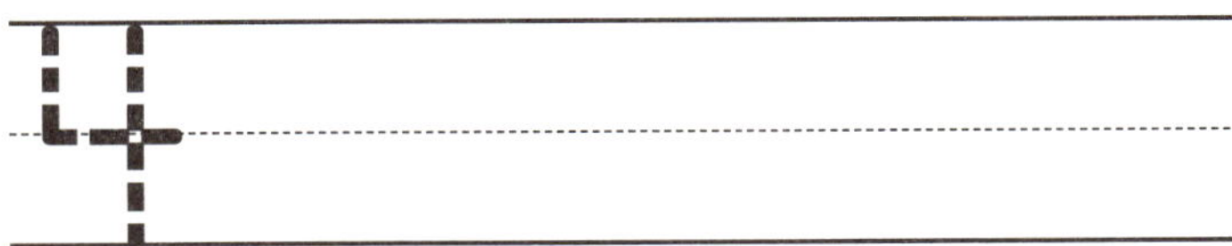

Color each dog with 4 spots.

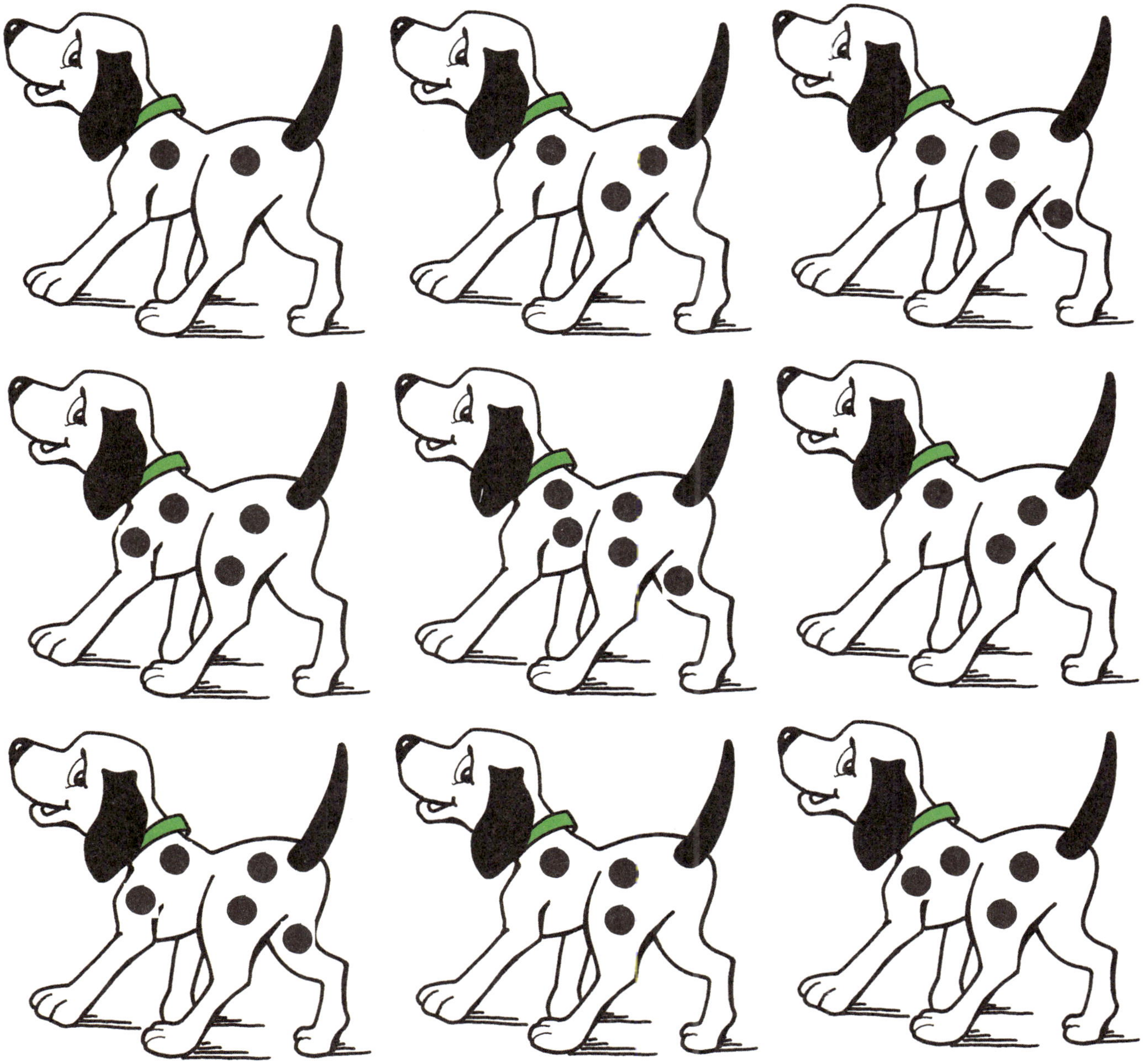

Name ______________________________

Climb to the Top

Count the objects on each step. Circle the matching number.

How many steps have 4 objects? __________

Name ___________________________________ 

Five Friendly Frogs

Trace and write.

5

Color each lily pad with 5 flies.

Name ___________________________________ 

Fast Frogs

Color each rock with 5 bugs to find which frog finishes first.

How many rocks have 4 bugs? ___________

Name ___________________________________

Six Smelly Shoes

Trace and write.

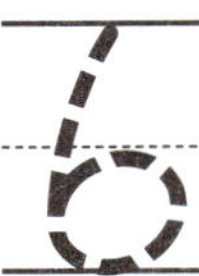

Circle 6 shoes in each box.

Draw more shoes to make 6.

Count the socks. Circle the right number. 5 6 7

Name ____________________

Two Make a Pair

Count the shapes on each shoe. Draw a line to the matching number.

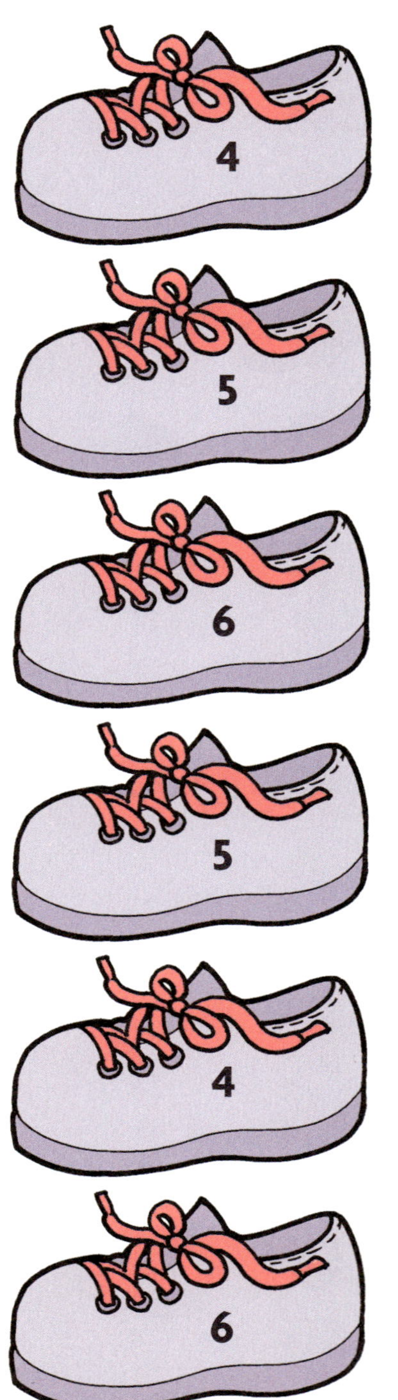

Count the shoes in your closet. How many shoes did you count?

Name ______________________________

Seven Seashells

Trace and write.

7

Color 7 shells in each box.

Name ______________________________  **Counting to 7**

Seashells by the Seashore

Count each kind of shell in the picture. Write the total number next to the correct shell. Circle the shells that total 7.

How many?  ________ How many?  ________

How many?  ________ How many?  

Circle the number that tells how many.

Name ______________________

Eight Electric Eels

Trace and write.

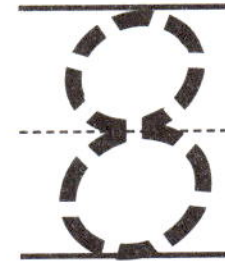

Draw more eels to make 8.

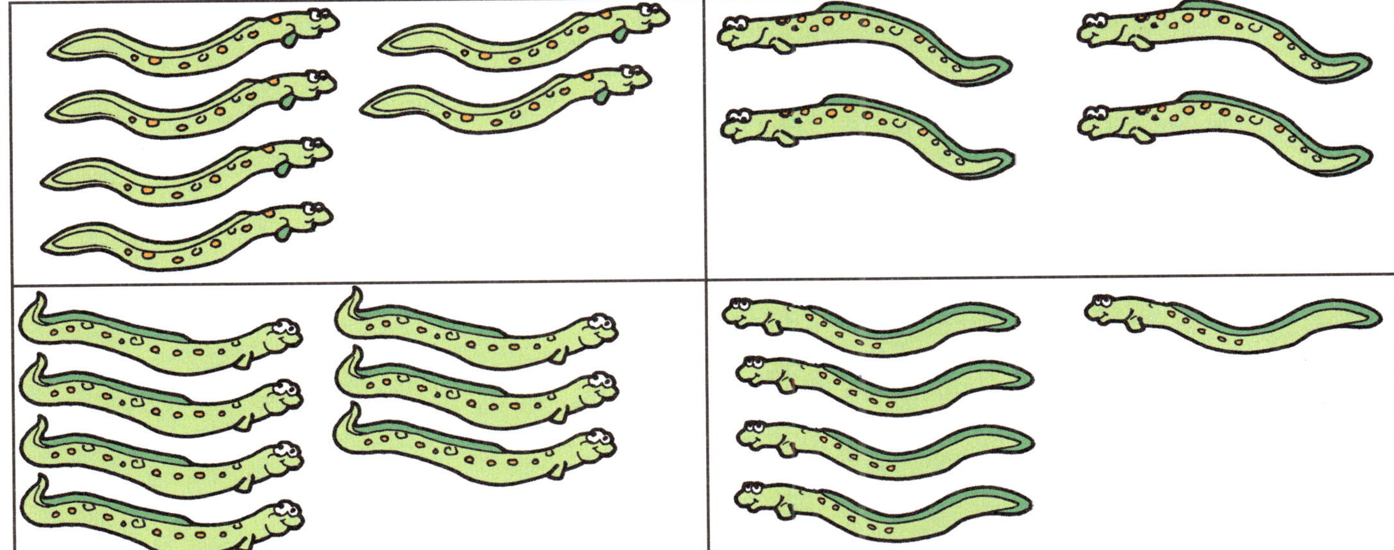

Count the eels. Color the matching number.

Eddie Eel Is Lost

Help Eddie Eel find his way back to the cave. Trace the path that goes in order from 1 to 8.

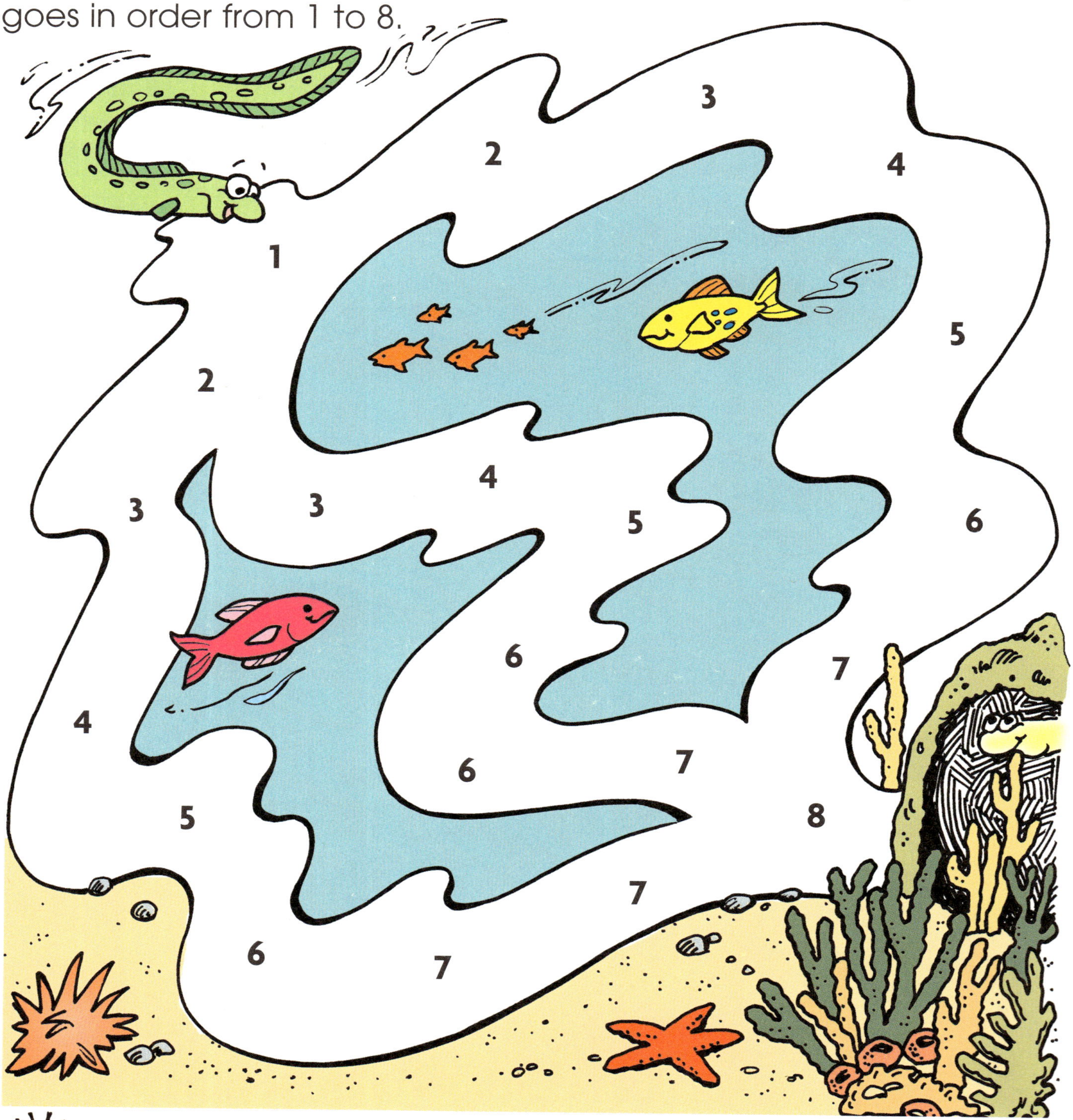

On another sheet of paper, draw a picture of 8 different sea creatures.

Name ______________________________

Nine Nice Nectarines

Trace and write.

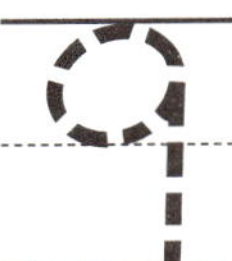

Color each basket that has 9 pieces of fruit.

Going to the Market

FRESH FRUIT

Count. Write how many. Color each fruit with 9.

 ________

 ________

 ________

 ________

 ________

 ________

On another sheet of paper, draw 9 pieces of your favorite fruit.

Name ___

Ten Railroad Ties

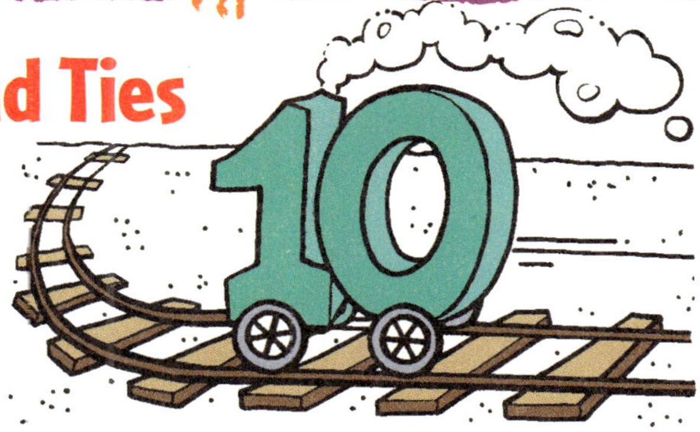

Trace and write.

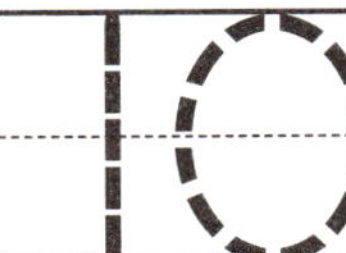

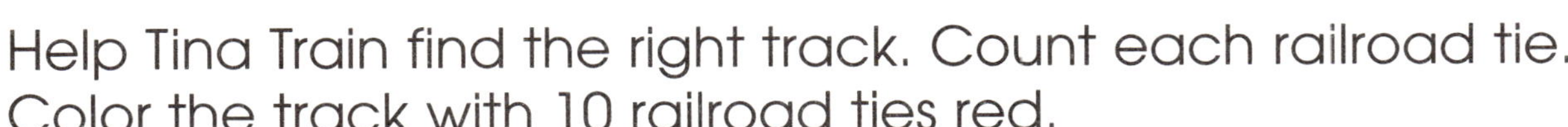

Help Tina Train find the right track. Count each railroad tie.
Color the track with 10 railroad ties red.

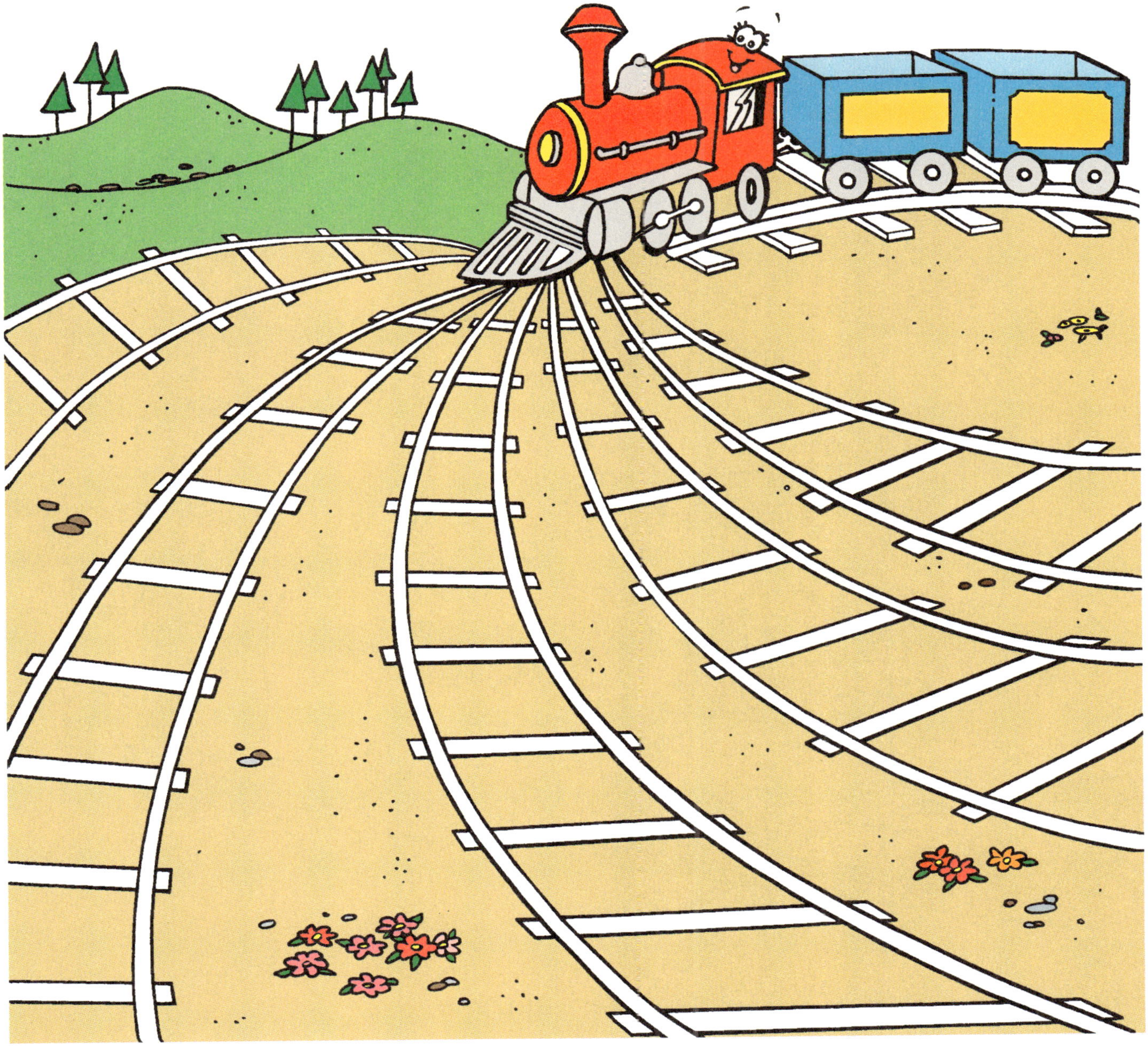

All Aboard

Color each train car with 8 barrels red.
Color each train car with 9 barrels blue.
Color each train car with 10 barrels green.

On another sheet of paper, draw a train with 10 train cars.

Name ______________________________ 

1, 2 . . . Presents for You

Draw a circle around each group of 1.

Draw a square around each group of 2.

Name ____

3, 4 . . . Let's Read More!

Draw a triangle around each group of 3.

Draw a diamond around each group of 4.

Name ____

5, 6 . . . Flowers to Pick

Draw an oval around each group of 5.

Draw a rectangle around each group of 6.

Name ____________________

7, 8 . . . Time to Skate

Color each group of 7 red.

Color each group of 8 yellow.

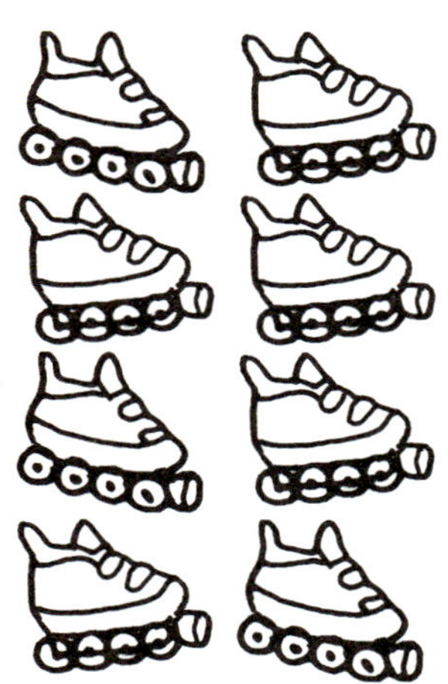

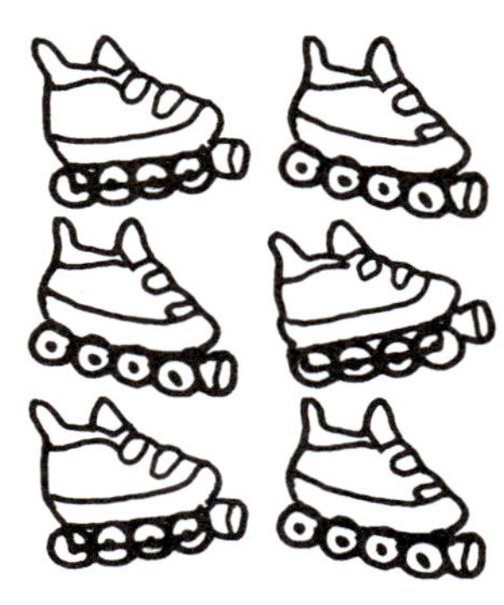

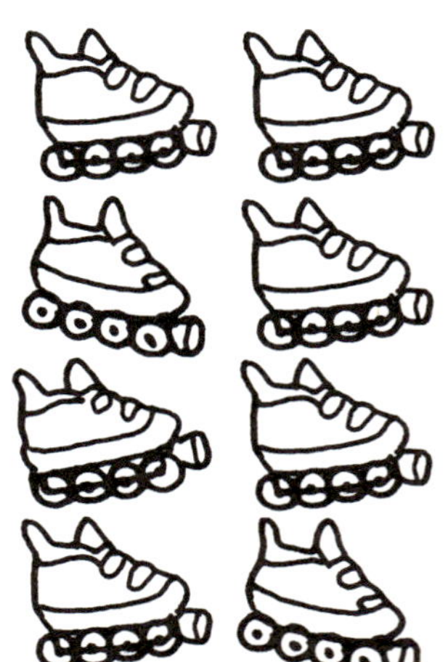

Name ____________________

9, 10 . . . It's Fun to Win!

Color each group of 9 blue.

Color each group of 10 green

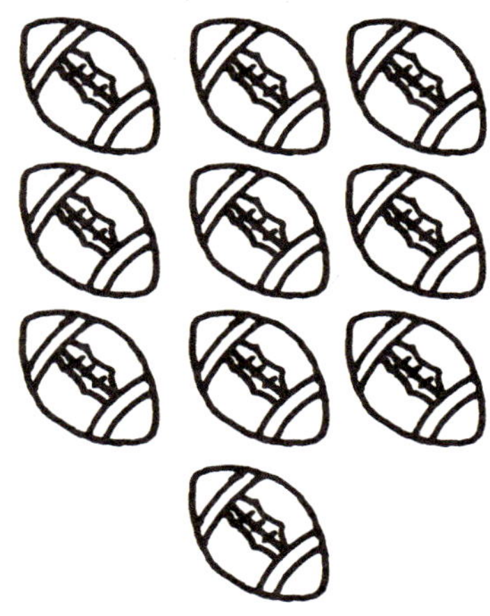

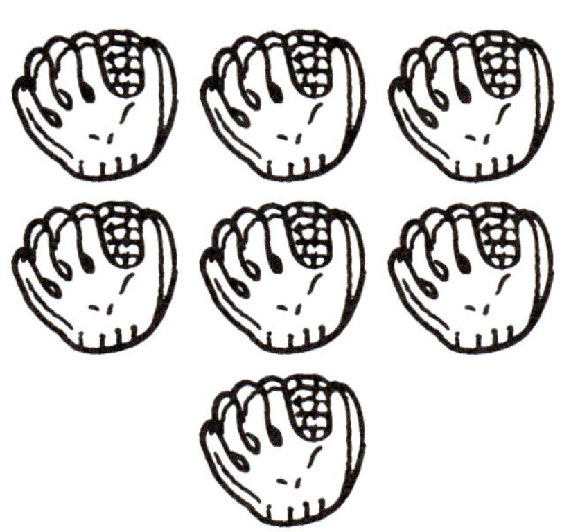

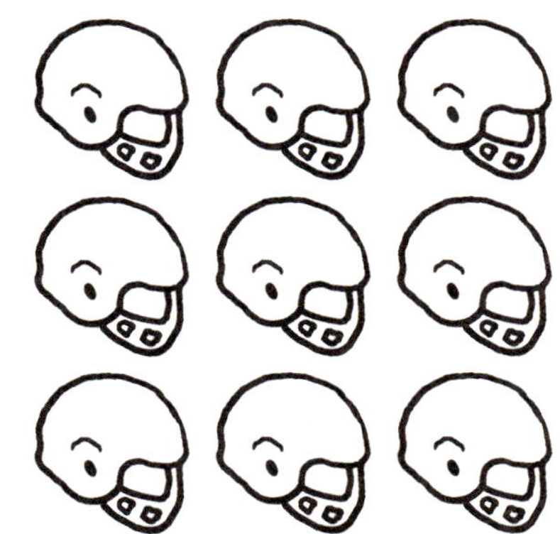

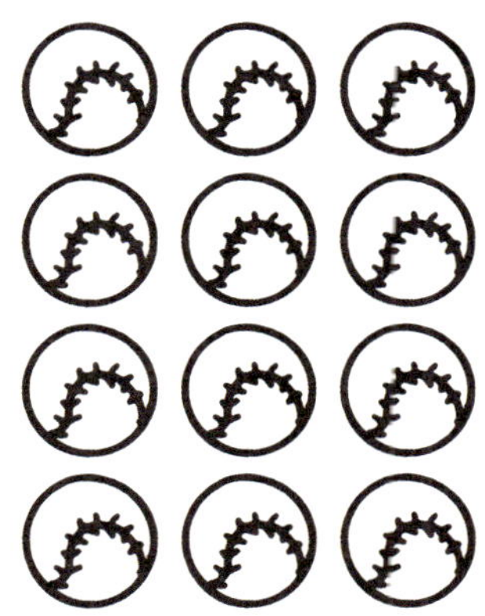

Name ___________________________________

Bunny Number Fun

Color.

1 = pink	2 = green	3 = blue
4 = red	5 = brown	6 = yellow
7 = purple	8 = black	9 = orange

Name ______________________________

A Colorful Garden

•	yellow	:	pink	⋮	red
∷	black	⁙	orange	⠿	purple
⁝•⁝	blue	∷∷	green	⋮⋮⋮	brown

Name ______________________________

Gumball Goodies

Color.

	blue		red		green
	orange		purple		black
	brown		white		yellow

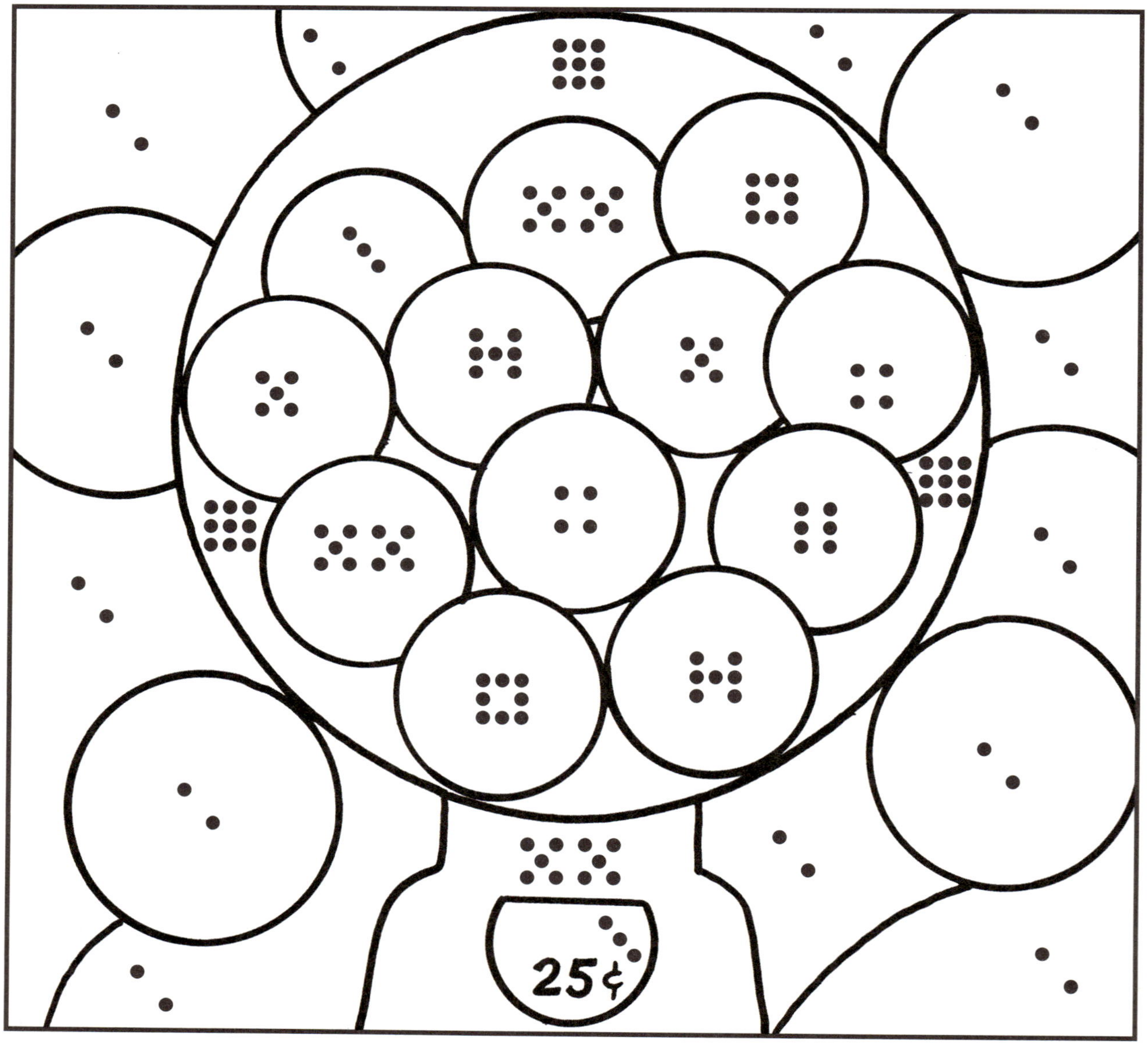

25¢

Name ______________________________

Count and Color

Color the correct number of objects.

1	
6	
4	
10	
5	
2	
7	
8	
3	
9	

Name ______________________________________

Ordering numbers from 1 to 10

Lighten Things Up!

Connect the dots from **1** to **10**. Color.

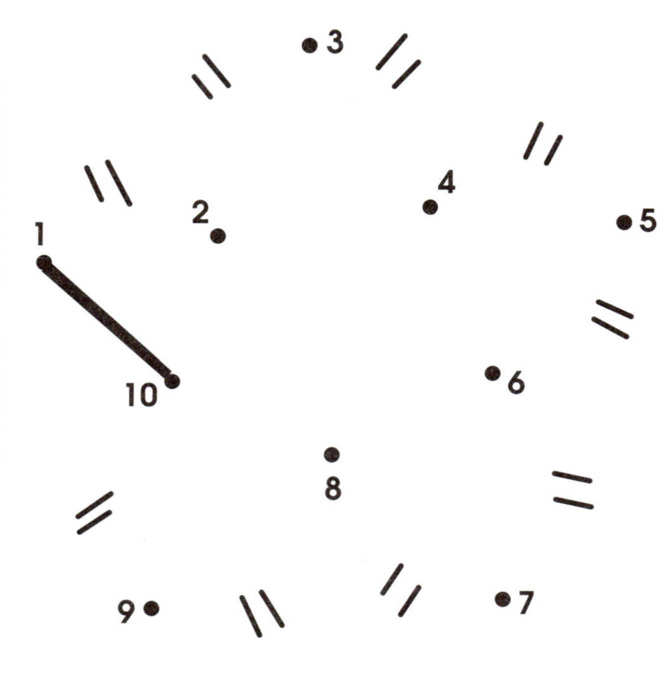

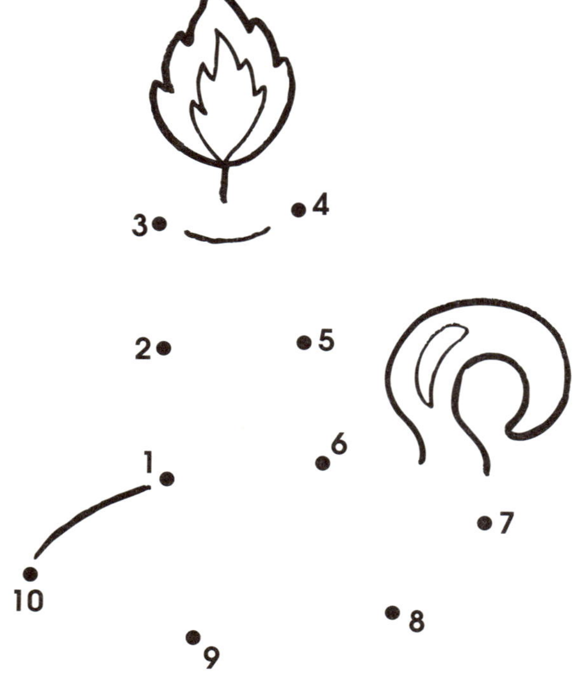

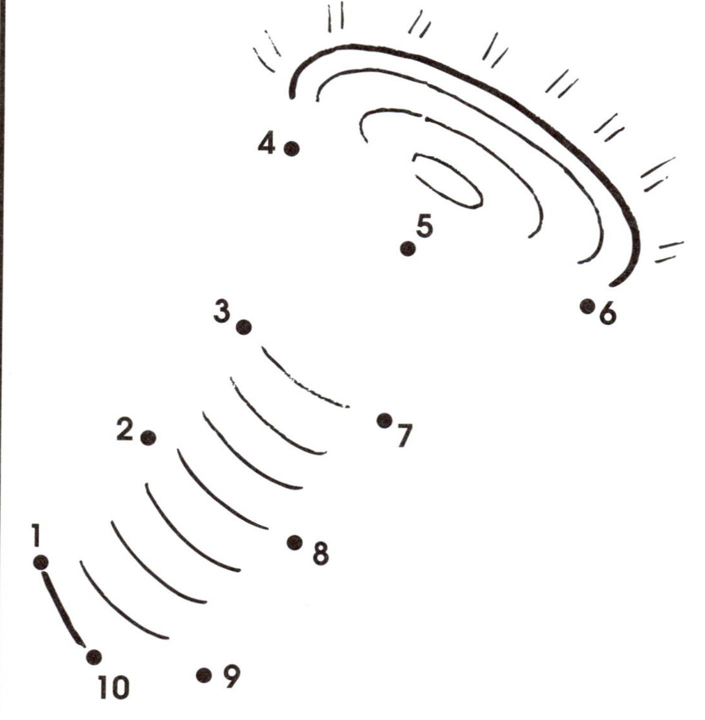

Name ____

Calling All Alarms

Help the fire truck get to the fire. Color the path that goes in order from **1** to **10**.

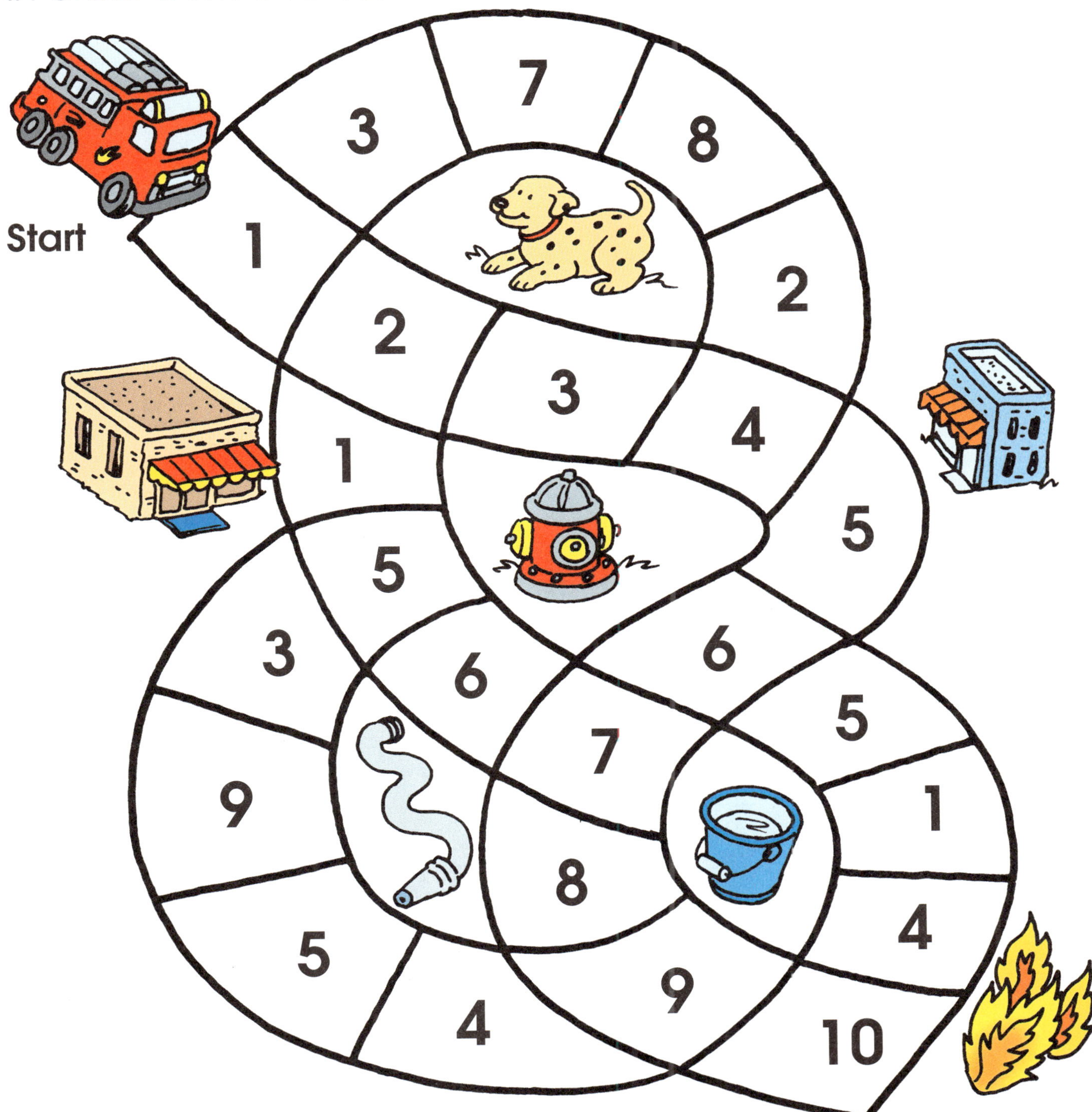

Name ______________________________________

Home Sweet Home

Write each missing number.

5 6 8

1 2 3

3 5 6

7 9 10

Name ______________________________

Eleven Excited Earthworms

Trace and write.

11

Color each set of 11 earthworms.

Name ______________________________

Betty Bookworm

Count each stack of books. Draw a line to match each stack to the correct number.

Color the stack with 11 books.

Name ________________________________

Twelve Tasty Treats

Trace and write.

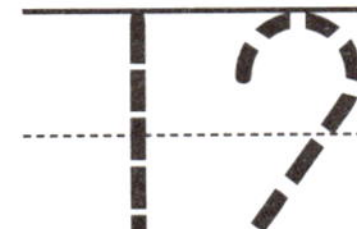

Count the candy in each jar. Color each jar with 12.

Gingerbread Man

Help the Gingerbread Man find his gingerbread house. Color the path that goes in order from 1 to 12.

Count the lollipops in the picture. Draw more lollipops to make 12.

Name ___________________________

Thirteen Tasty Bones

Trace and write.

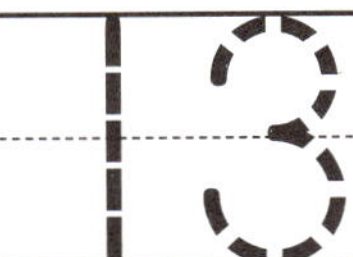

Circle 13 bones in each picture.

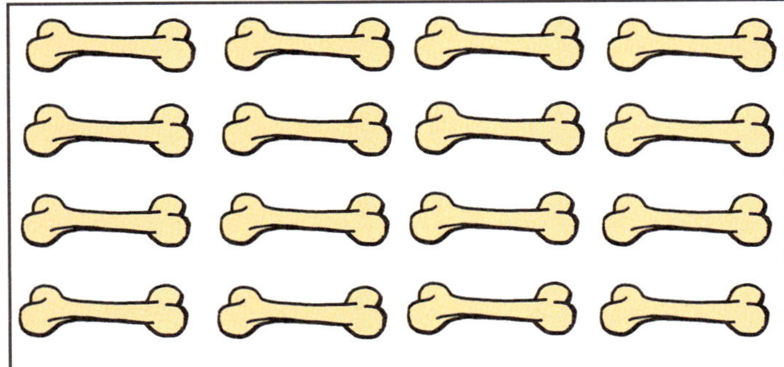

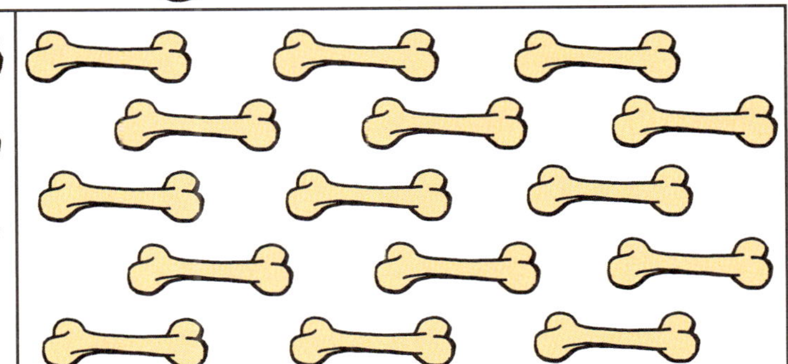

Draw more bones to make 13.

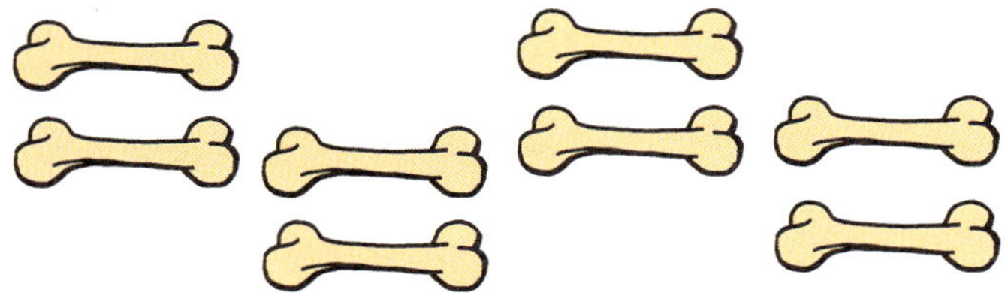

Count the bones. Circle the correct number. 12 13 14

Name ______________________________  **Counting to 13**

Where, Oh Where, Has My Puppy Gone?

Help the puppy find its home. Trace the path that goes in order from 1 to 13.

Write the number that comes next in each bone.

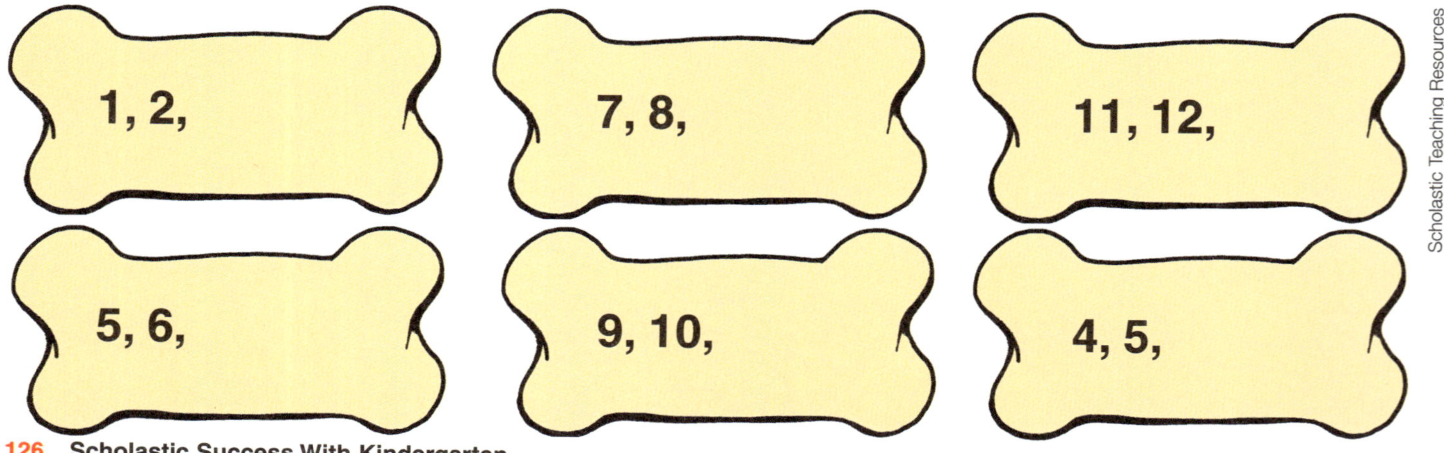

Name ___________________________

Juggling Fourteen Balls

Trace and write.

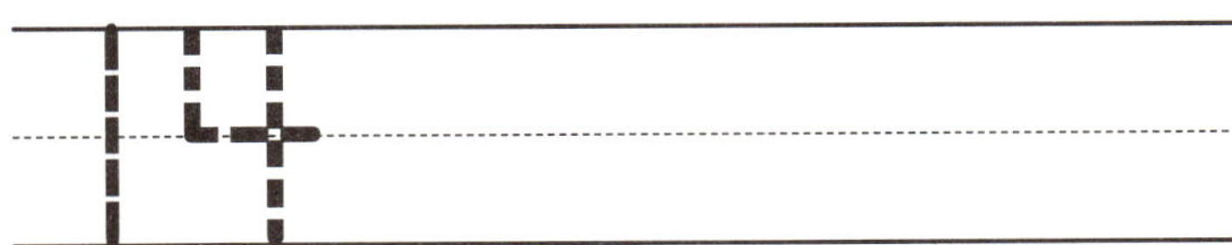

Color each ball with 14 dots.

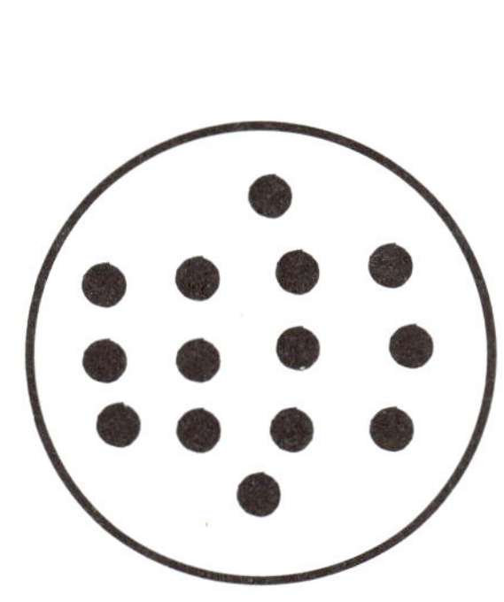
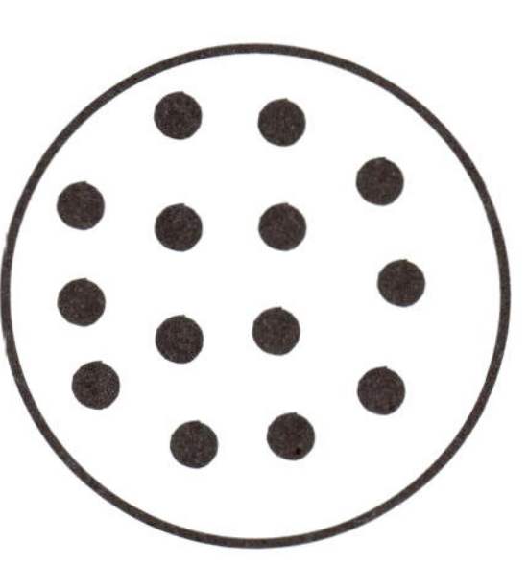
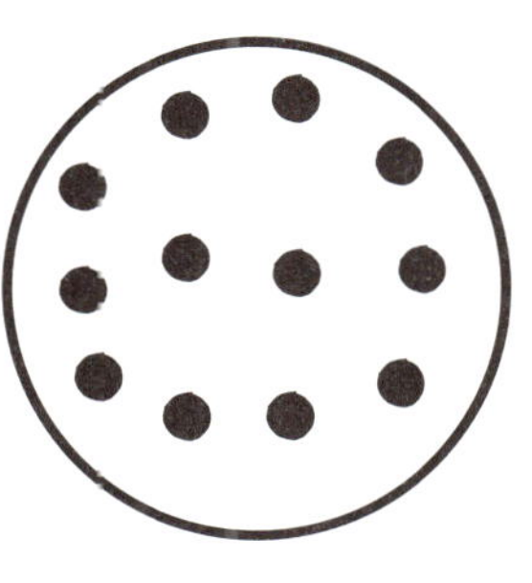
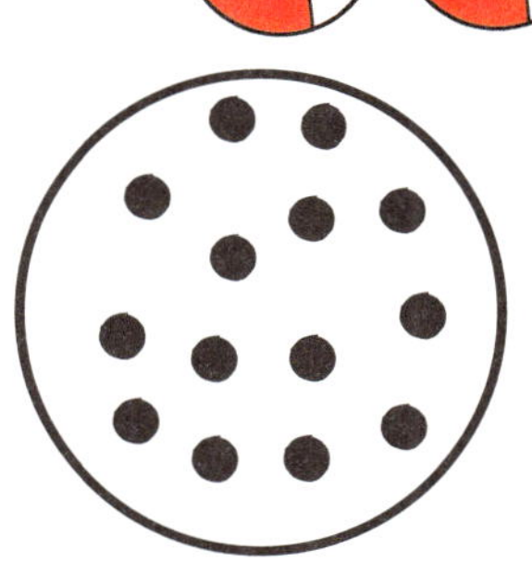

Name ______________________________

Catch the Ball!

Count. Write how many.

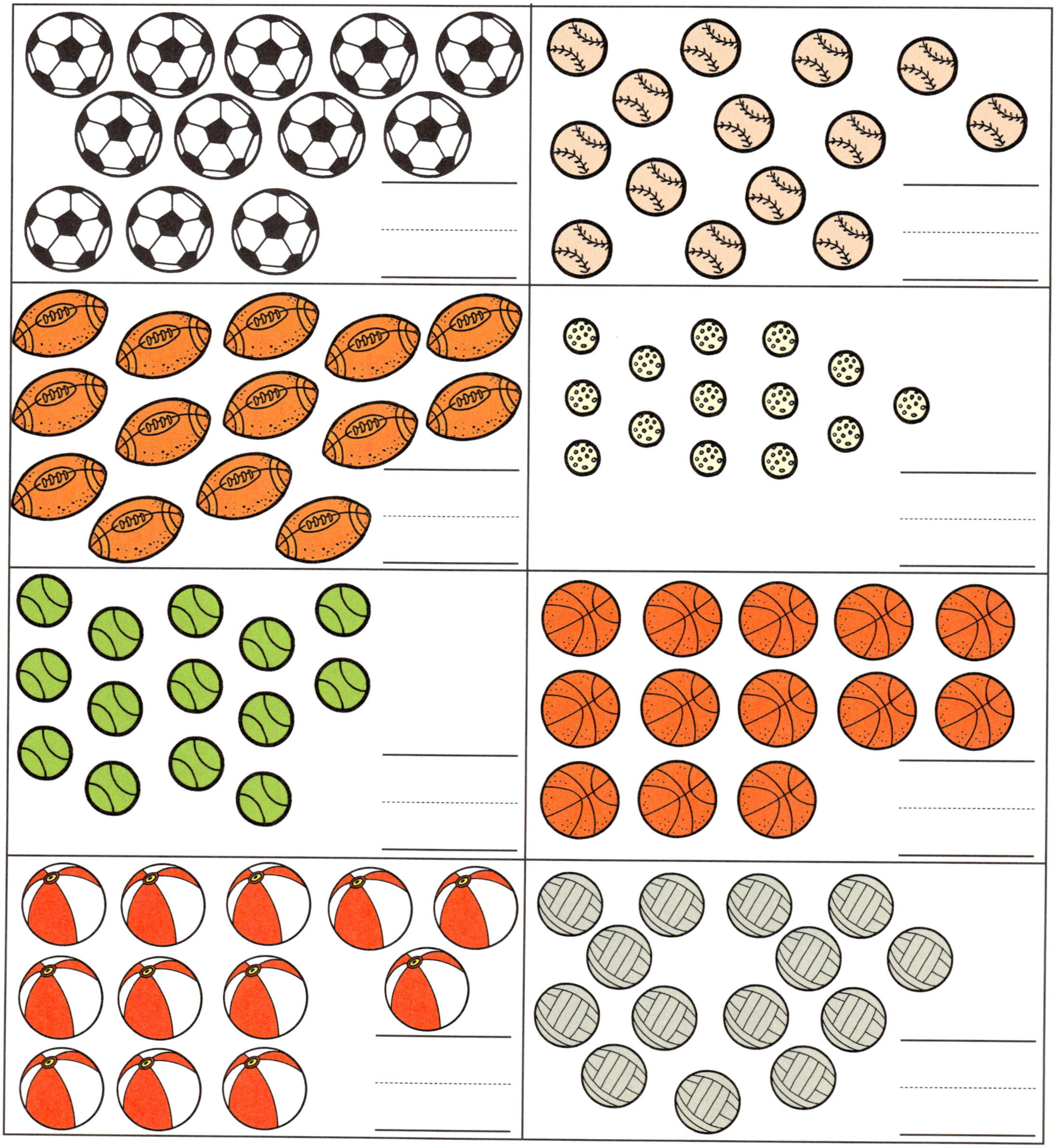

Name ______________________________

Fifteen Pennies

Trace and write.

15

Count the pennies in each bank. Color each bank with 15.

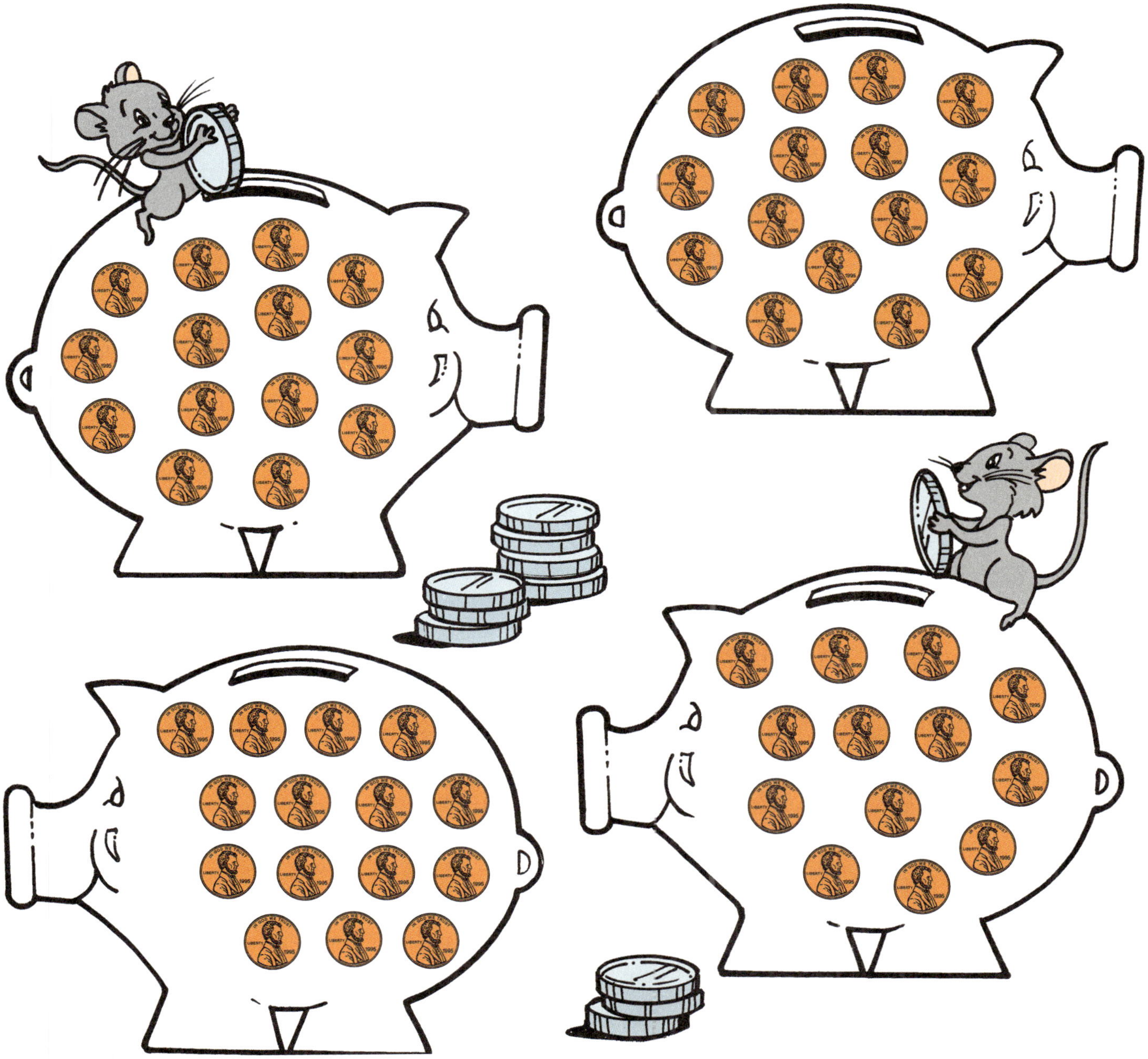

Name ______________________________ 

A Penny in Your Pocket

A penny equals 1¢. Count the pennies in each pocket. Write the total.

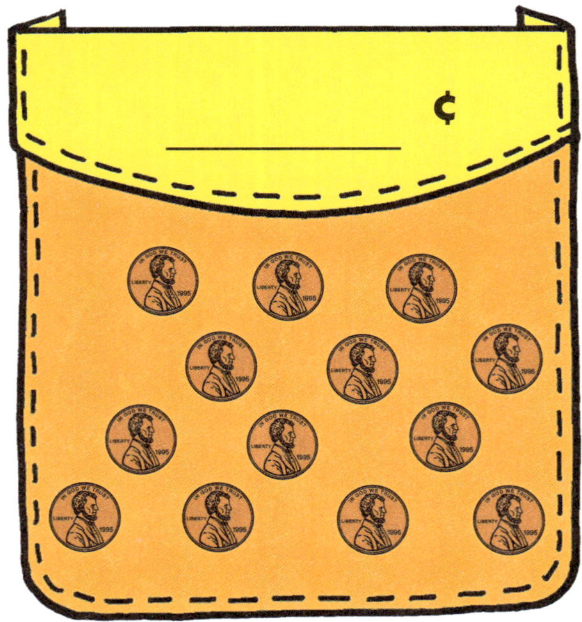

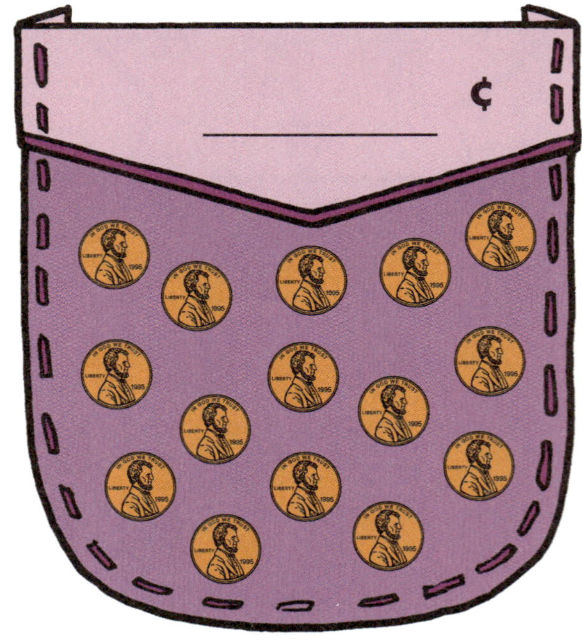

Find 15 pennies at home. Count them as you put them in your bank.

Name ______________________________

Sixteen Kites

Trace and write.

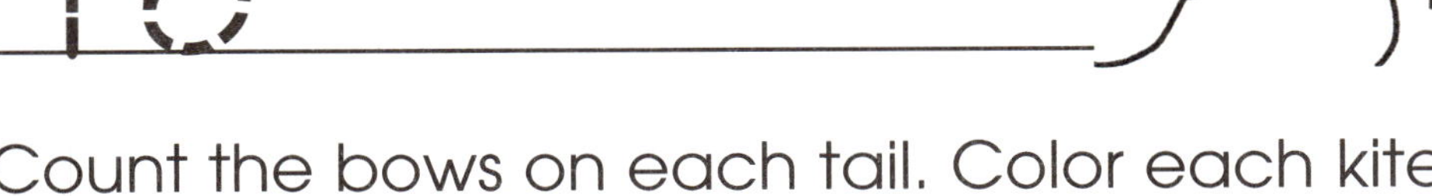

Count the bows on each tail. Color each kite with 16 bows.

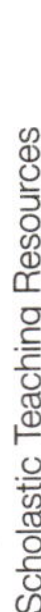

Flying High

Connect the dots from 1 to 16. Color the picture.

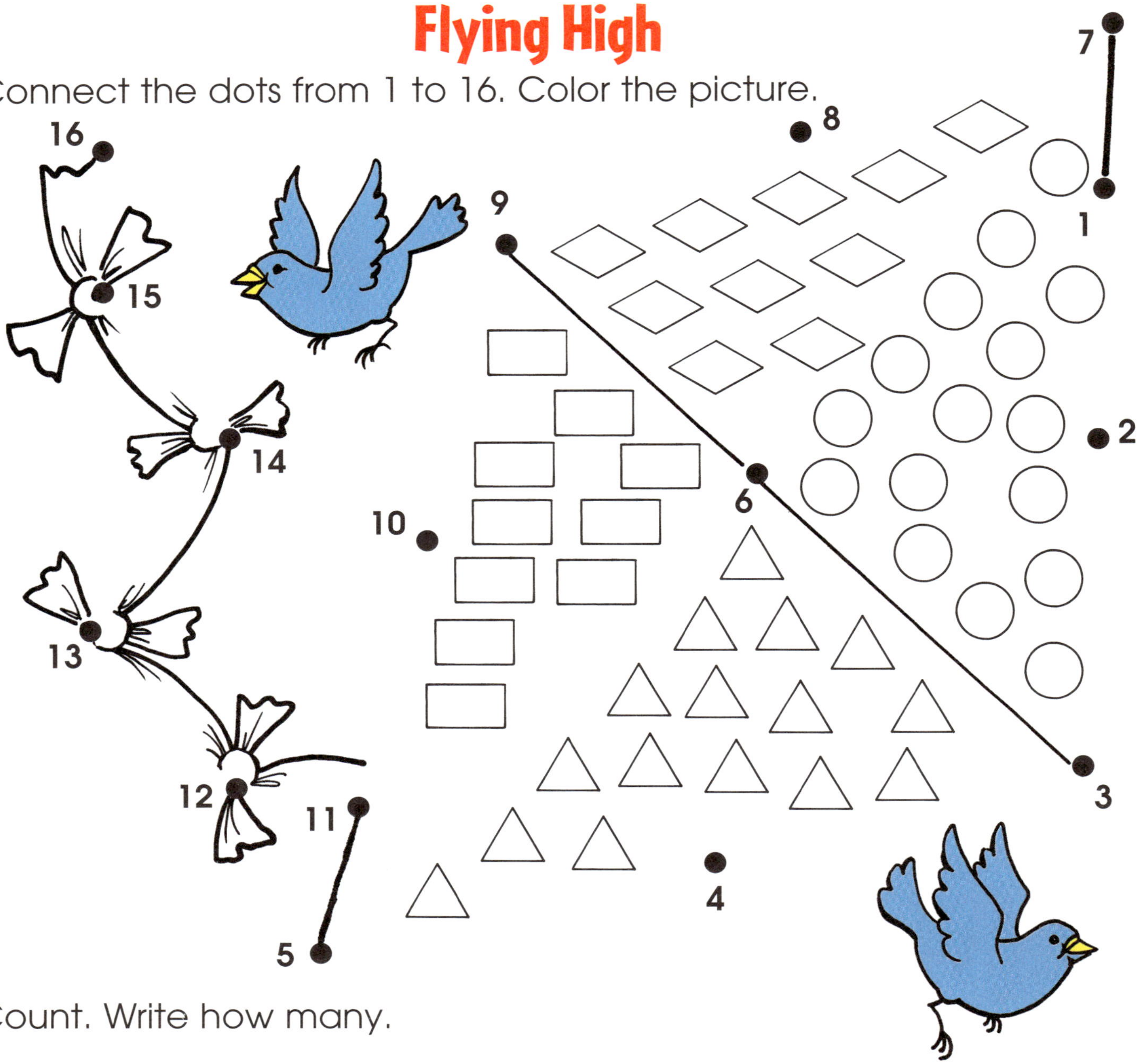

16 15 14 13 12 11 10 9 8 7 1 2 6 3 4 5

Count. Write how many.

Name ______________________________________

Seventeen Gallons of Gas

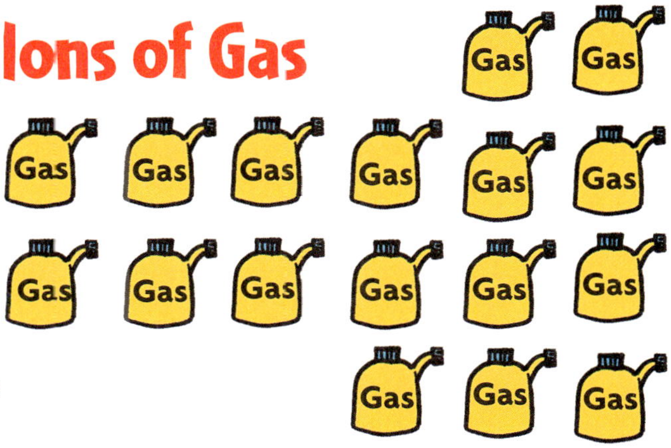

Trace and write.

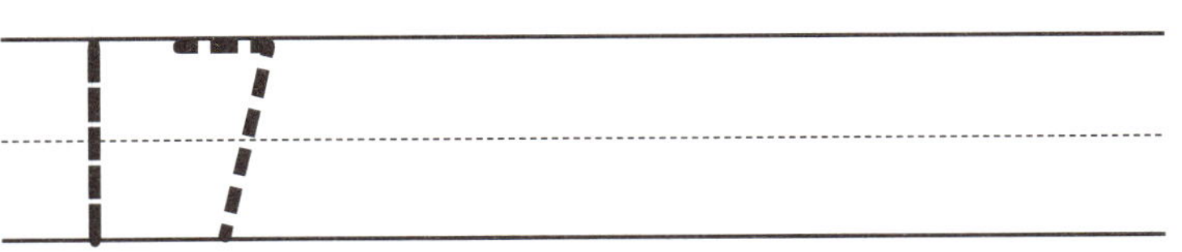

Find the gas pump by following the numbers in order from 1 to 17.

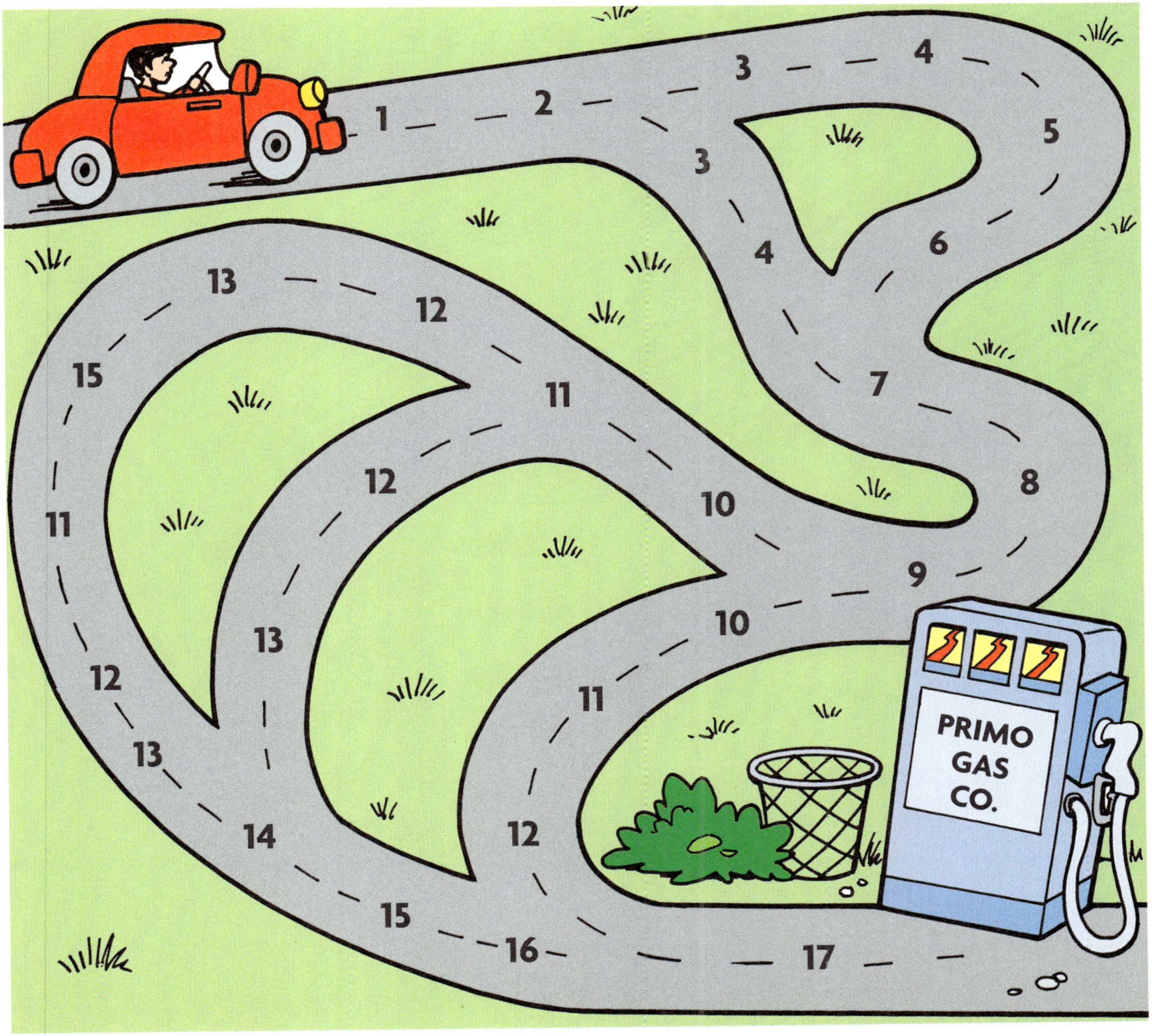

Name ______________________ 

Way to Go!

Count. Write how many.

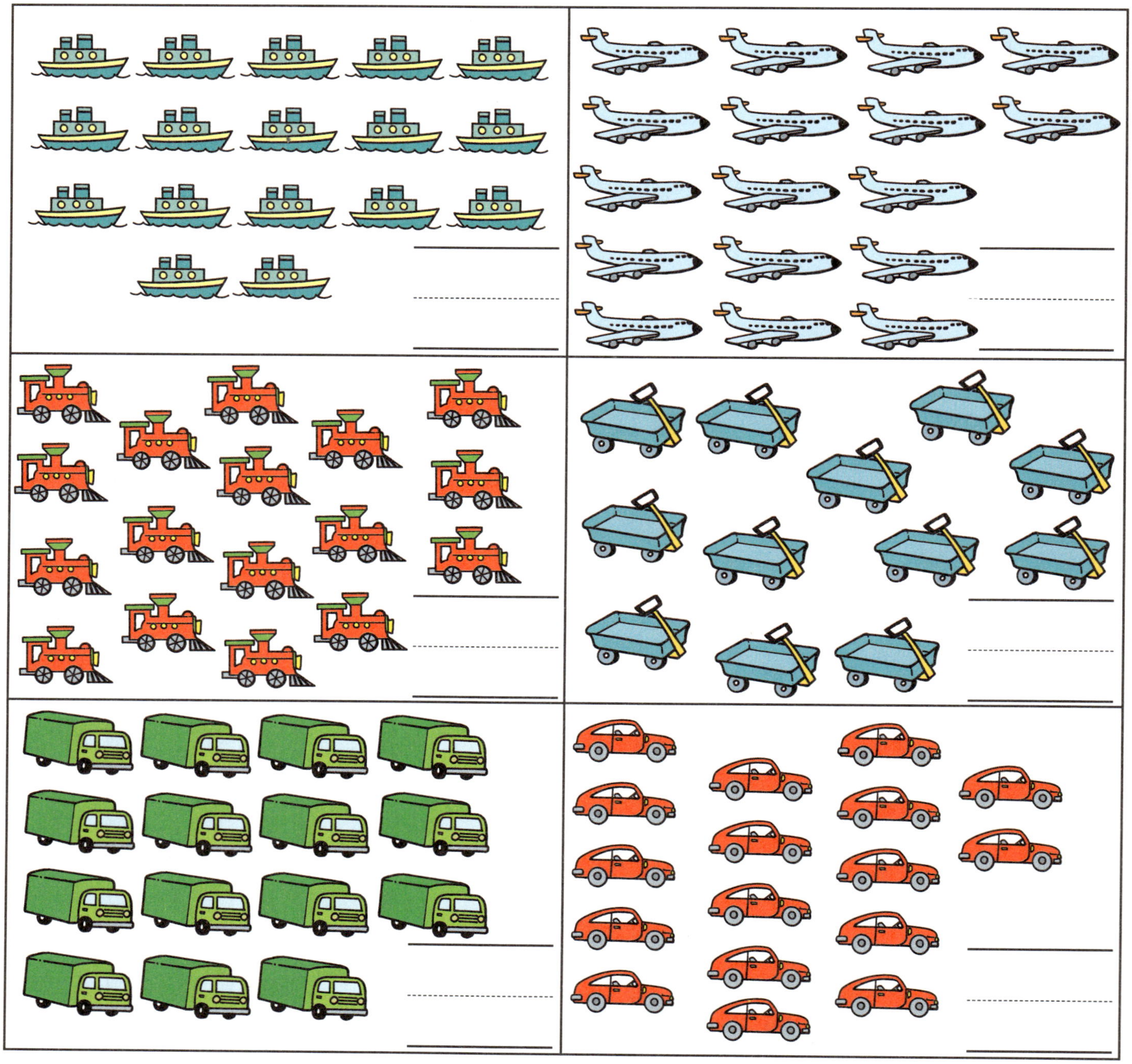

 **On another sheet of paper, draw a train with 17 cars.**

Name ___________________________ 

Eighteen Stars

Trace and write.

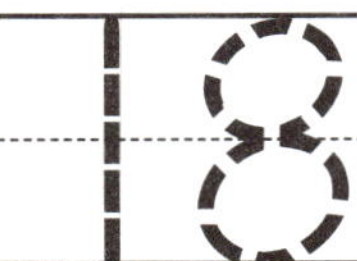

Circle 18 stars in each picture.

Draw more stars to make 18.

Count the planets. Write the number. __________

Name ______________________________ 

Out of This World

Count. Write how many. Color each group of 18 objects.

Name ______________________________

Nineteen Marbles

Trace and write.

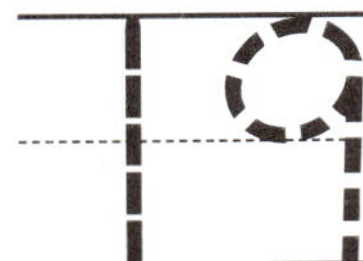

Circle the number that tells how many. Color each group with 19 marbles.

17 18 19

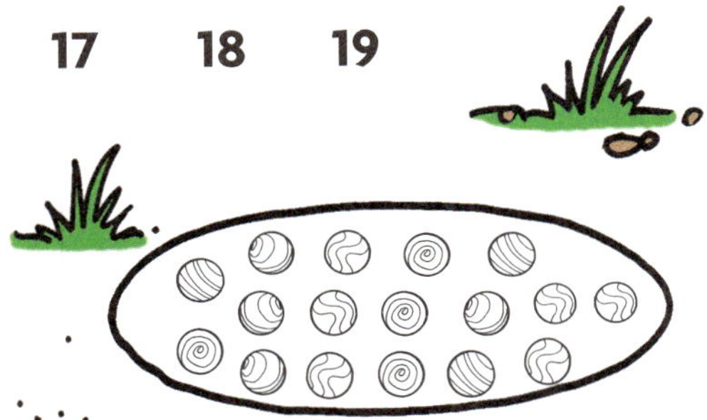

17 18 19

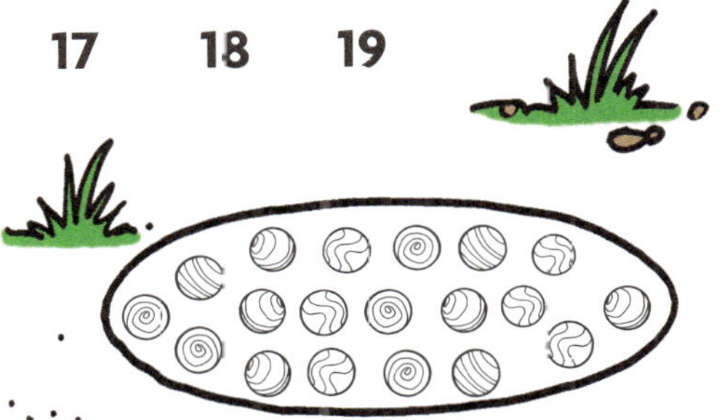

17 18 19

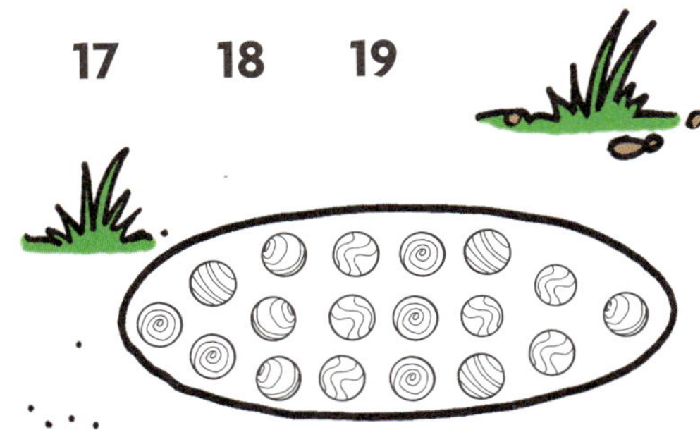

17 18 19

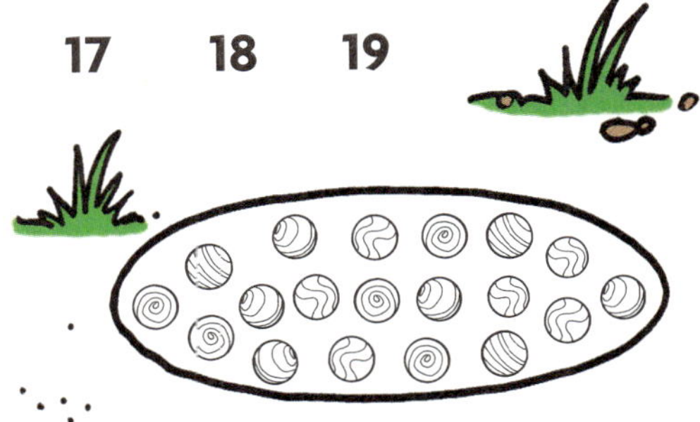

17 18 19

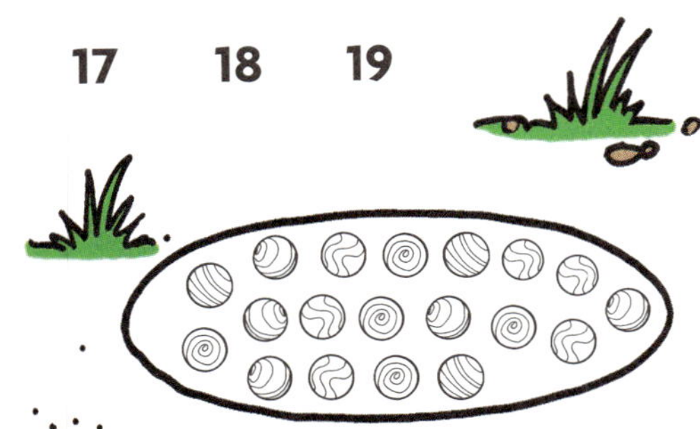

17 18 19

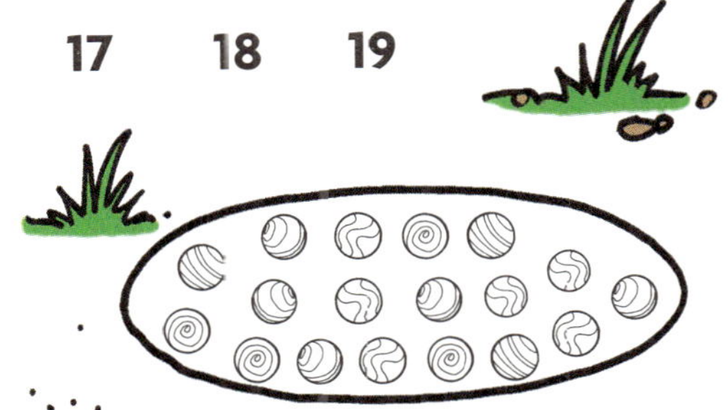

Name ________________________________

Let's Play Marbles

Circle 19 marbles.

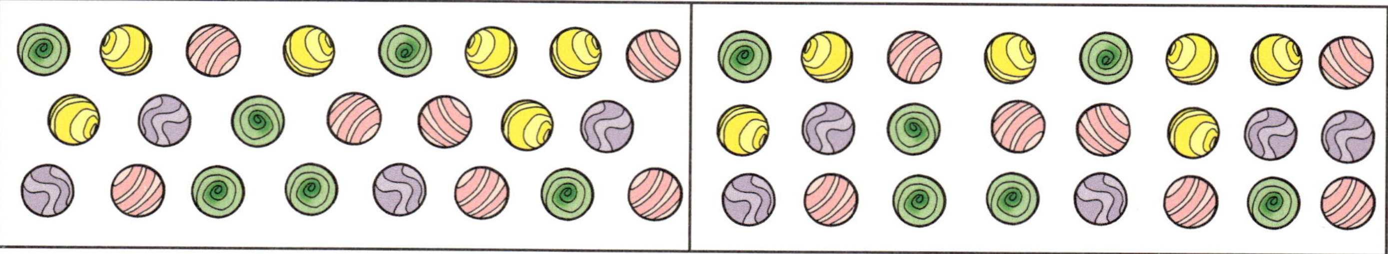

Draw more marbles to make 19.

Count the marbles. Write the number.

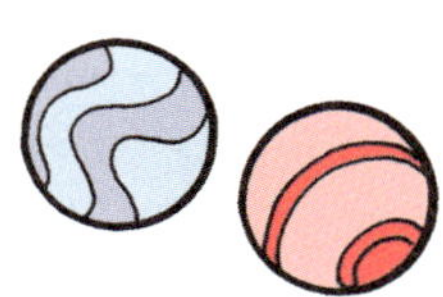

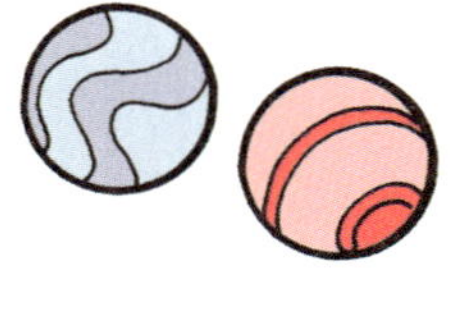

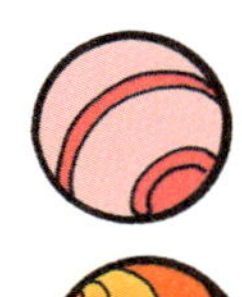

____

Name ____________________

Twenty Butterflies to Count

Trace and write.

20

Write the numbers 1 to 20 on the trail.

Start

Find and color 20 butterflies in the picture.

Name ____________________

Don't Bug Me!

Count each group of bugs. Draw a line to the matching number.

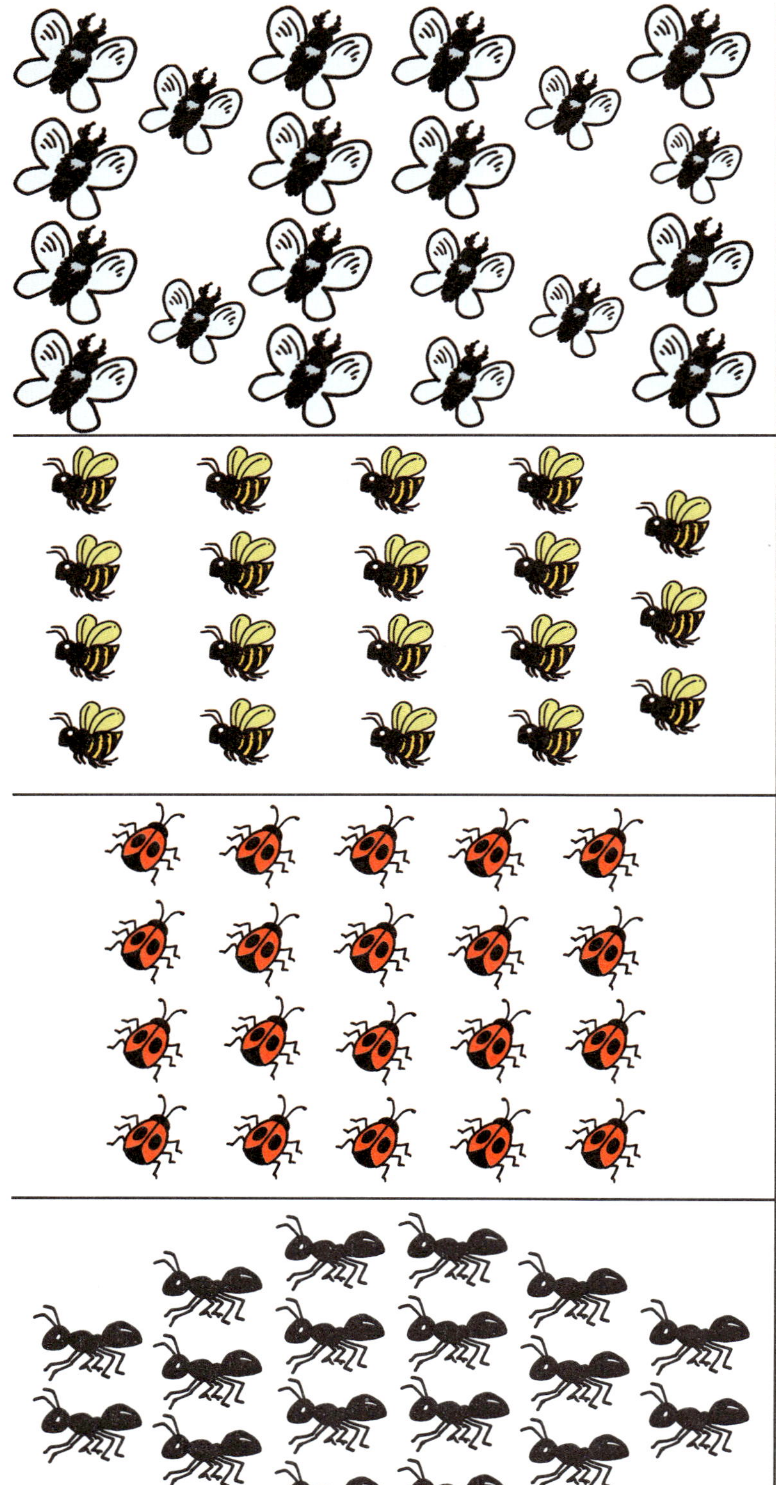

Name ____

11, 12 . . . It's on the Shelf!

Draw a circle around each group of 11.

Draw a square around each group of 12.

13, 14 . . . Let's Play the Tambourine!

Draw an oval around each group of 13.

Draw a rectangle around each group of 14.

Name ______________________________________

15, 16 . . . Eat Each Green Bean!

Draw a circle around each group of 15.

Draw a rectangle around each group of 16.

Name ____

17, 18 . . . Don't Forget the Sunscreen!

Draw a circle around each group of 17.

Draw a square around each group of 18.

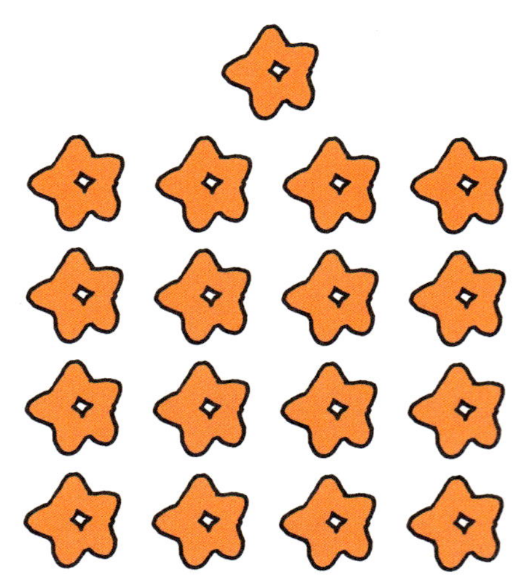

Name ______________________________________

19, 20 . . . There Are Plenty!

Draw a circle around each group of 19.

Draw a square around each group of 20.

Name ______________________________

Time to Build

Color. 11 = yellow 12 = black 13 = blue
14 = white 15 = orange 16 = green
17 = red 18 = purple 19 = brown
20 = pink

Name ____________________

Let's Count!

Color the correct number of objects.

14	
12	
16	
11	
18	
15	
17	
13	

Name ______________________________

Fun Fruits

Match.

13

14

15

16

17

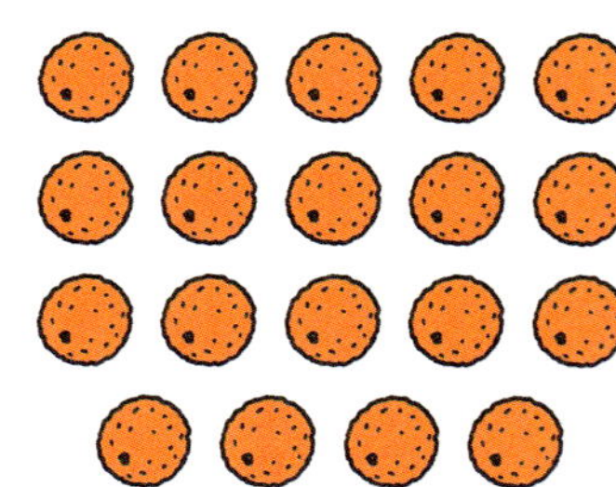

18

19

20

Name ____

Flying High

Color the bows on the tails to match the number above each kite.

20 16 15 17 14 11 12 13

Juggling Act

Write each missing number.

9

12

5

15

1

18

Name ______________________________________

Each Number in Its Spot

Write each missing number.

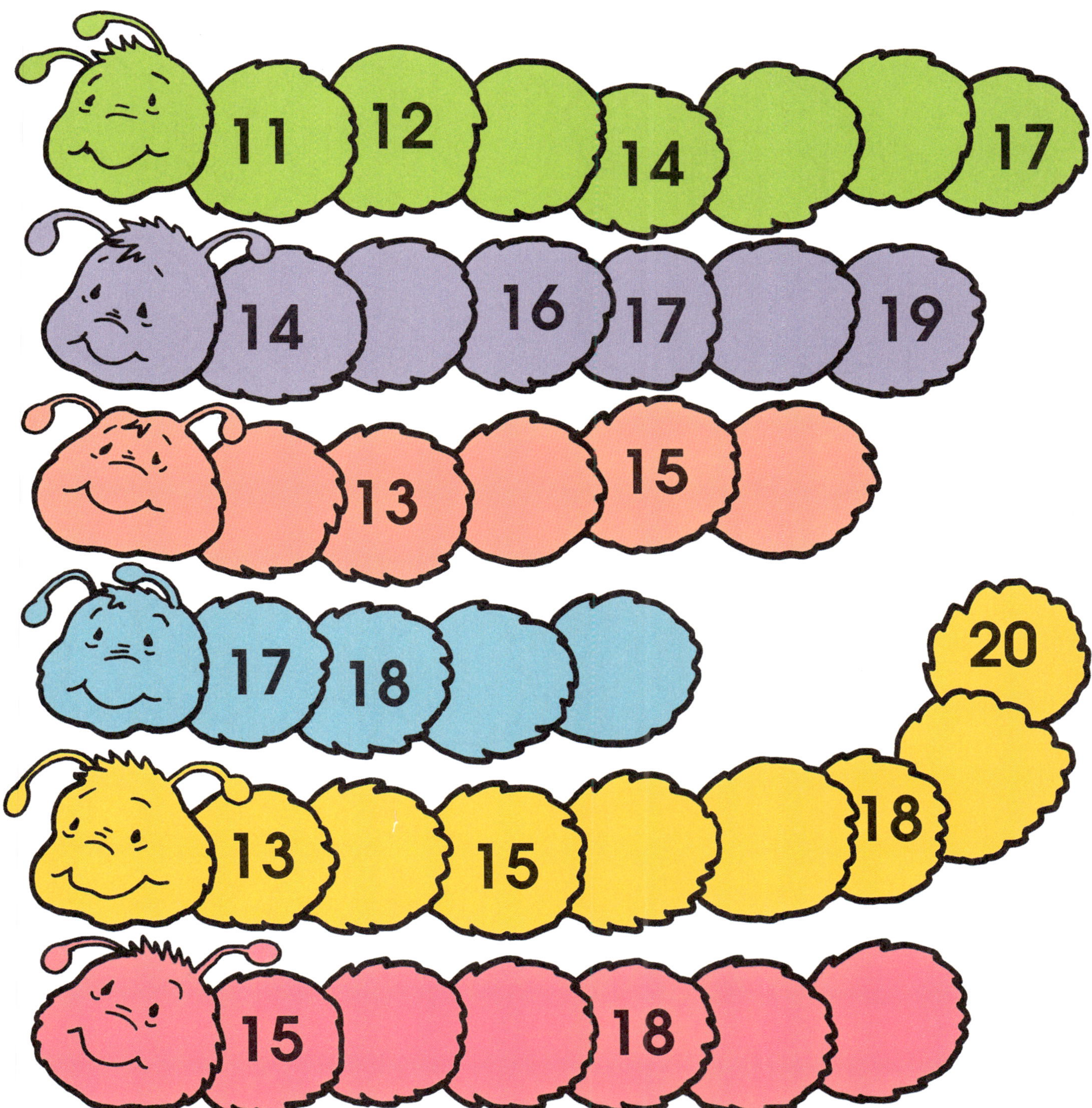

Name ______________________________ 

Pick Up Trash!

Help the trash collector find his way to the trash can. Color a path in order from **1** to **20**.

Start

1 1 2 3 3 4 4 5 5 2 4 5 6 7 8 8 9 10 11 12 13 14 15 16 17 18 19 20

Name ____

Keep On Trucking

Connect the dots from **1** to **20**.

Look Alikes

Color the pictures with the same number as in the first picture.

Name ___________________________

Just the Same

Match the groups with the same number.

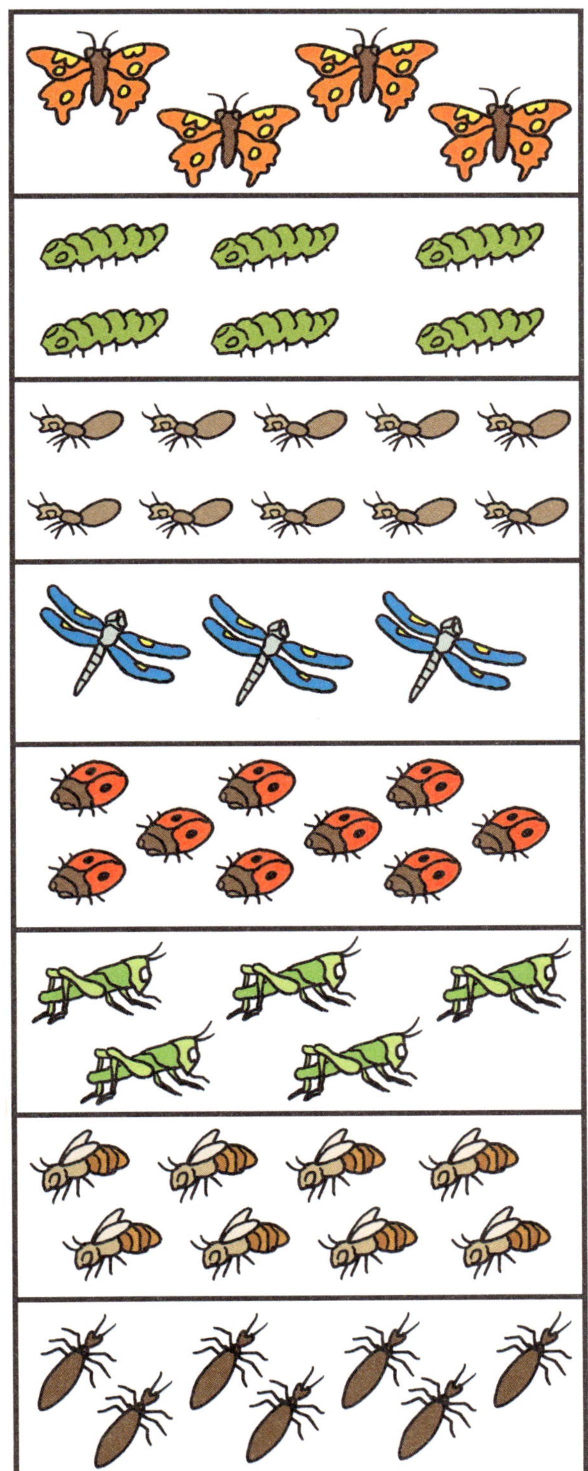

Tasty Treats

Circle the one with more.

A Little Snack

Circle the one with less.

Name ______________________________ 

Sweet Spotted Buddies

Color the dog with more spots in each picture.

Name ___

Moving Along

Look at the picture.

Write the number.

How many?   

How many in all?

 and    and  

 and    and  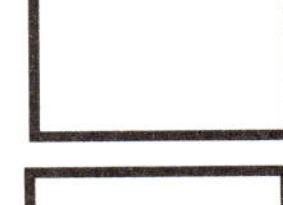

 and    and  

Name ______________________________________

A Perfect Day at the Park

Circle how many you see in the picture.

	1	5
	4	2
	8	5
	6	3
	7	10
	2	8
	9	7
	10	7
	3	1

Circle how many you see in all.

	+		=	8	9	10
	+		=	3	8	9
	+		=	6	2	4

Name ______________________________ 

Teeny Tiny Garden Friends

Look at the picture.

Write the number.

How many? ☐  ☐ 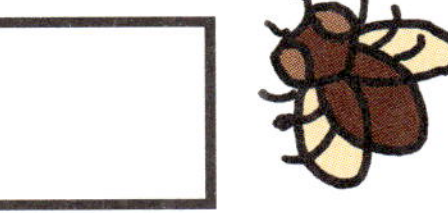 ☐ 

☐  ☐  ☐ 

How many in all?

 and   ☐  and   ☐

 and   ☐   and   ☐

 and   ☐   and   ☐

Name ______________________________

Easy as One, Two, Three

Color.

one = yellow two = black three = blue

four = white five = orange six = green

seven = red eight = purple nine = brown

ten = pink

one one one
six four four
nine six nine
six six
ten eight one three
ten six one
six
nine three six
eight
ten ten
seven seven four
three
five five
one one
two two

Name ___________________________

Busy Bees

Count the bees in each picture.
Circle the correct number word.

Name ______________________________

Identifying number words 1–20

Lovely, Little Ladybugs

Count the spots on each picture.
Circle the correct number word.

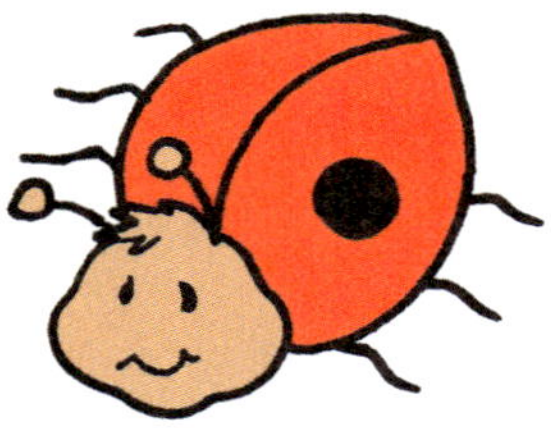	one five	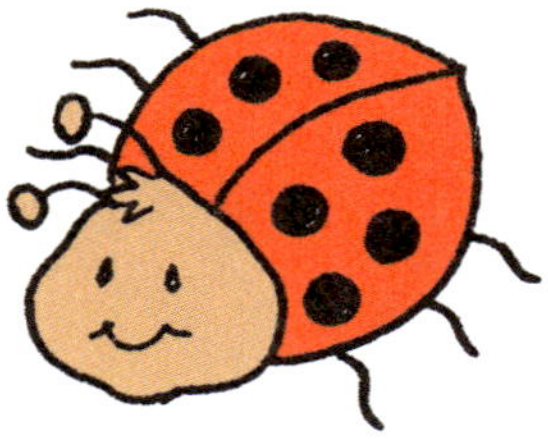	two seven
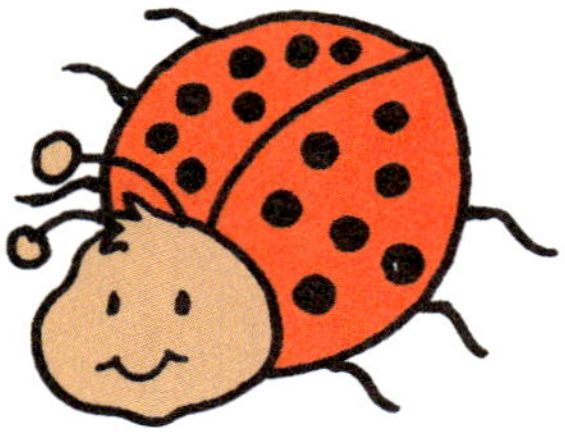	fourteen sixteen	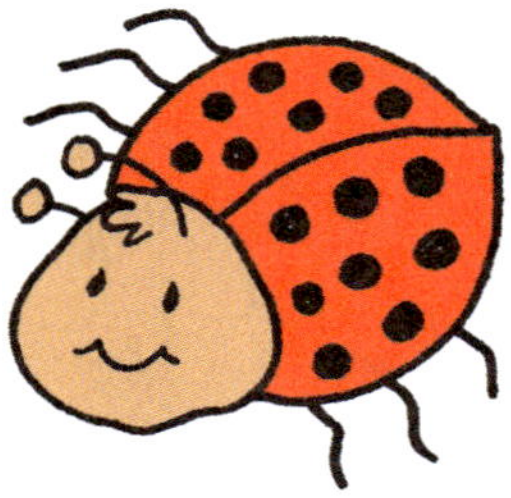	nineteen fifteen
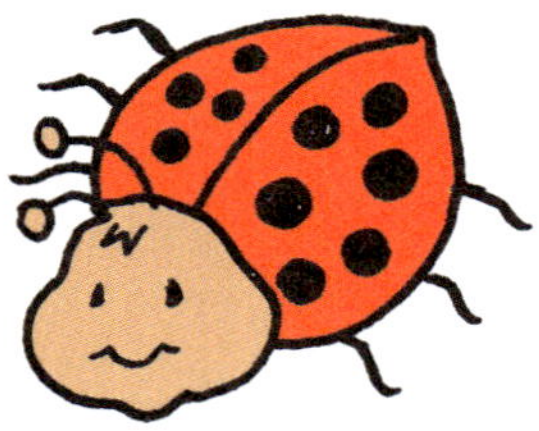	ten eleven	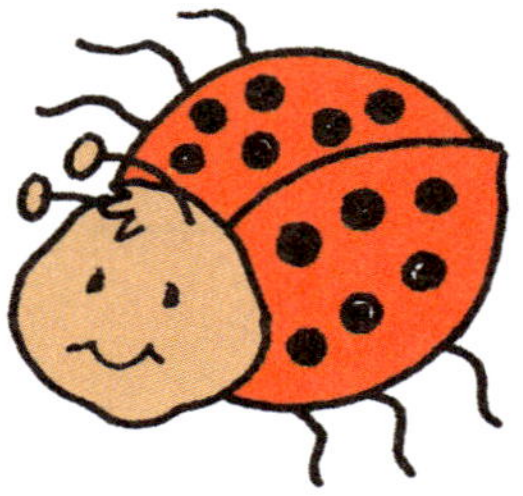	twenty twelve
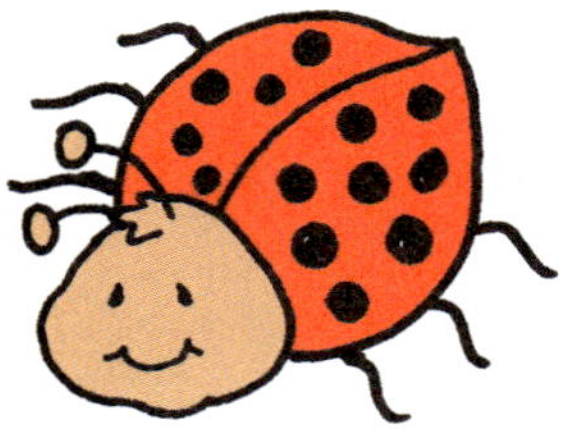	eighteen thirteen	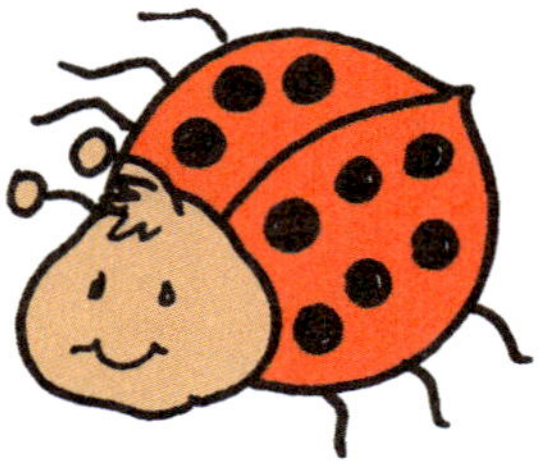	nine eight
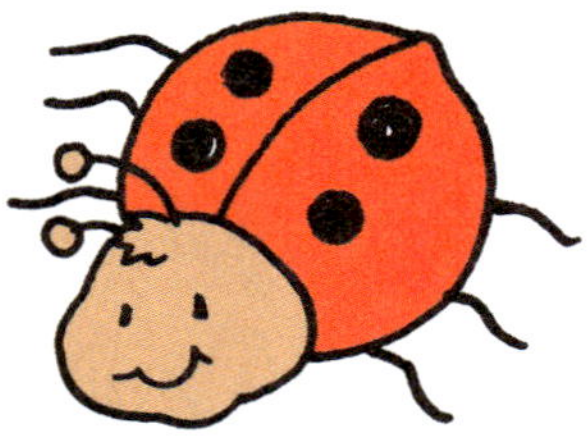	seven four	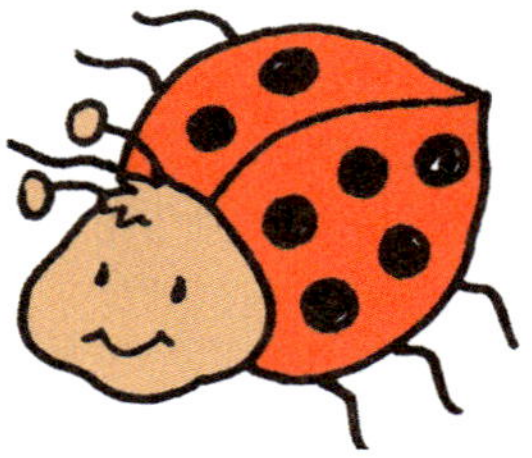	seven three

Scholastic Success With

HANDWRITING

Name ______________________________

Petting-Zoo Pairs

Trace each line from a baby animal to its mother.

Name ____ 

Pretty Ponies

Trace each line from a pony to its child.

Name ____________________

A Rainy Day

Trace each line from top to bottom.

Big Balloons

Trace each line from bottom to top.

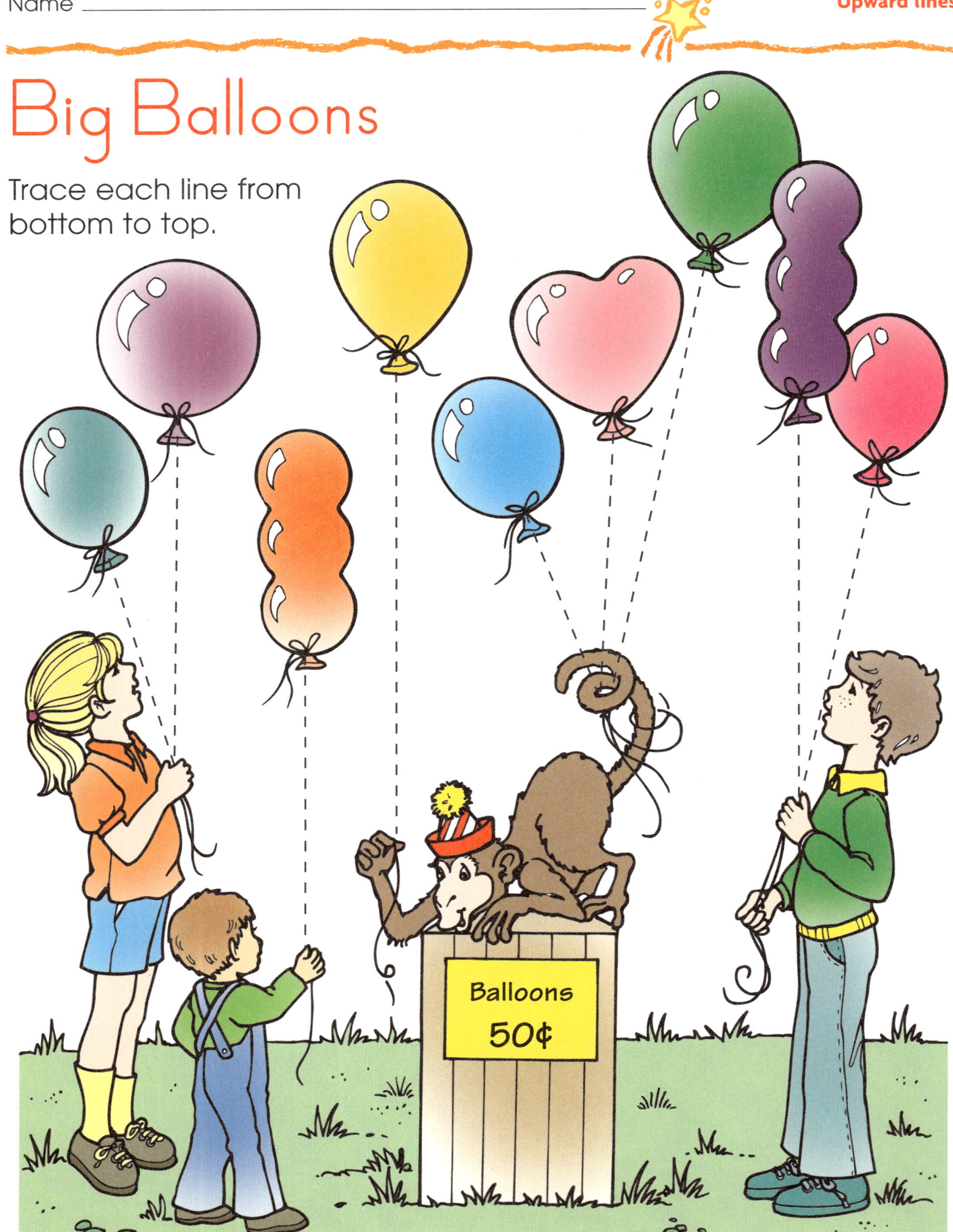

Name ____

Out Comes the Sun

Trace each line from top to bottom.

Name ______________________________

Colorful Kites

Trace each line from bottom to top.

Name ______________________________________

Blowing Bubbles

Trace each circle. Start at the ●. Follow the ⟶ .

Name ______________________________

Clowning Around

Trace each circle. Start at the ●. Follow the ⟶.

Name ____________________

Wonderful Watermelons

Trace each curved line. Start at the ●. Follow the →.

Name ___________________________

Fun at the Fair

Trace each line. Start at the ●. Follow the →.

Name ______________________________ 

Lots of Licks

Trace and write.

Name ______________________________

Ticket Time

Trace and write.

1
2

If the weather is nice, go outside and draw straight lines on a sidewalk with large pieces of chalk.

Name ______________________________

Ooh! Aah!

Trace and write.

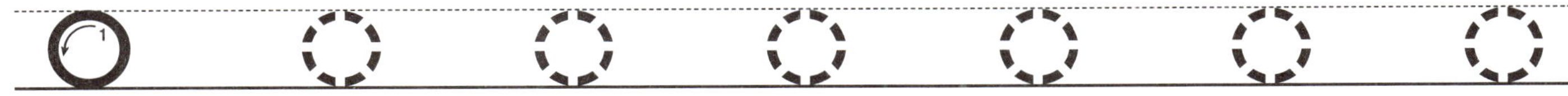

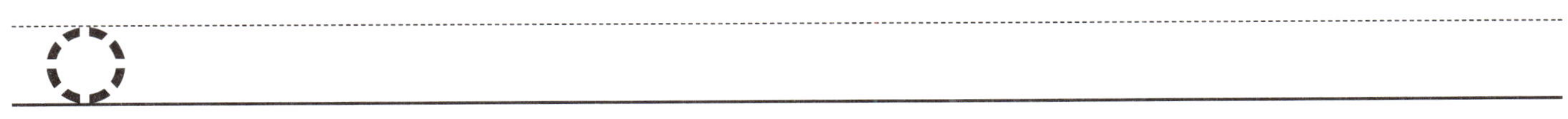

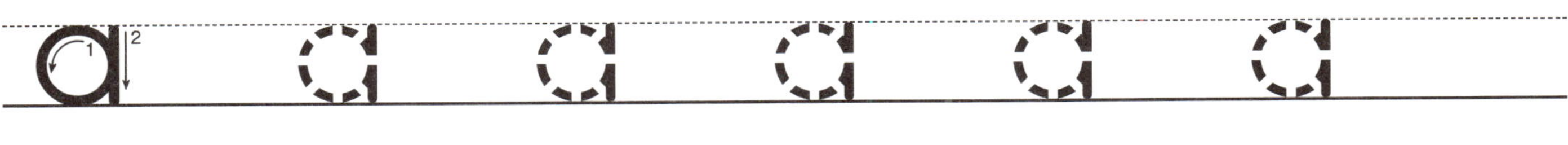

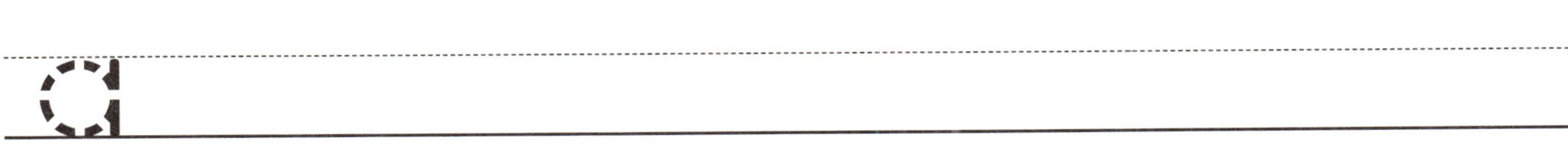

Name ______________________________ d, o, a

Dancing Dogs

Trace and write.

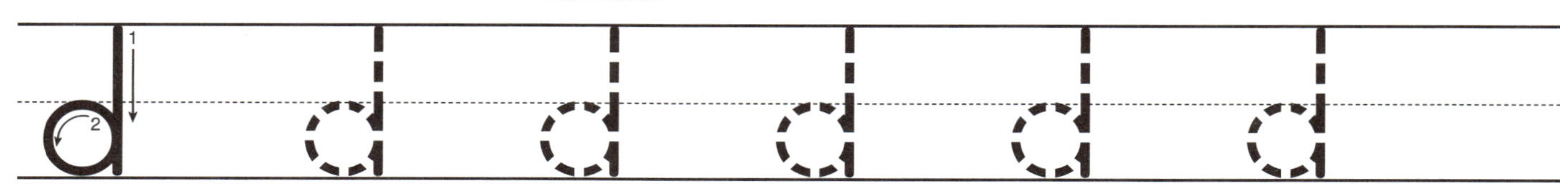

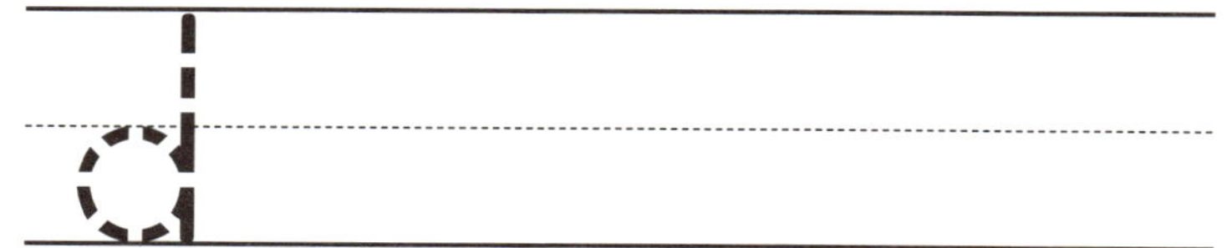

Practice drawing letters on an erasable tablet. You can erase letters by lifting the sheet of plastic film on the tablet.

Name ______________________________

Crack! Splat!

Trace and write.

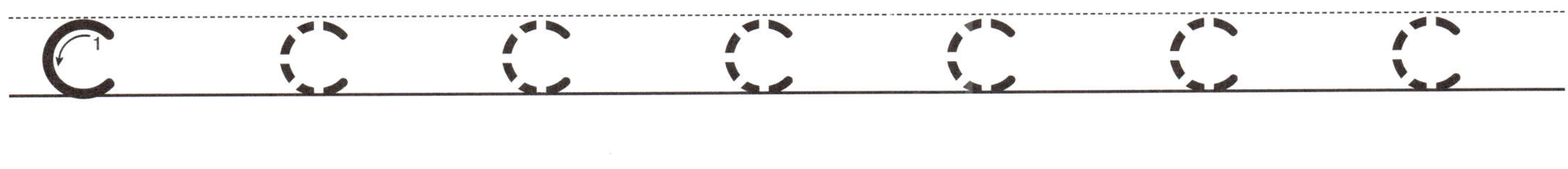

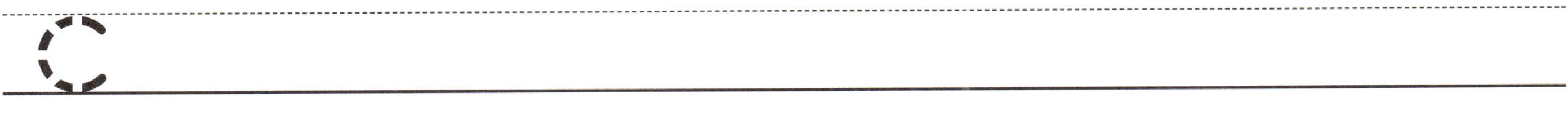

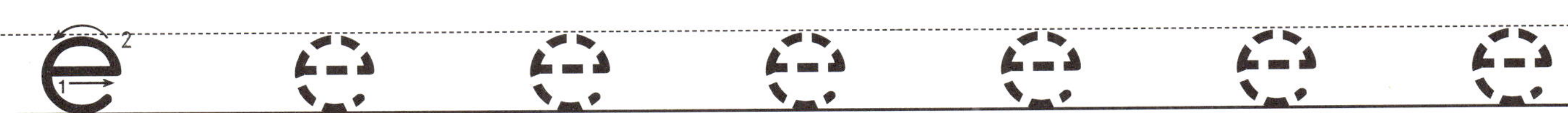

Name ___________________________

Fancy Fireworks

Trace and write.

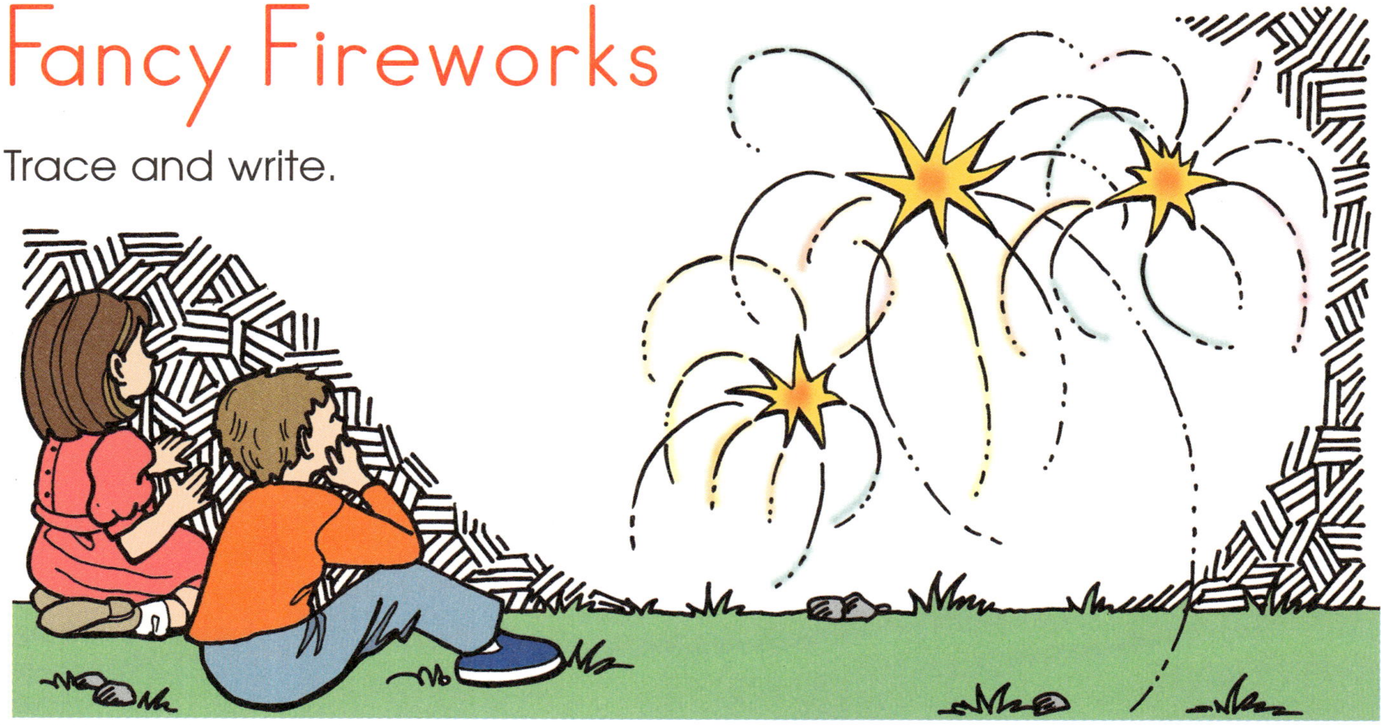

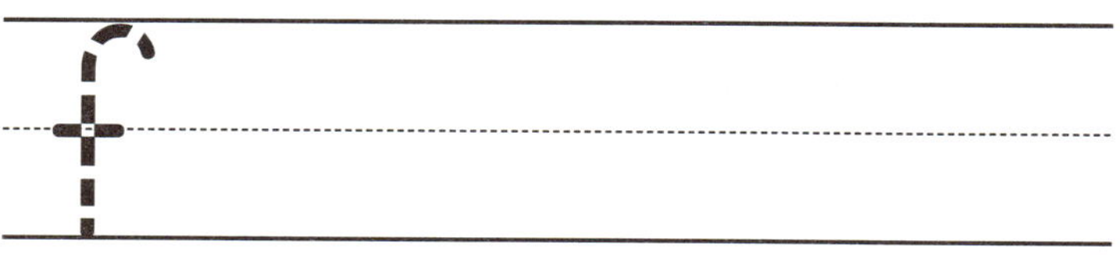

Spray some shaving cream on cookie sheets. Spread out the shaving cream with your hands and use your pointer finger to draw letters in it.

Name ______________________________ 

Radiant Rainbow

Trace and write.

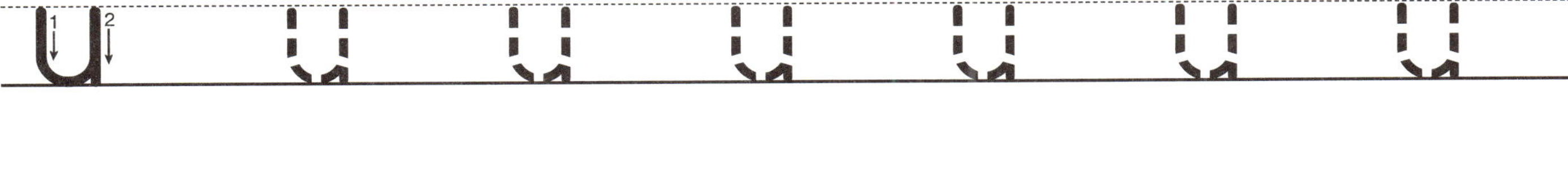

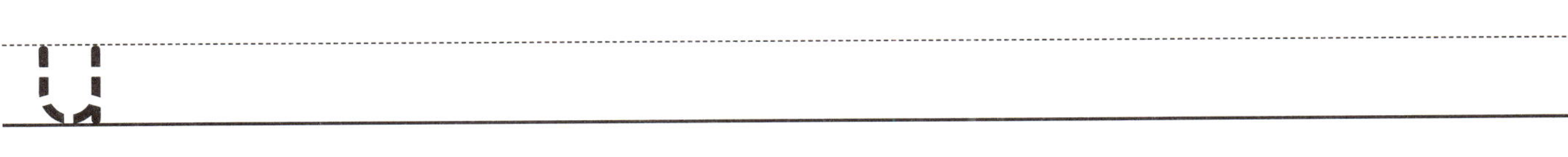

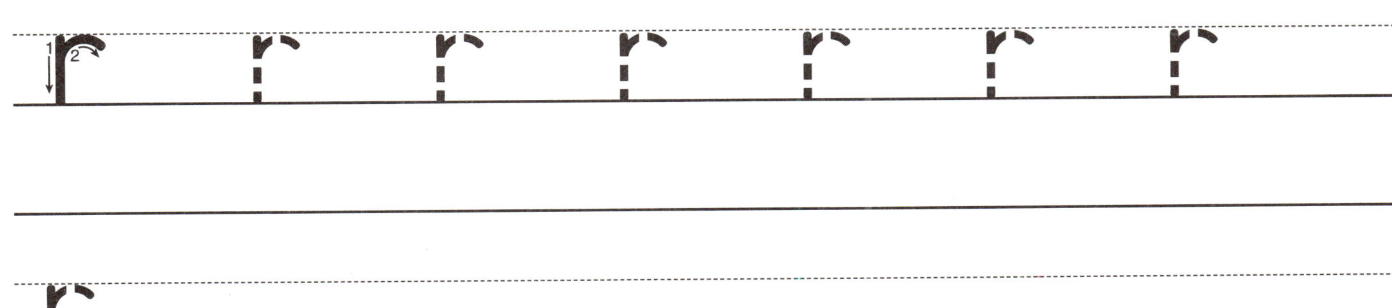

Name ______________________________

Time for a Nap

Trace and write.

n n n n n n n

n

u r

n

Go outside and practice writing letters in the sand or dirt with craft sticks.

Name ______________________________

Bouncing Balls

Trace and write.

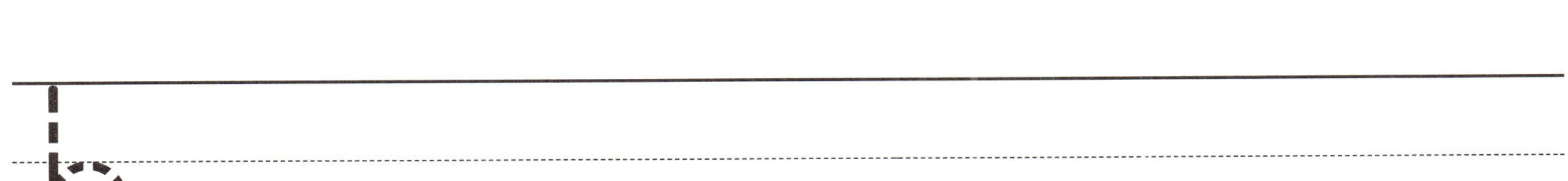

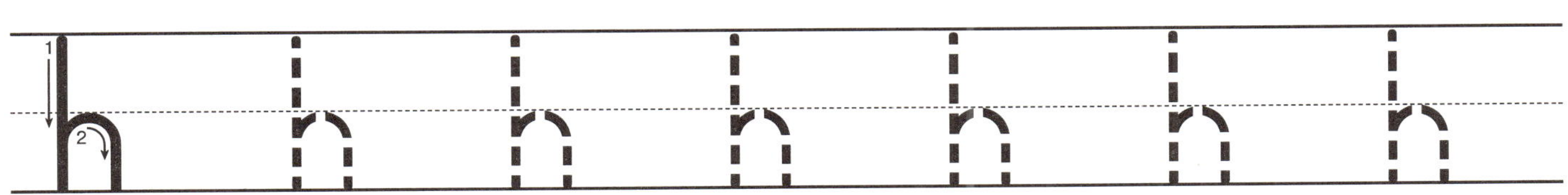

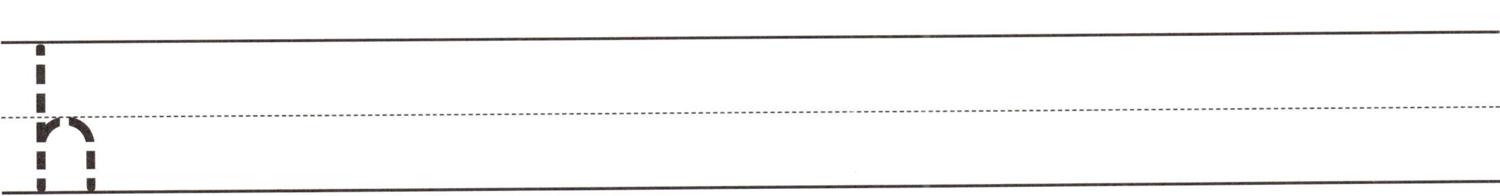

Name ________________________________

Perfect Pumpkins

Trace and write.

p p p p p p

p

b h

p

Fill plastic squeeze-type bottles with different colors of tempera paint. Squeeze the paint onto construction paper to create letters.

Name ______________________________

Jumping Goats

Trace and write.

Name ____

A Quarter a Quack

Trace and write.

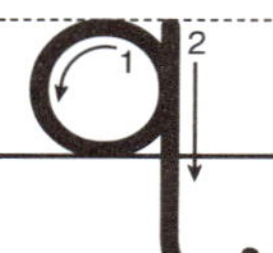

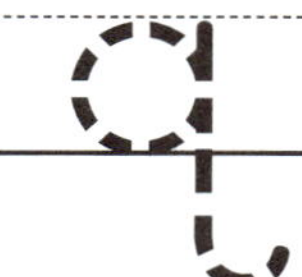

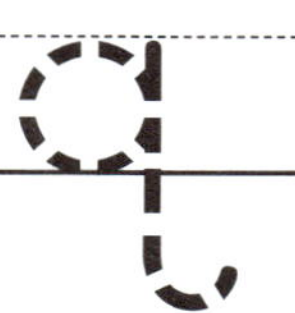

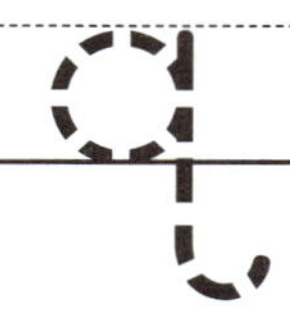

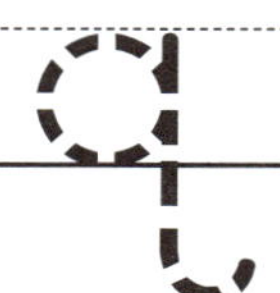

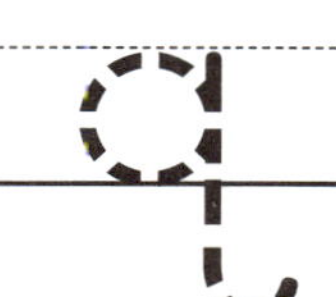

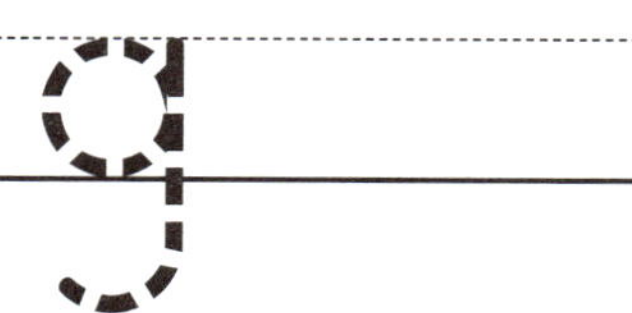

Print large letters on pieces of paper. Press your thumb on an inkpad. Trace over the letters on the paper by stamping on your thumbprint.

Name ______________________________

Music Makers

Trace and write.

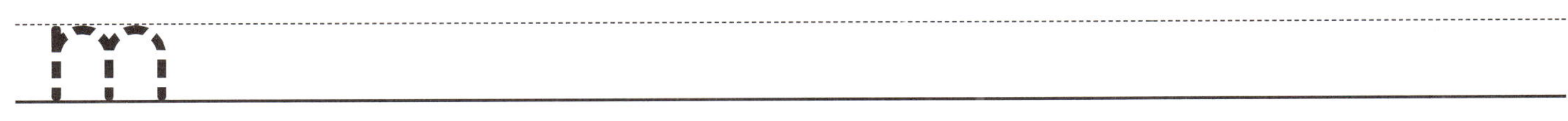

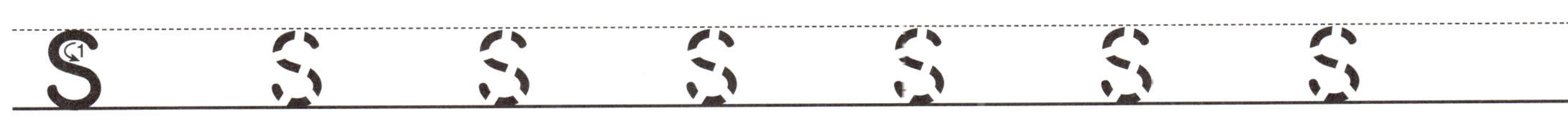

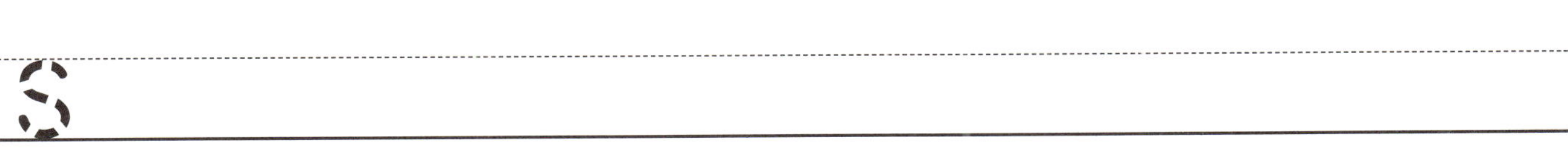

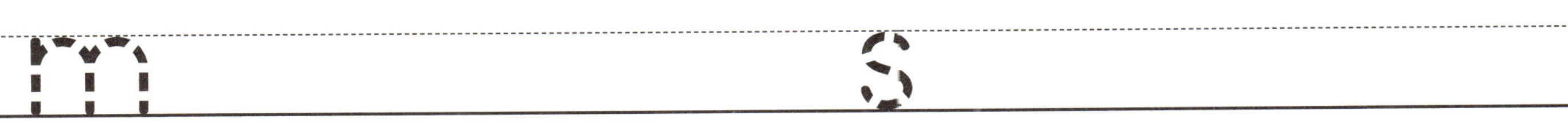

Name ______________________________

A Vulture's Yo-Yo

Trace and write.

v v v v v v v

v

y y y y y y y

y

Name ___________________________________

What Time Is It?

Trace and write.

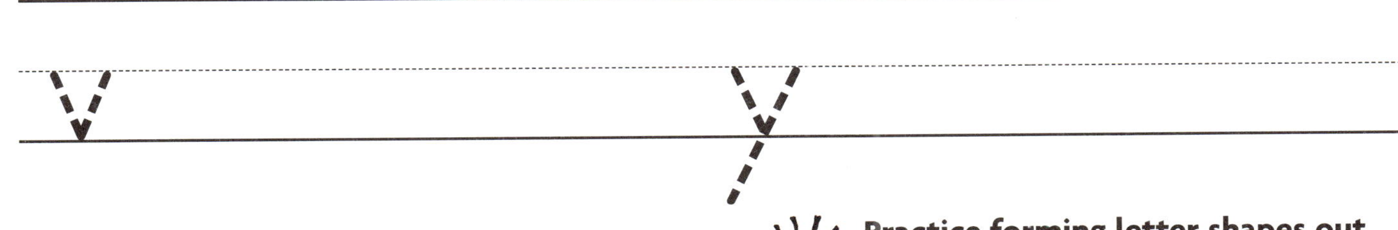

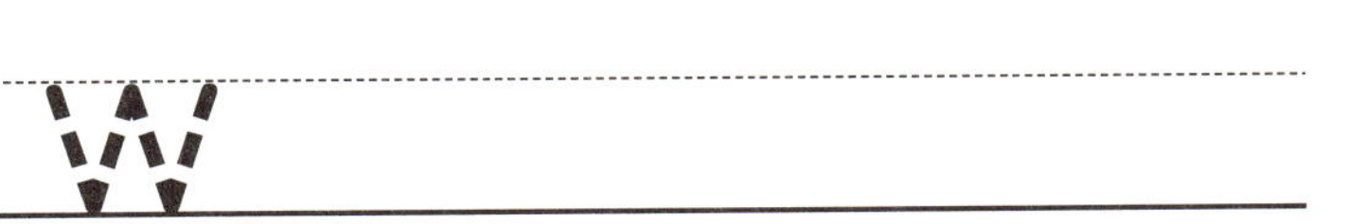

Practice forming letter shapes out of clay. Roll the dough into long strips and twist and turn the strips to form different letters.

Name ________________________________

Box Kites

Trace and write.

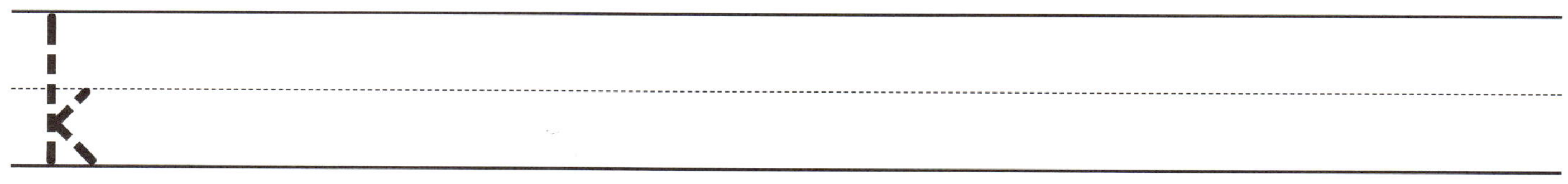

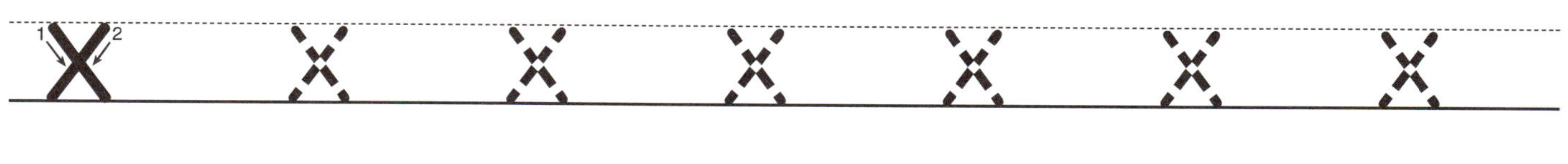

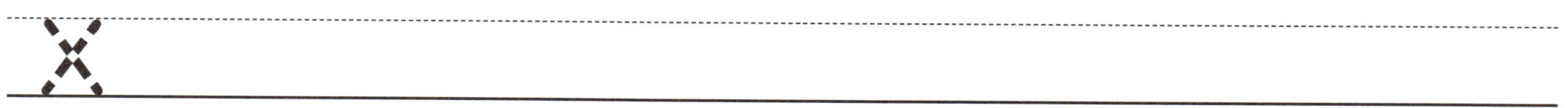

Name ______________________________

Zooming Along

Trace and write.

Z Z Z Z Z Z Z

Z

k x

Z

Practice forming letters using craft sticks. Glue your stick letters to construction paper.

Name ______________________________

Ice-Cold Lemonade

Trace and write.

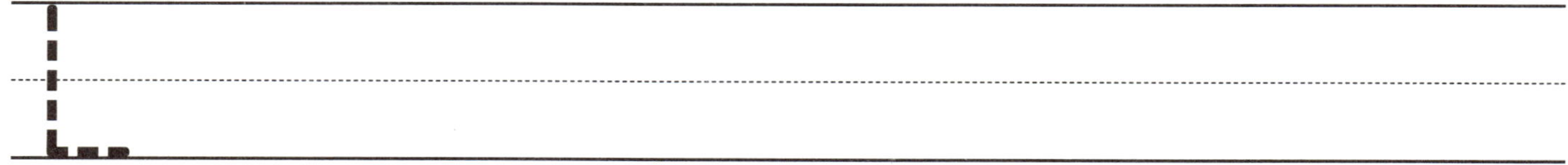

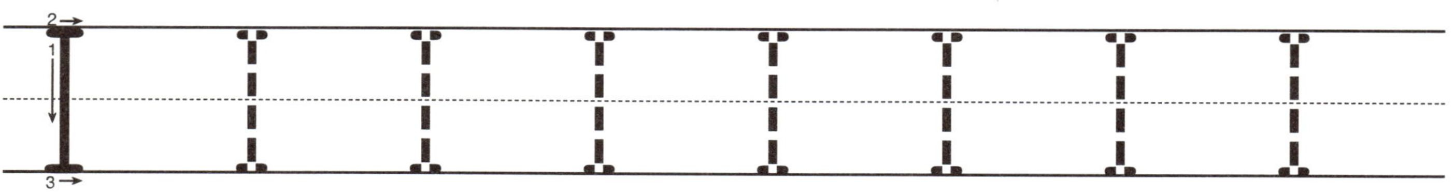

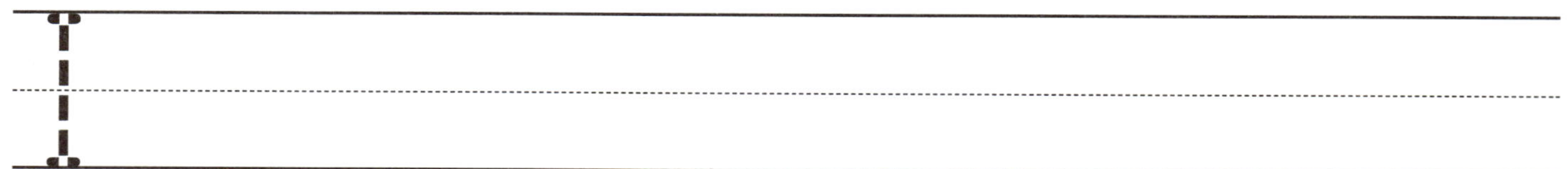

Name ____________________

Toot-Toot!

Trace and write.

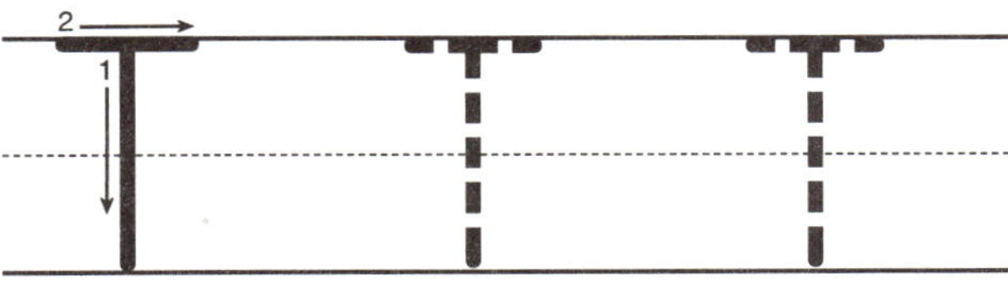

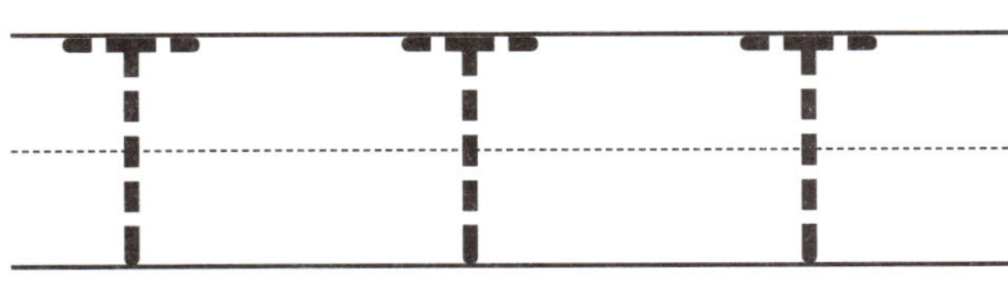

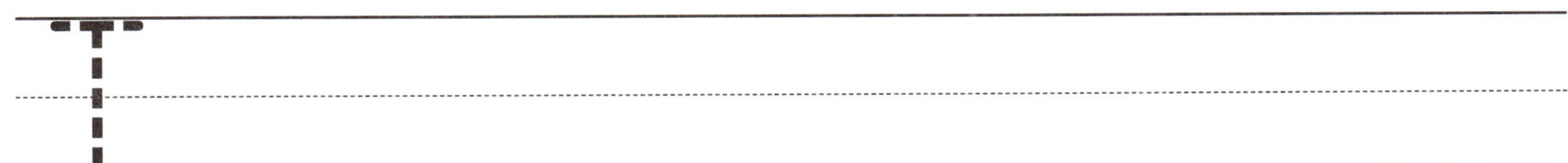

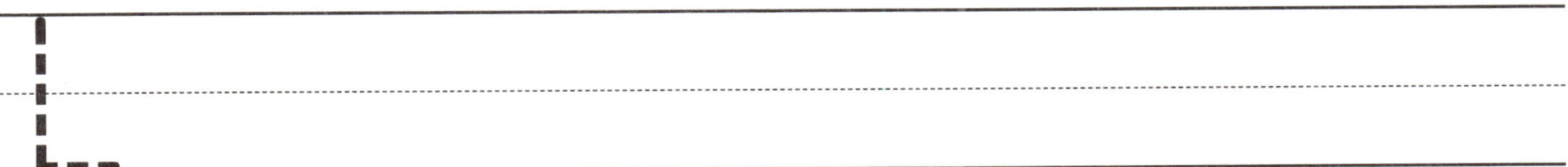

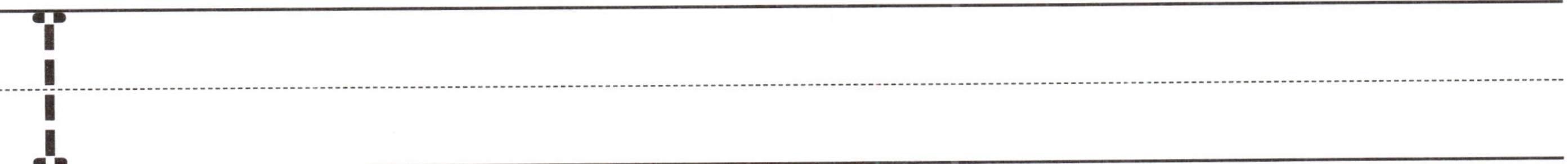

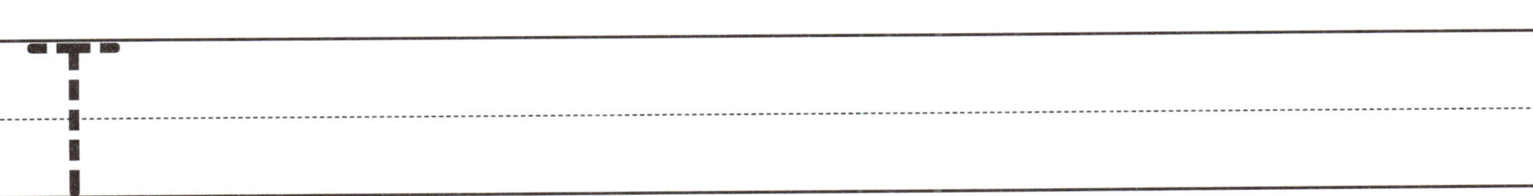

Name ______________________________________

Making Friends at the Fair

Trace and write.

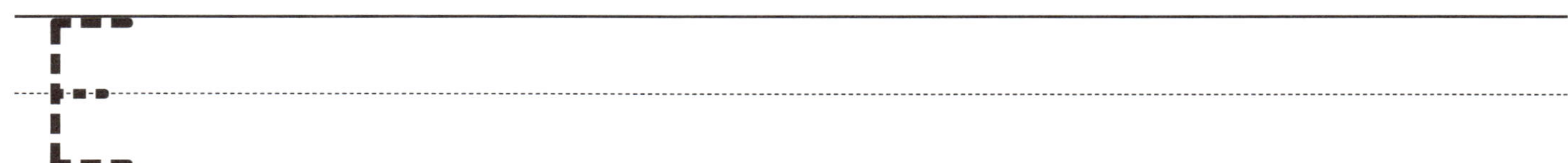

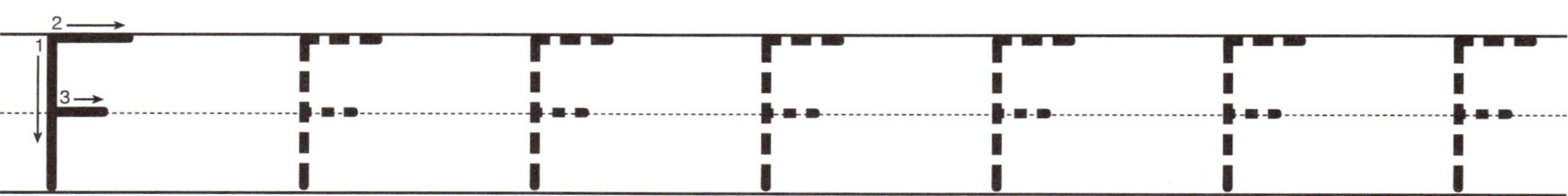

Name ______________________________

Hungry for Hot Dogs

Trace and write.

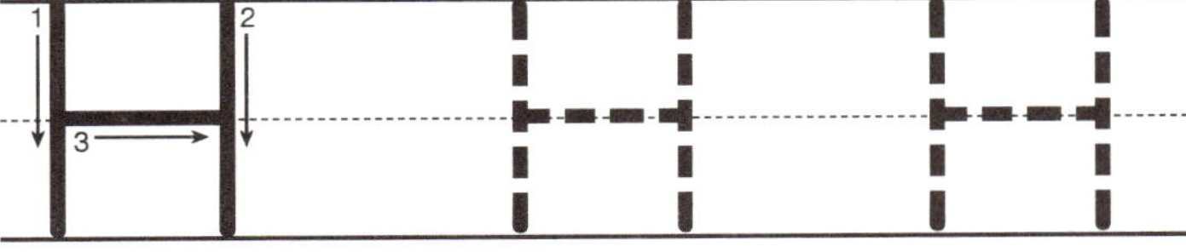

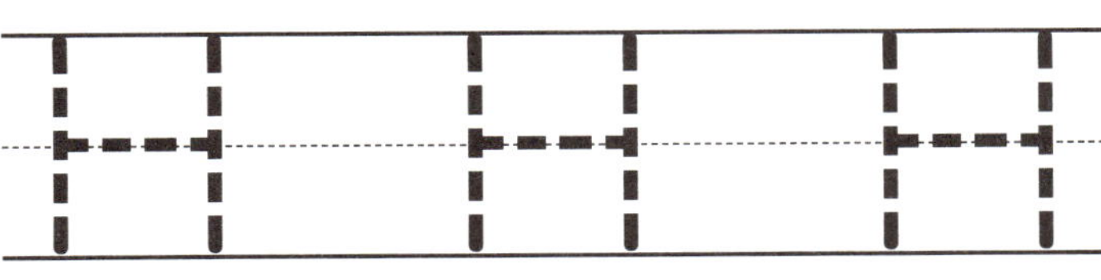

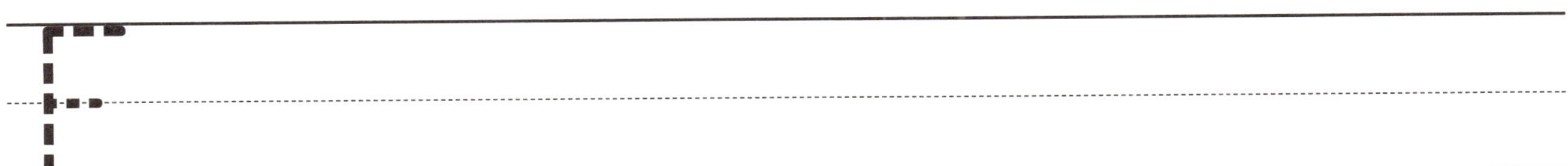

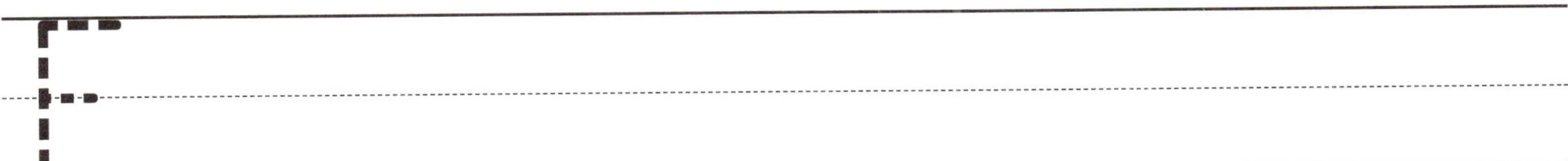

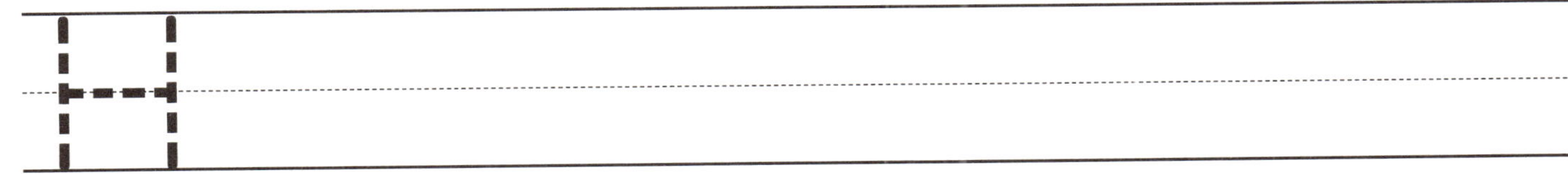

Name ____

A Cozy Quilt

Trace and write.

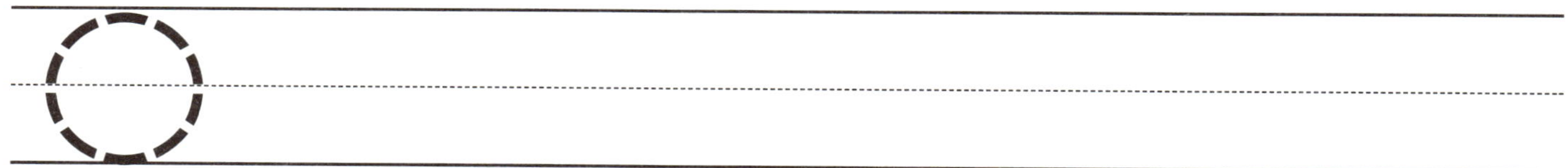

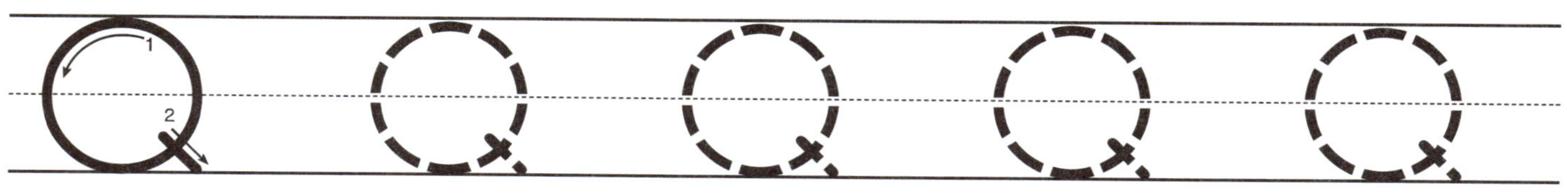

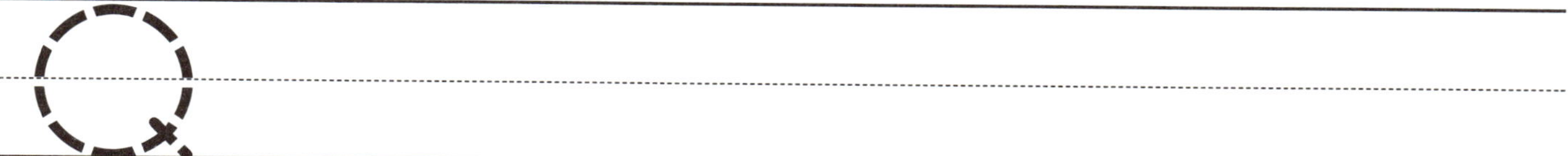

Cotton Candy

Trace and write.

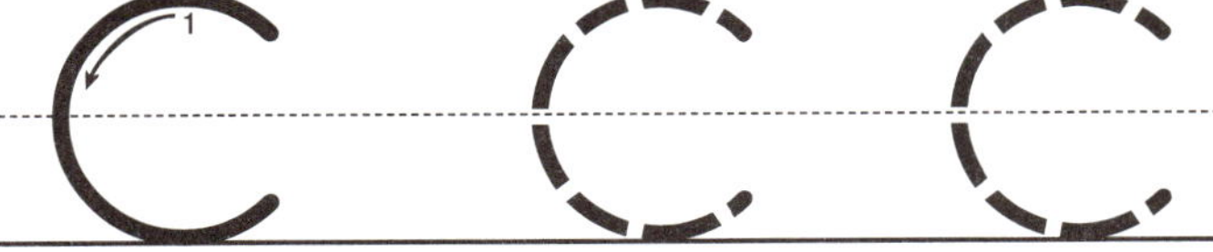

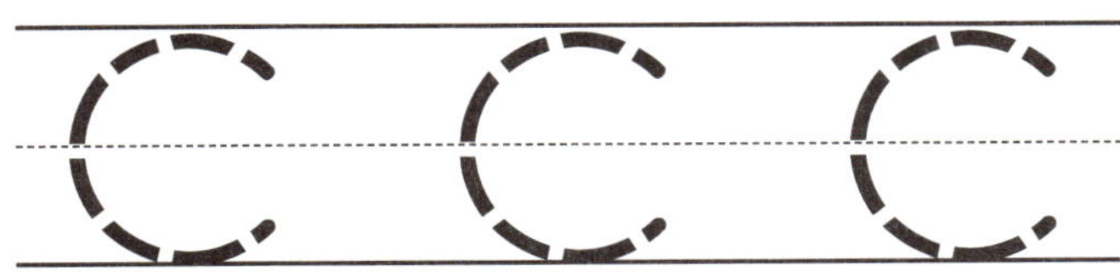

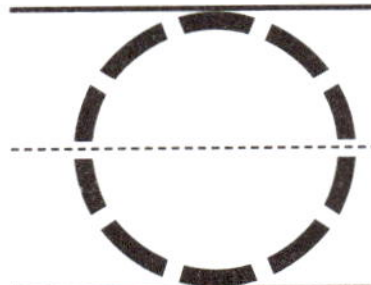

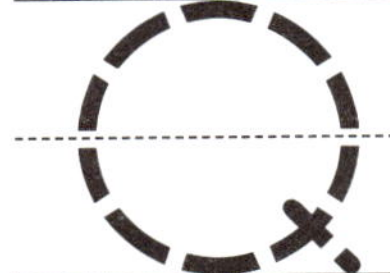

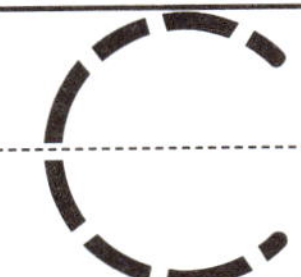

Name ______________________________

The Dunking Booth

Trace and write.

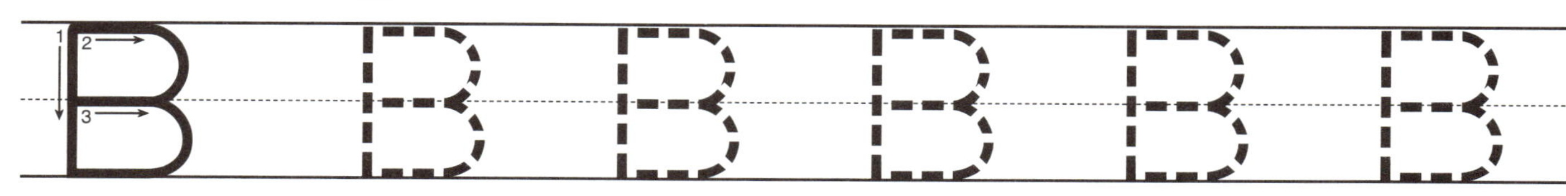

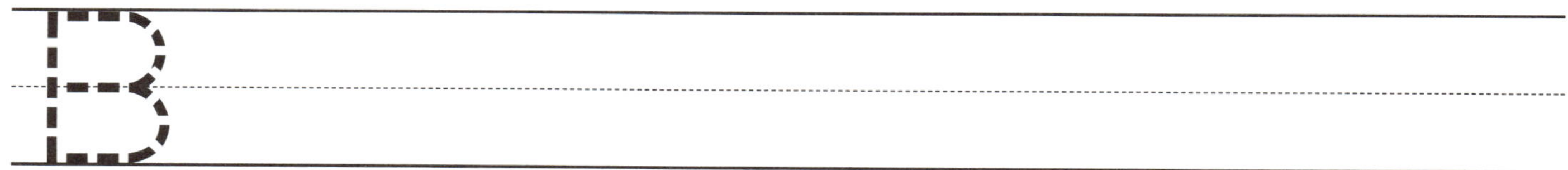

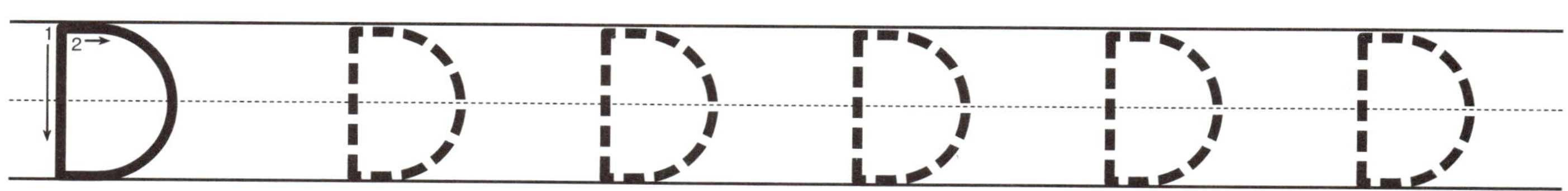

Name ______________________________ 

Feeding Time

Trace and write.

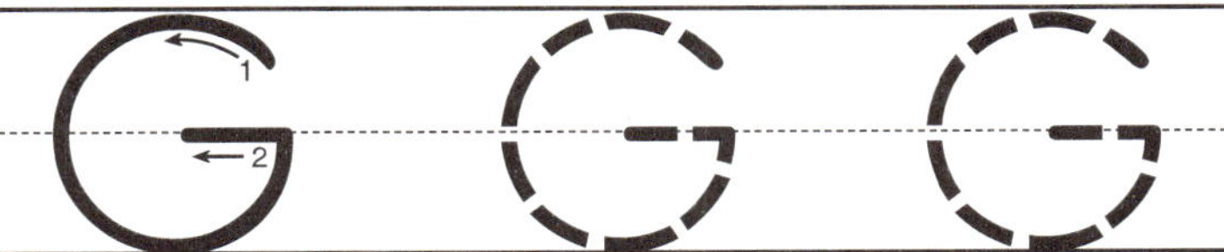

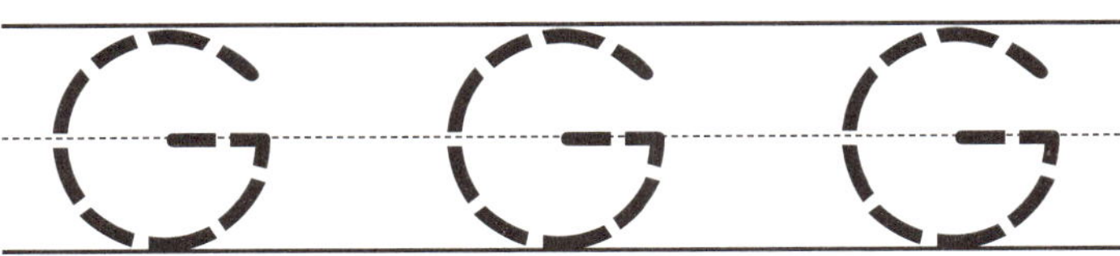

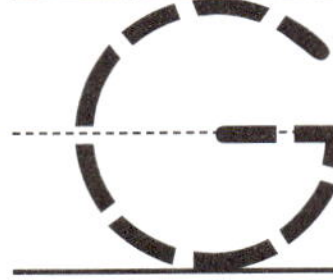

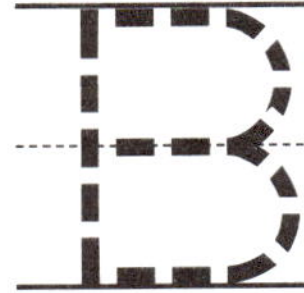

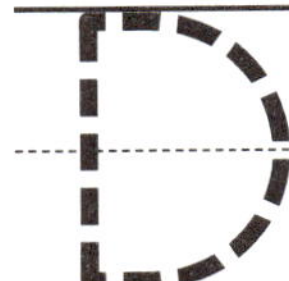

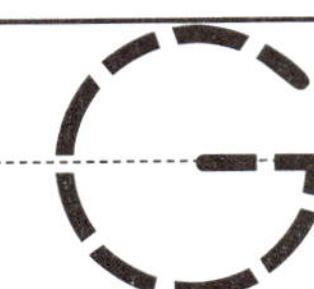

Name ____________________

Rolling Roller Coaster

Trace and write.

P P P P P P

P

R R R R R R

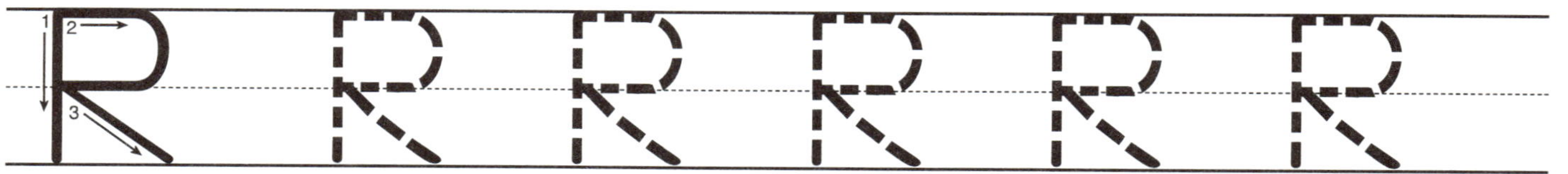

R

Name ______________________

Up, Up, and Away!

Trace and write.

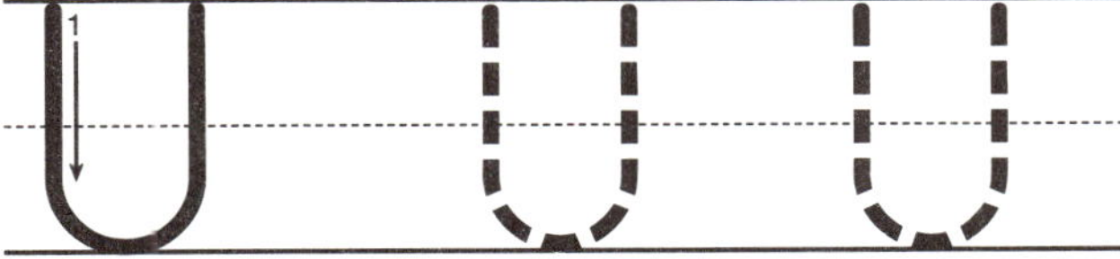

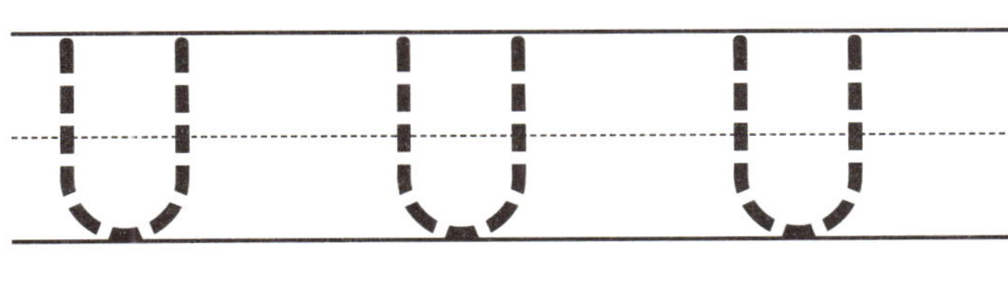

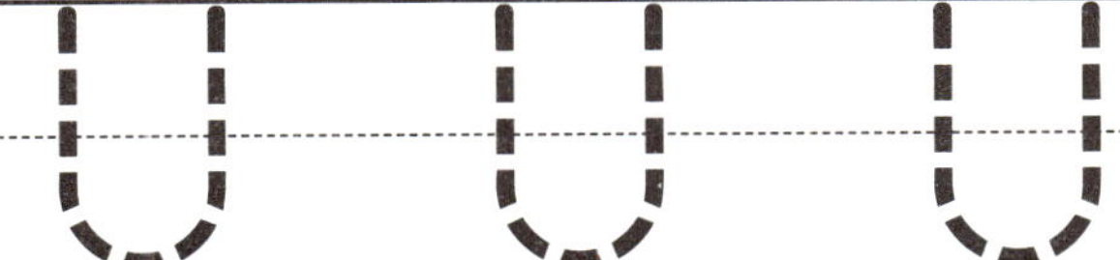

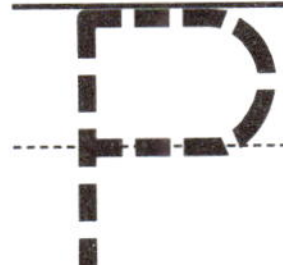

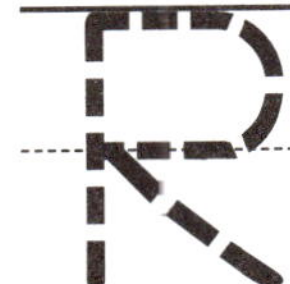

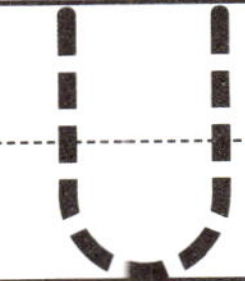

Name ______________________________

Sack-Jumping

Trace and write.

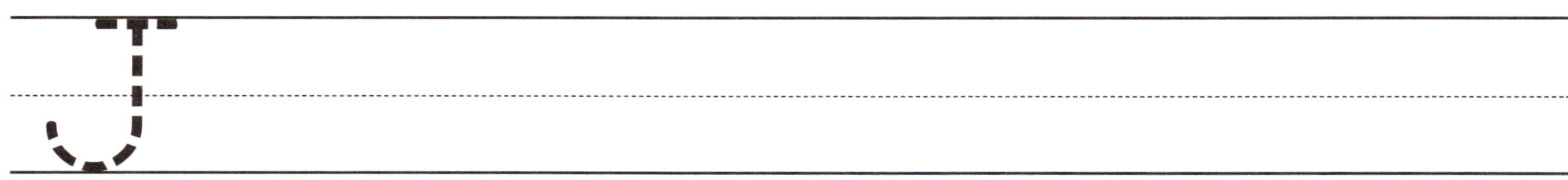

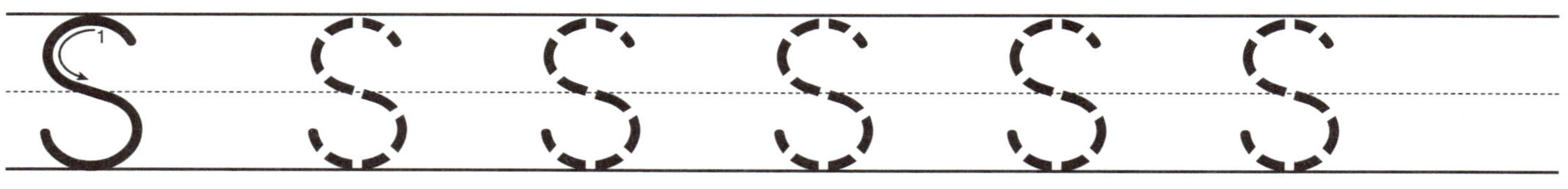

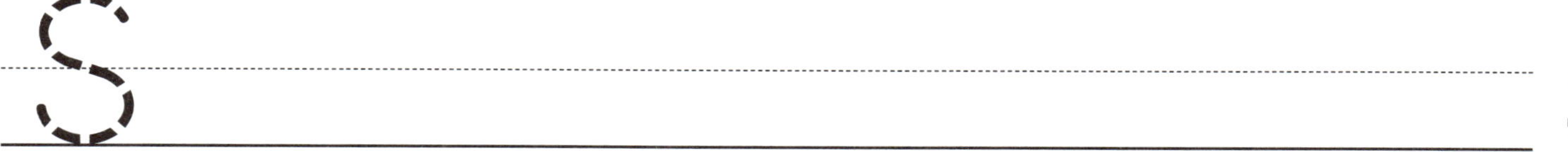

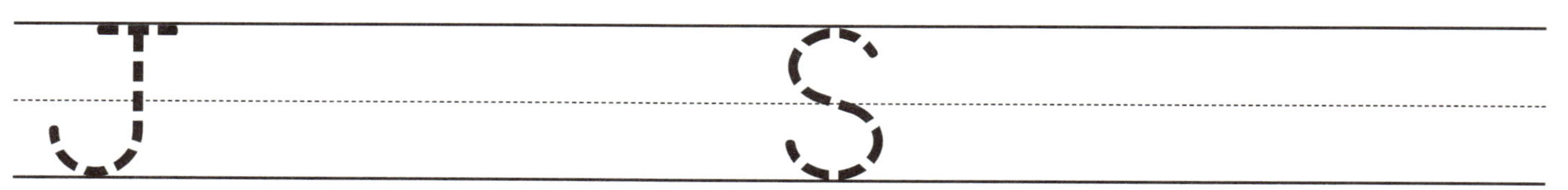

Name ______________________________

Ant Antics

Trace and write.

A A A A A

A

N N N N N N

N

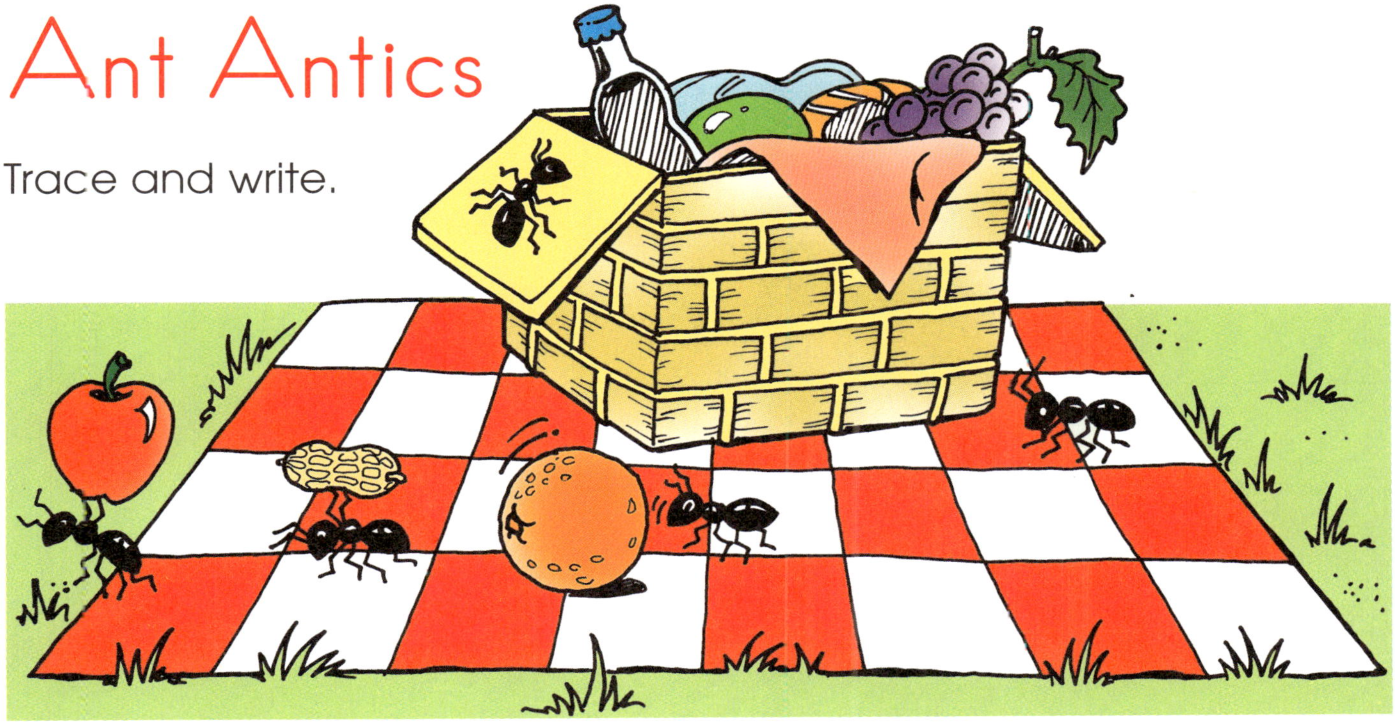

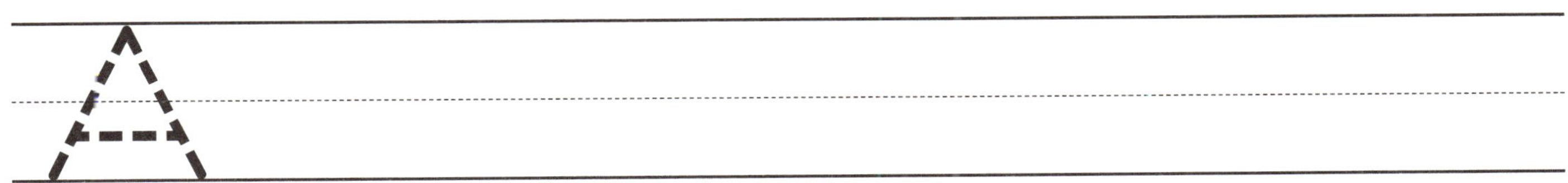

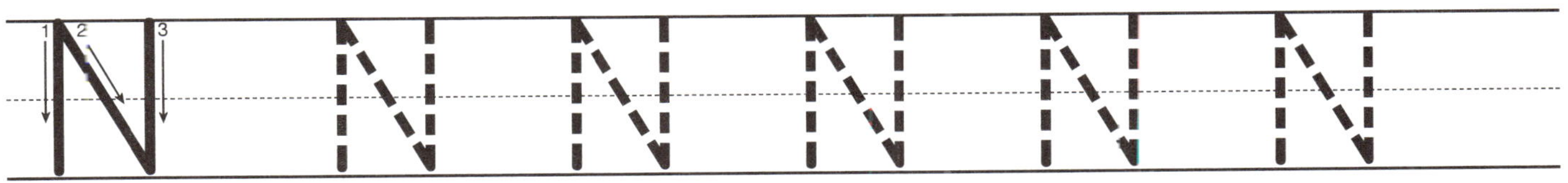

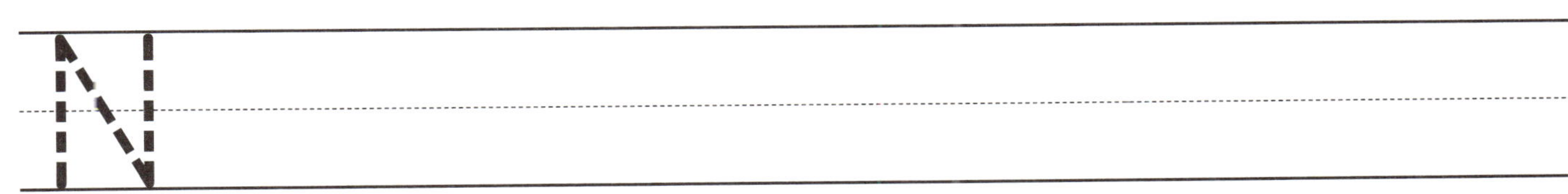

Name ______________________________

Merrily We Go Around!

Trace and write.

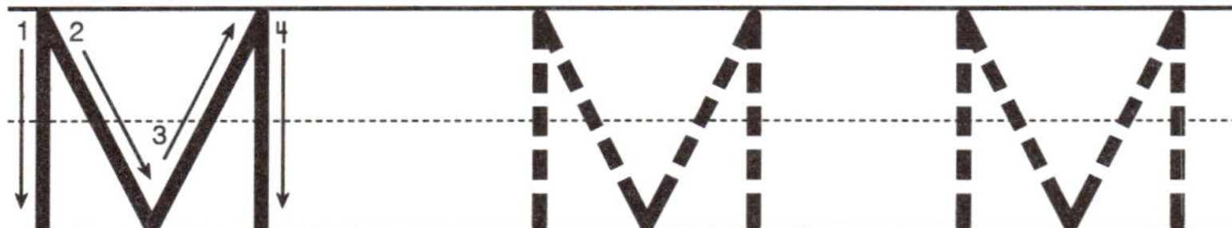

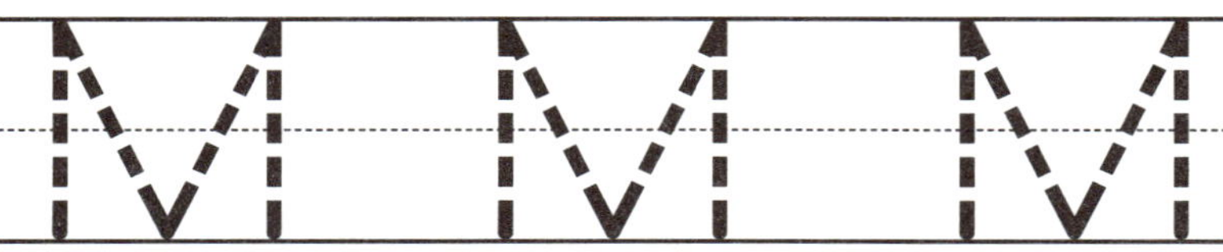

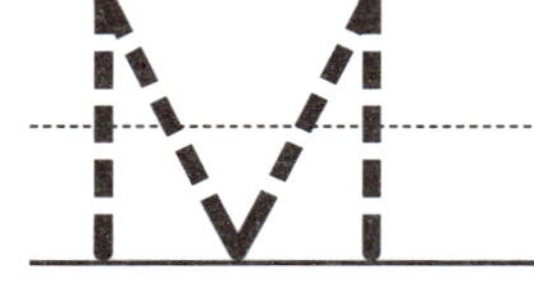

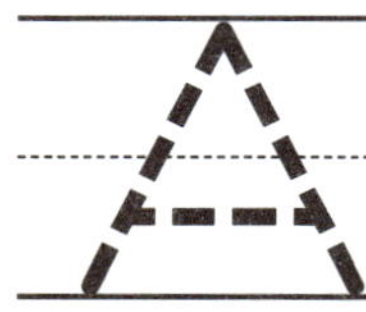

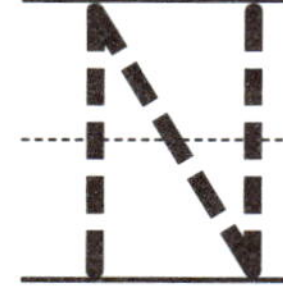

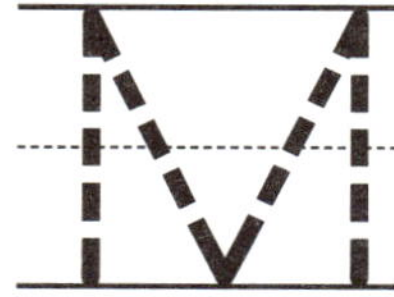

Name ___

What a Day!

Trace and write.

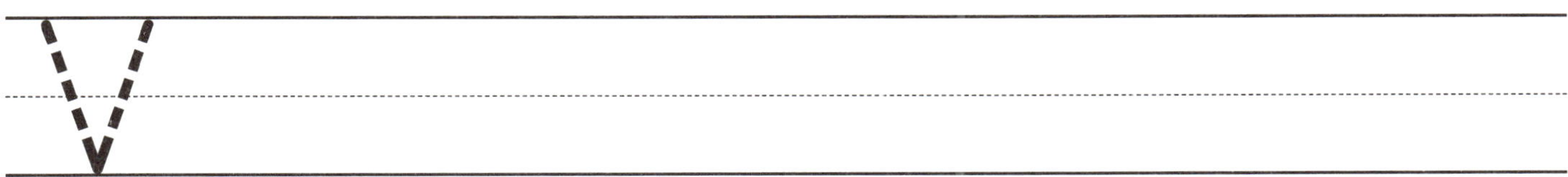

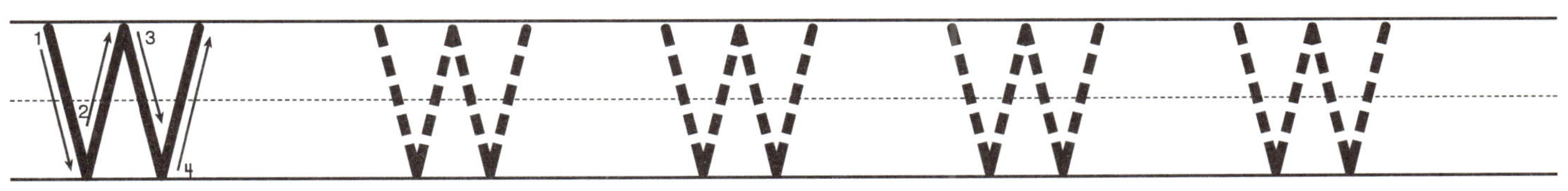

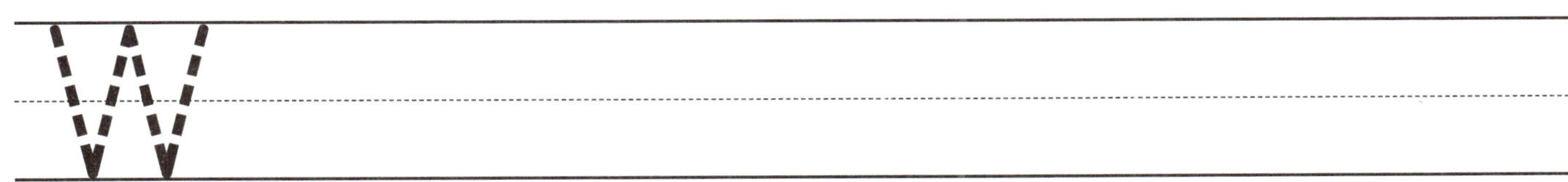

Name ____________________

A Youthful Yawn

Trace and write.

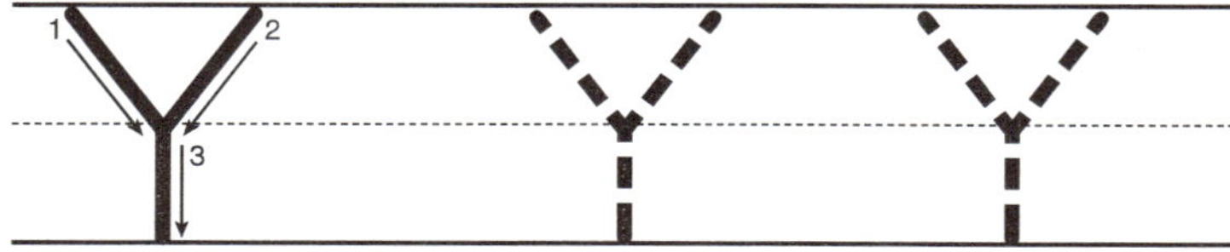

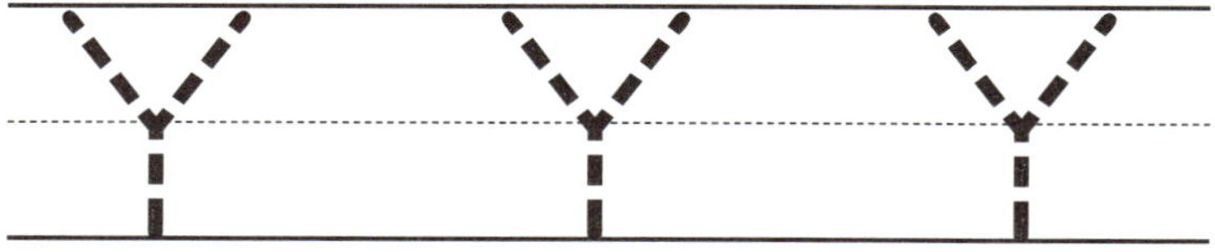

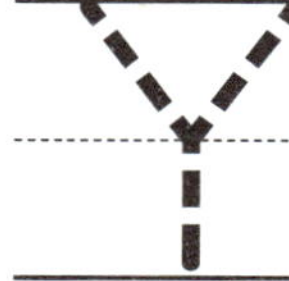

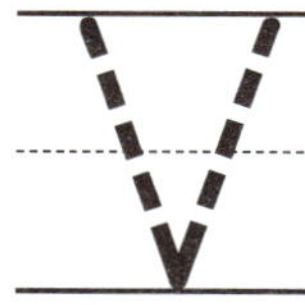

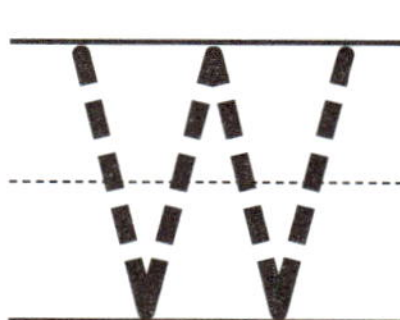

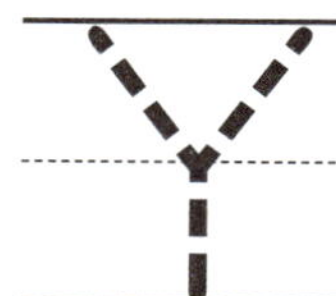

Name ________________________________

Can We Keep One?

Trace and write.

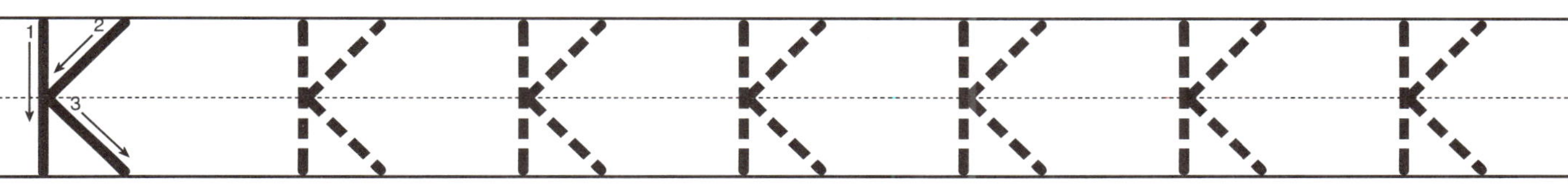

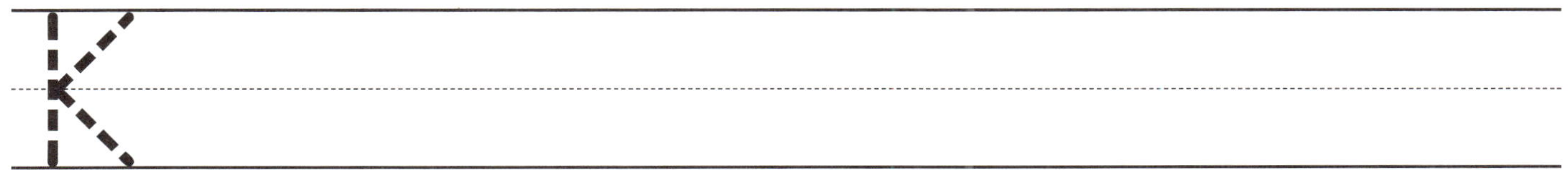

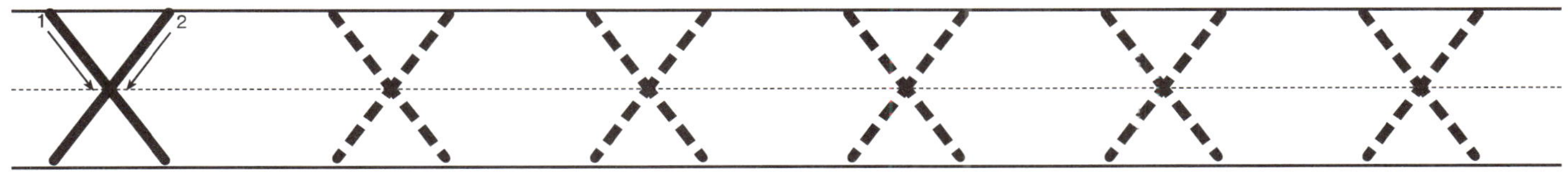

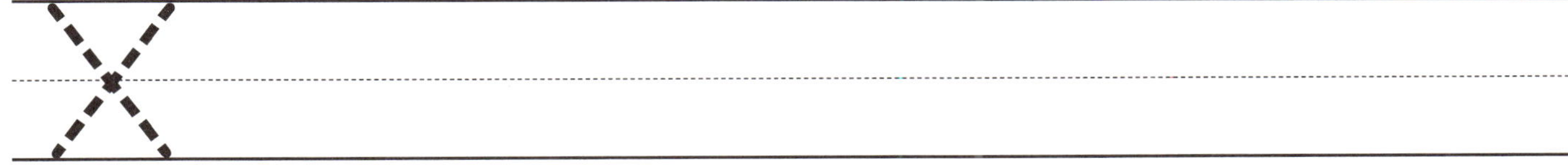

Name ______________________________

The Petting Zoo

Trace and write.

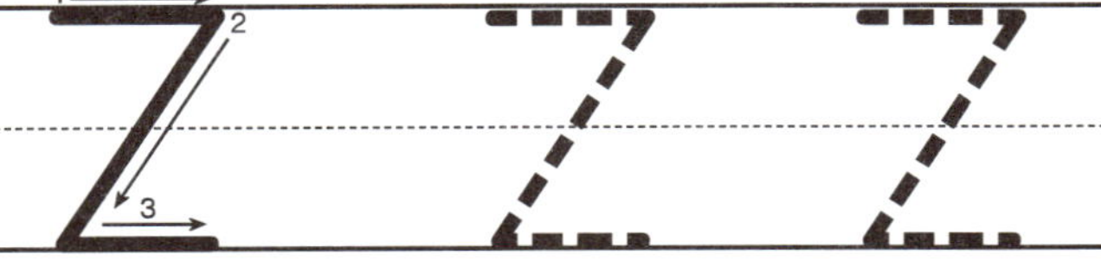

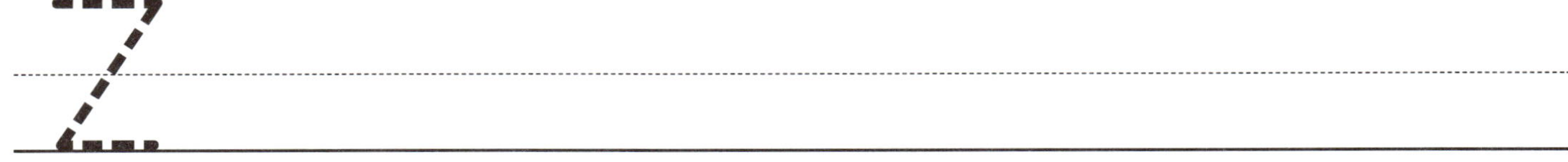

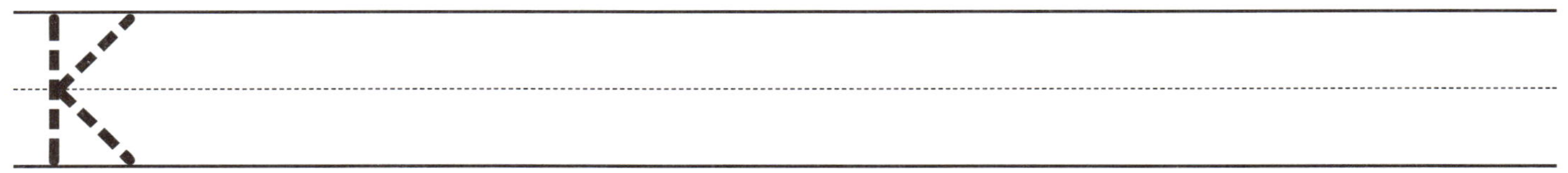

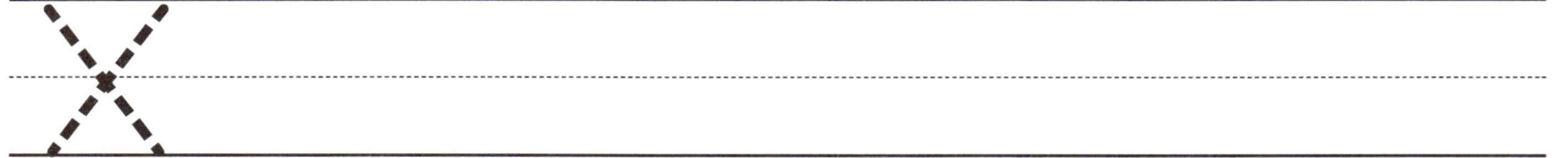

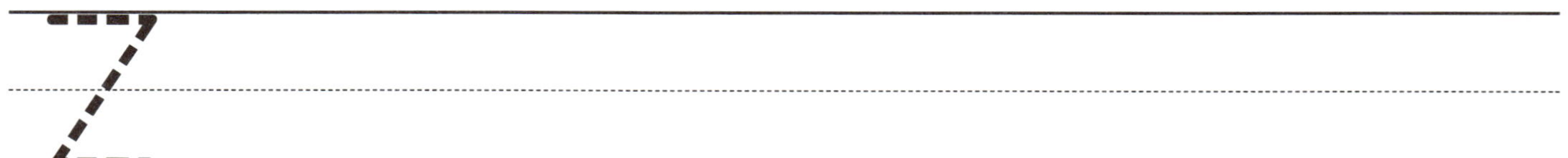

Name ______________________________ **Review**

A–Z

Trace and write.

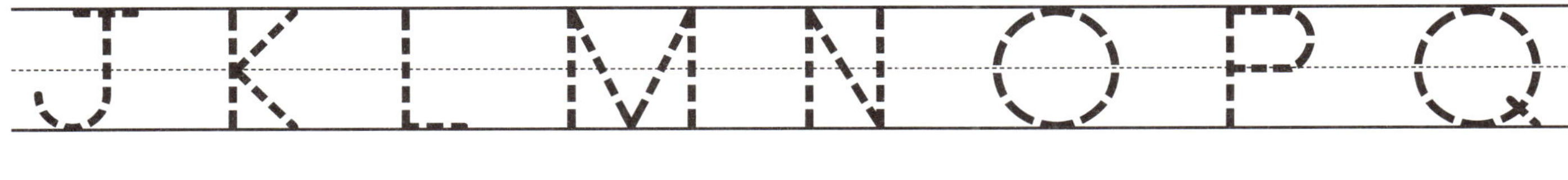

R S T U V W X Y Z

Name ______________________________ **Review**

a – z

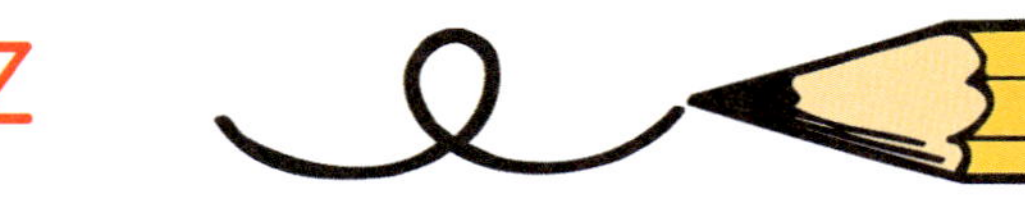

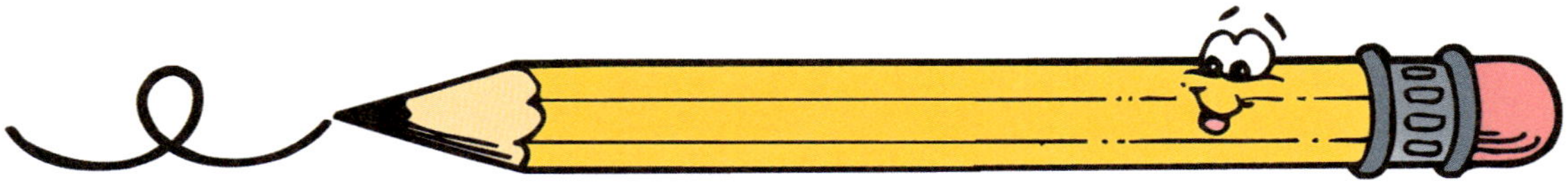

Trace and write.

a b c d e

f g h i j k

l m n o p

q r s t u

v w x y z

Scholastic Teaching Resources

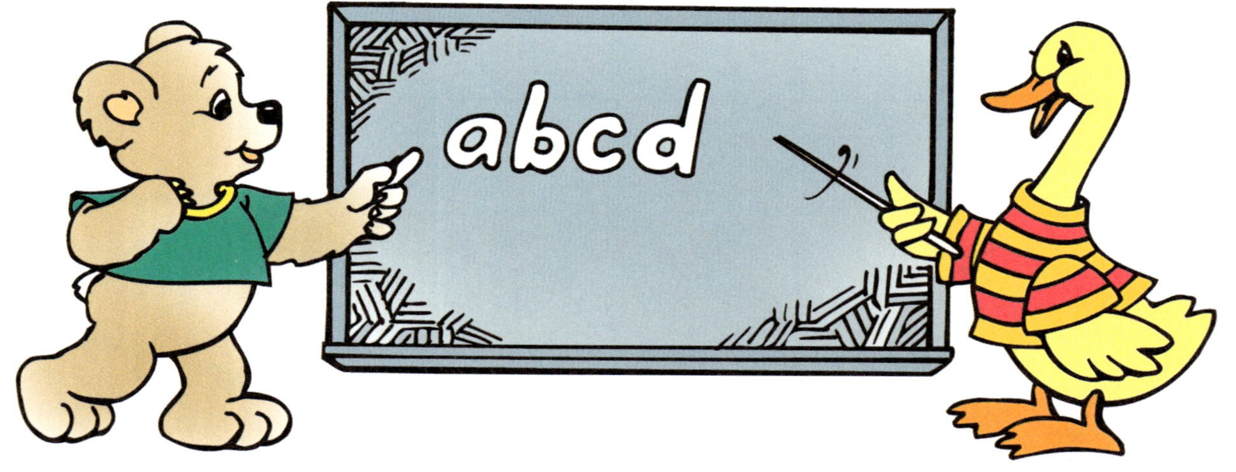

Name ______________________

1–5

Trace and write.

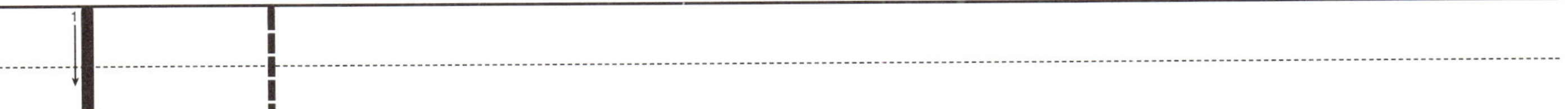

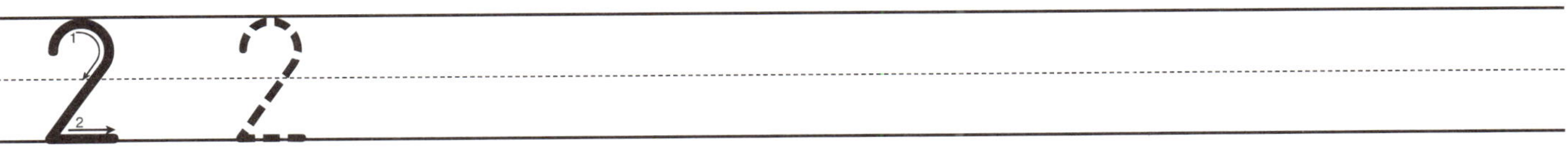

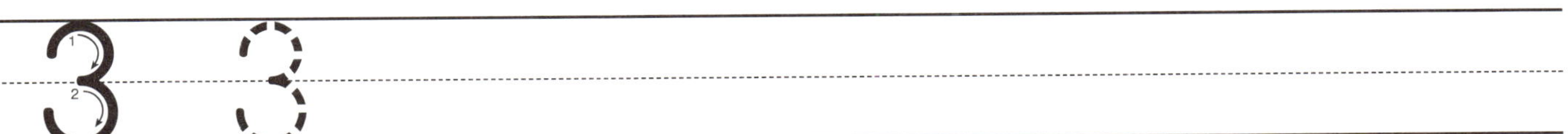

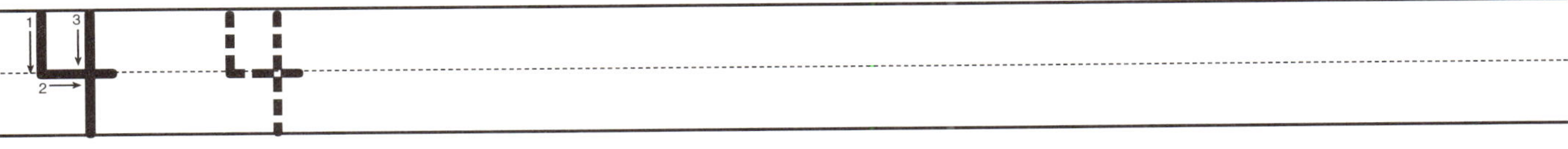

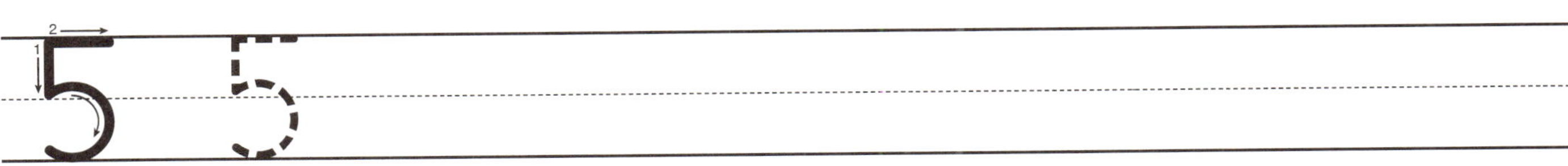

Name ___________________________________

6–10

Trace and write.

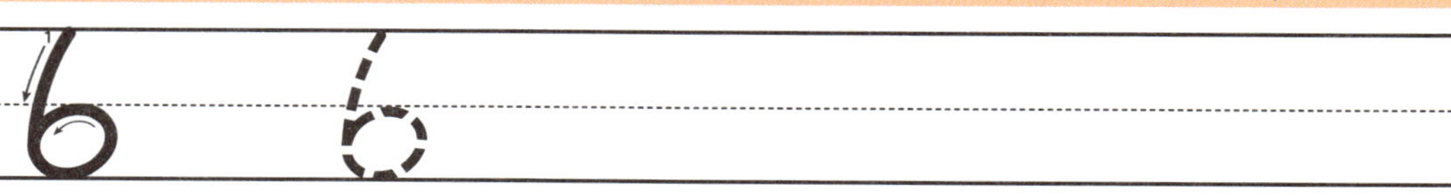

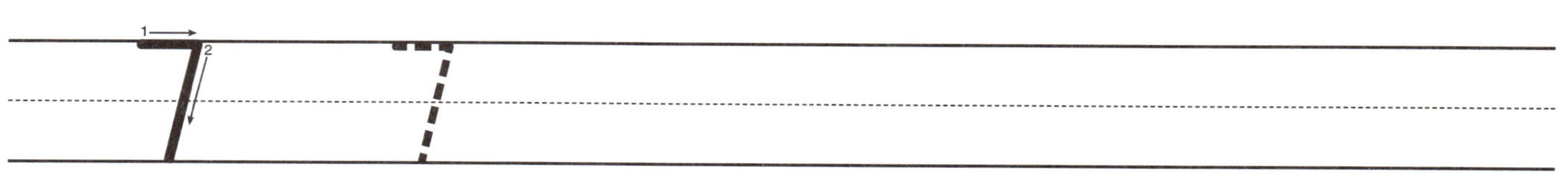

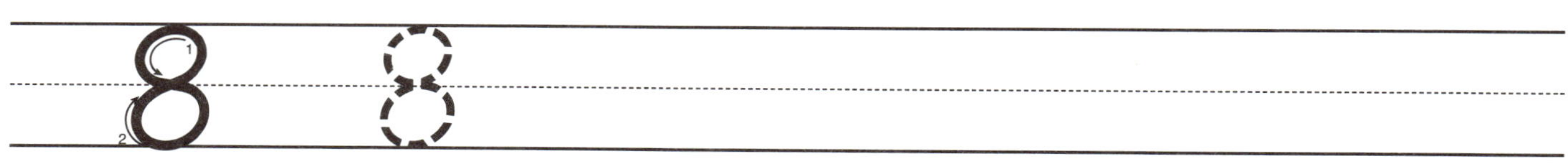

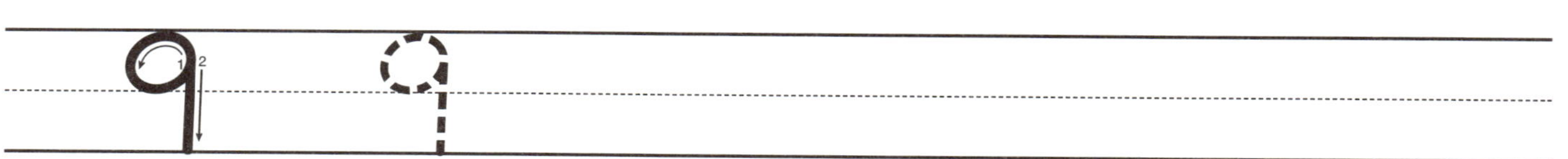

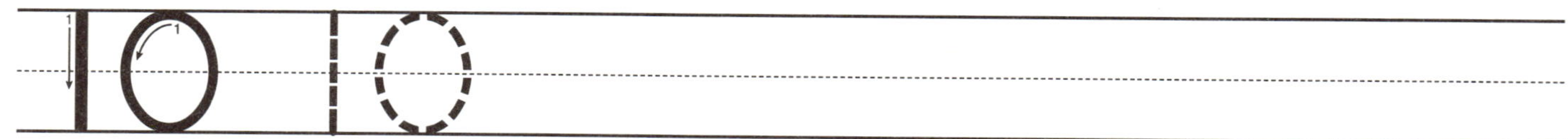

Name ______________________________

Color Words

Trace and write.

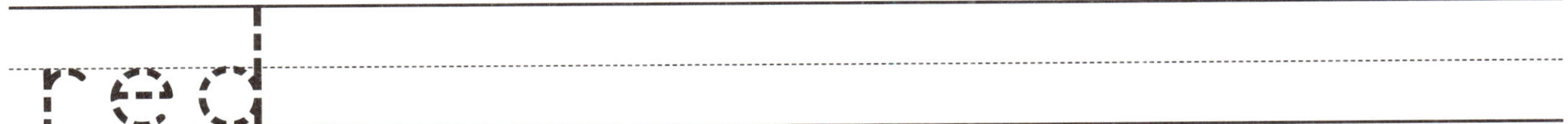

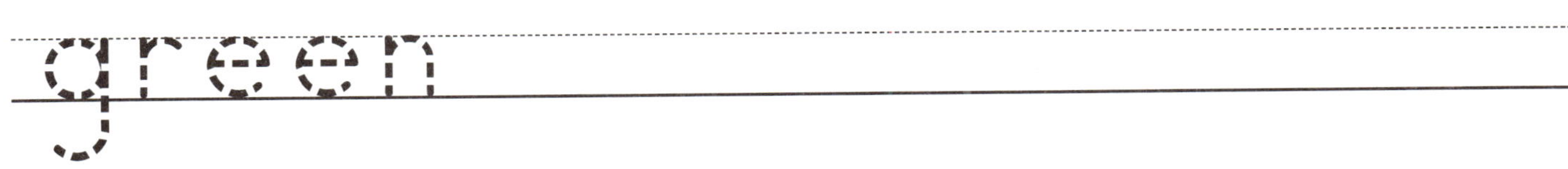

orange

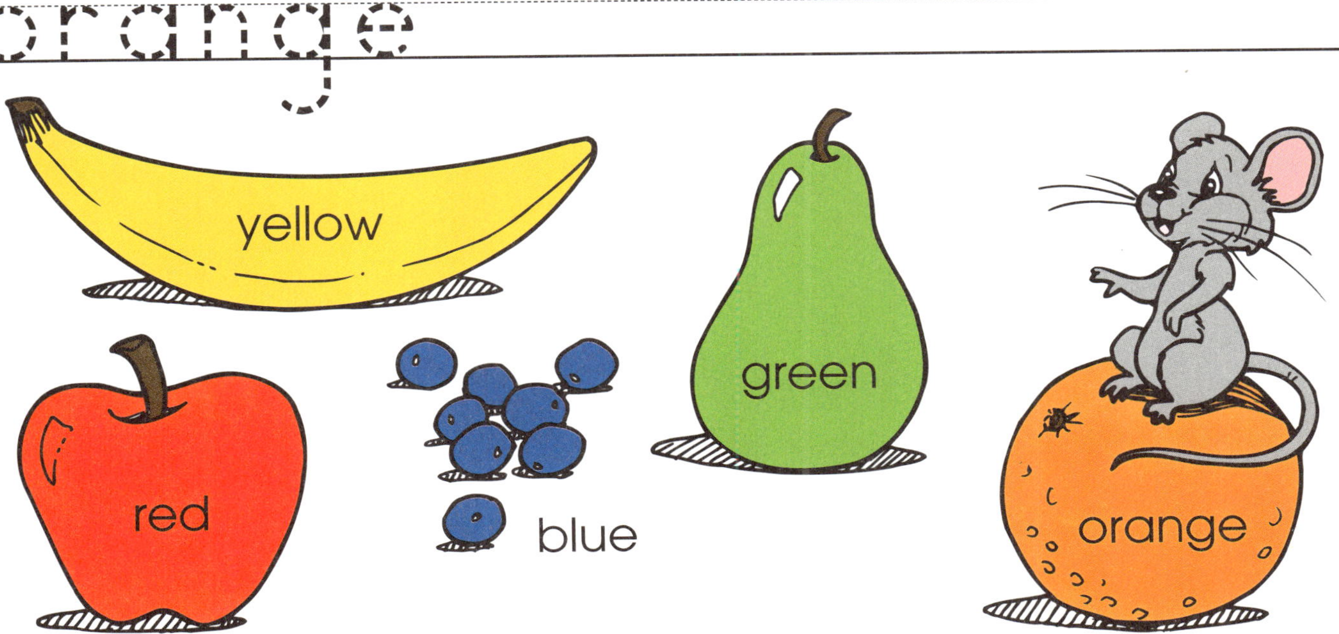

Name James

More Color Words

Trace and write.

purple purple

brown brown

black black

white whi

pink pink

Name ______________________________

Number Words

Trace and write.

1 one one

2 two two

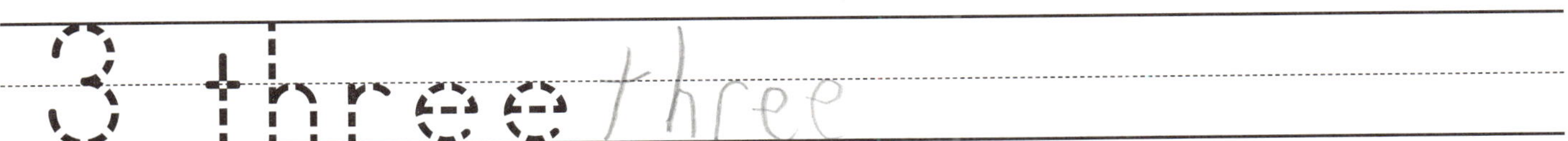

3 three three

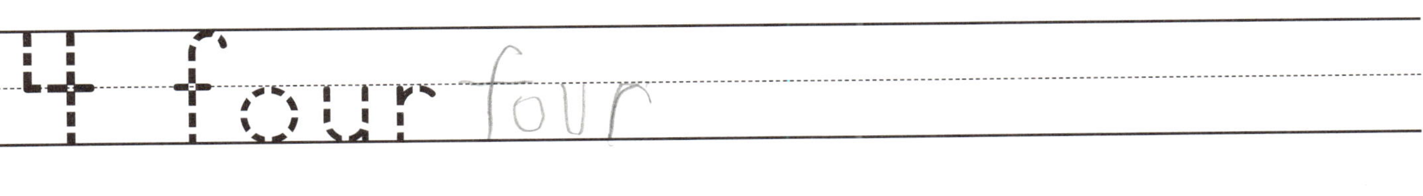

4 four four

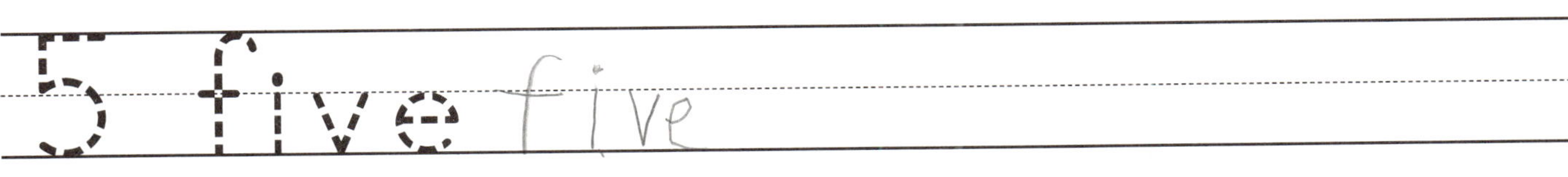

5 five five

Name ______________________________

More Number Words

Trace and write.

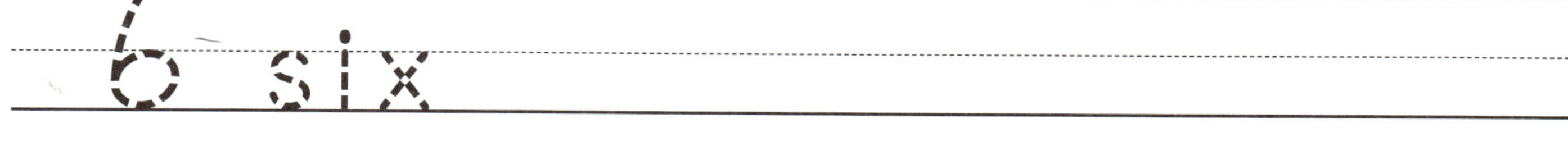

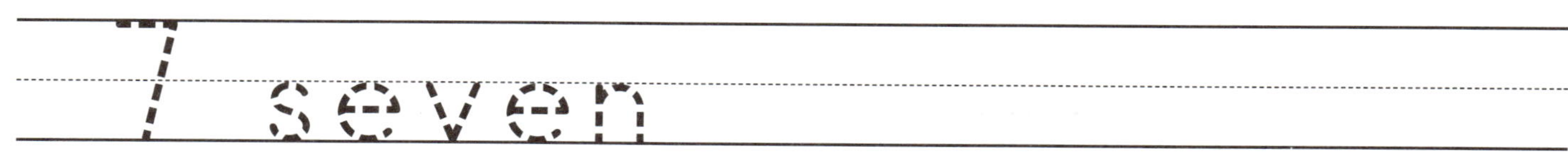

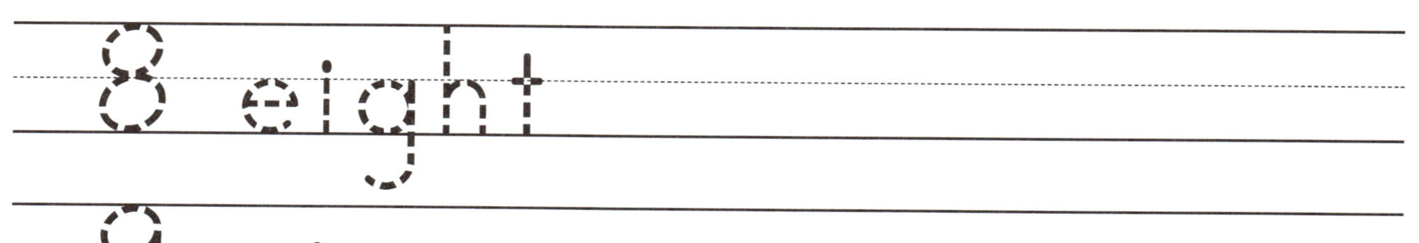

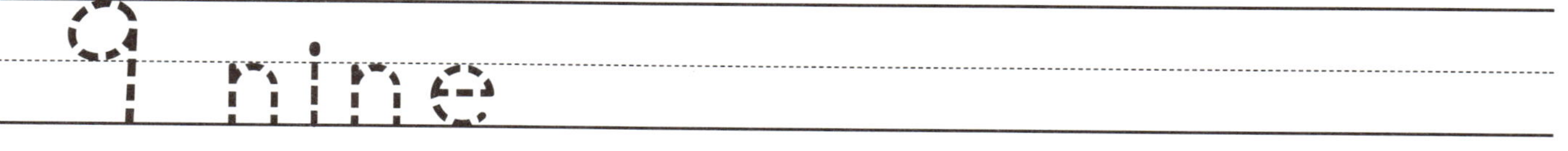

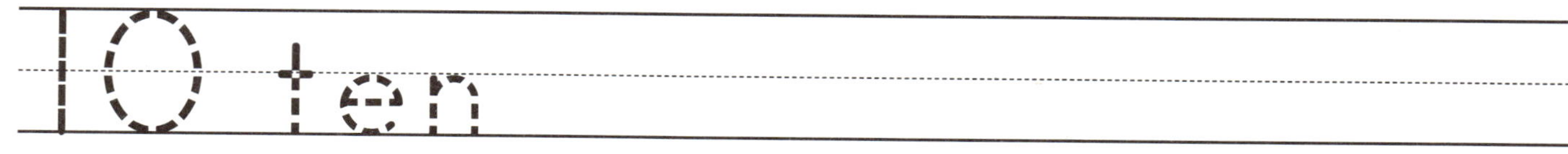

Shapes

Trace and write.

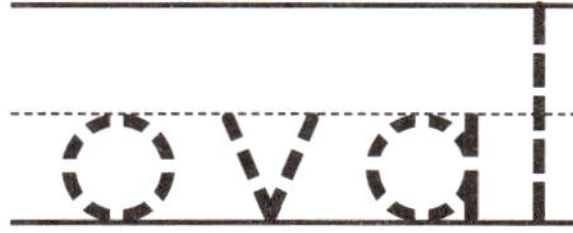

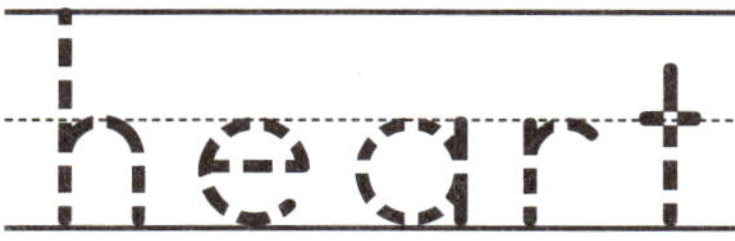

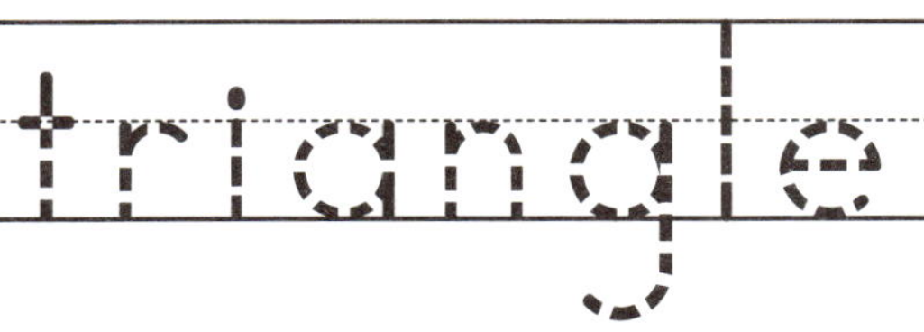

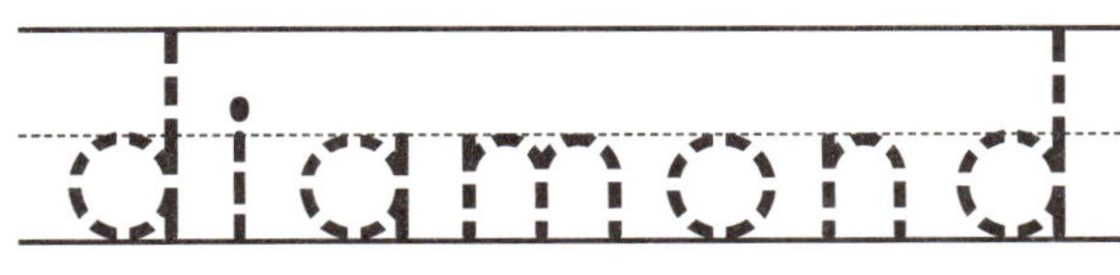

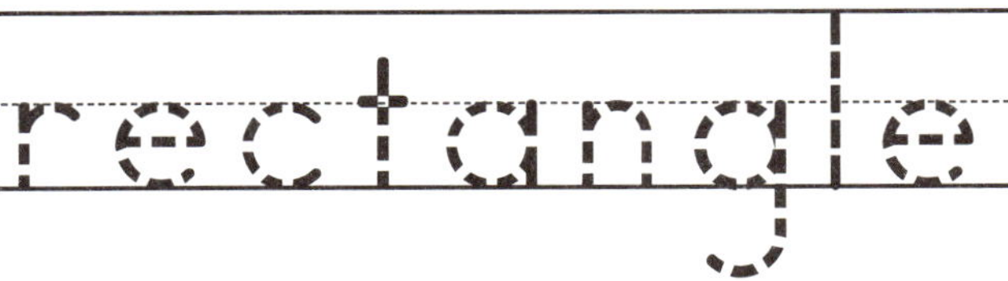

Name ______________________________

Writing practice

Days of the Week

Trace and write.

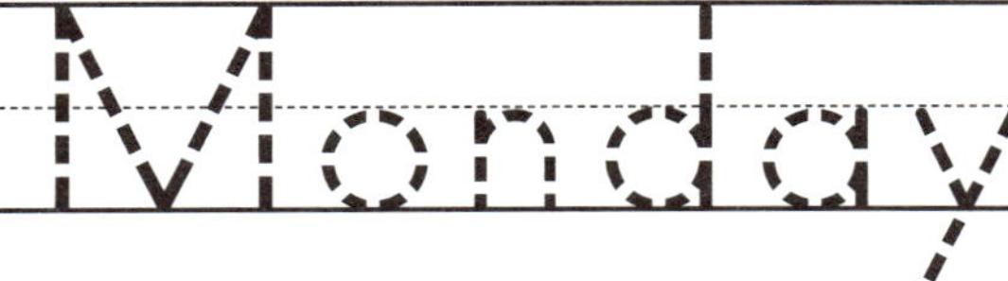

Tuesday

Thursday

Friday

Name ______________________________

Months

Trace and write.

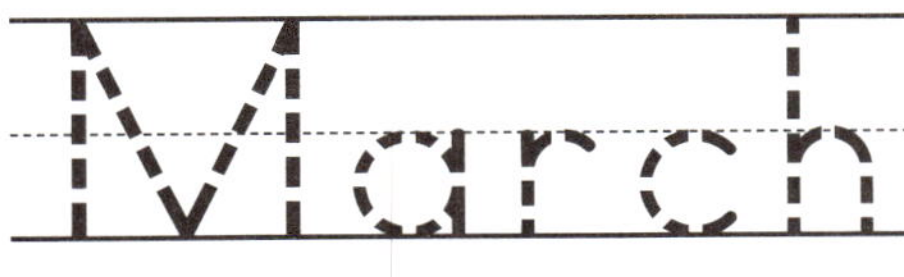

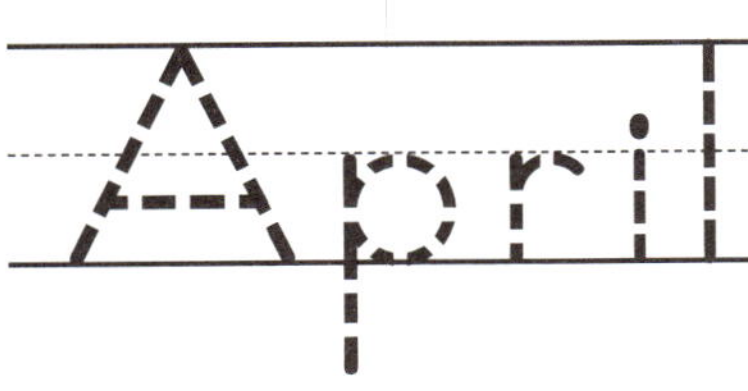

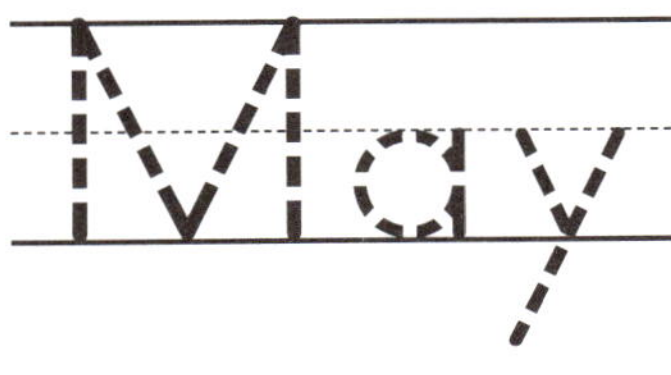

June

Name ______________________________ **Writing practice**

Months

Trace and write.

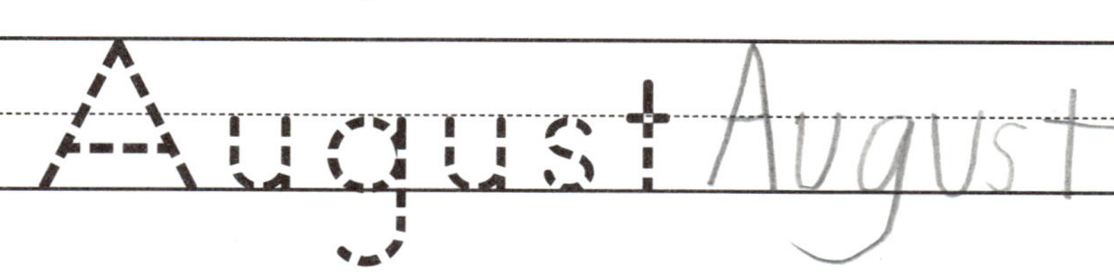

September

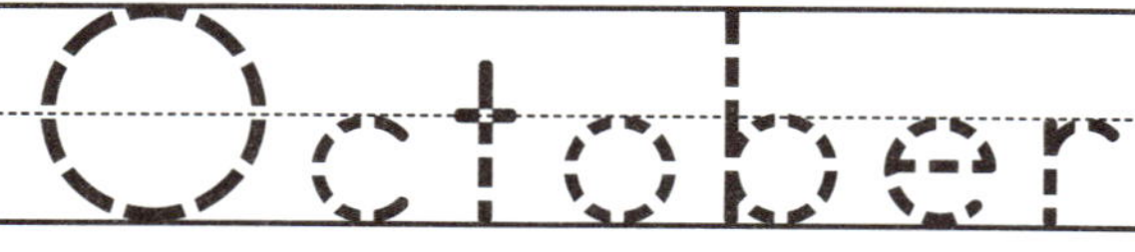

November

Name ____

Practice writing words.

has super handwriting!

Keep up the good work!

signed

date

Scholastic Success With

BASIC CONCEPTS

Name ____________________ 

Coloring Crayons

Color each crayon to show its color.
Draw a line from each crayon to its matching color word.

blue

orange

red

purple

yellow

green

red

yellow

orange

blue

green

purple

Name three things that are red.

Name ______________________________ 

What Color Am I?

Say the color words. Color the pictures.

yellow

red

green

blue

orange

black

purple

brown

On another sheet of paper, draw four things that are green.

Name ______________________________

Color Train

Draw a line to match each picture to the correct color.
Color.

blue

yellow

black

red

Name ___________________________

Color Train

Draw a line to match each picture to the correct color.
Color.

Name ____

Clowning Around

Color.

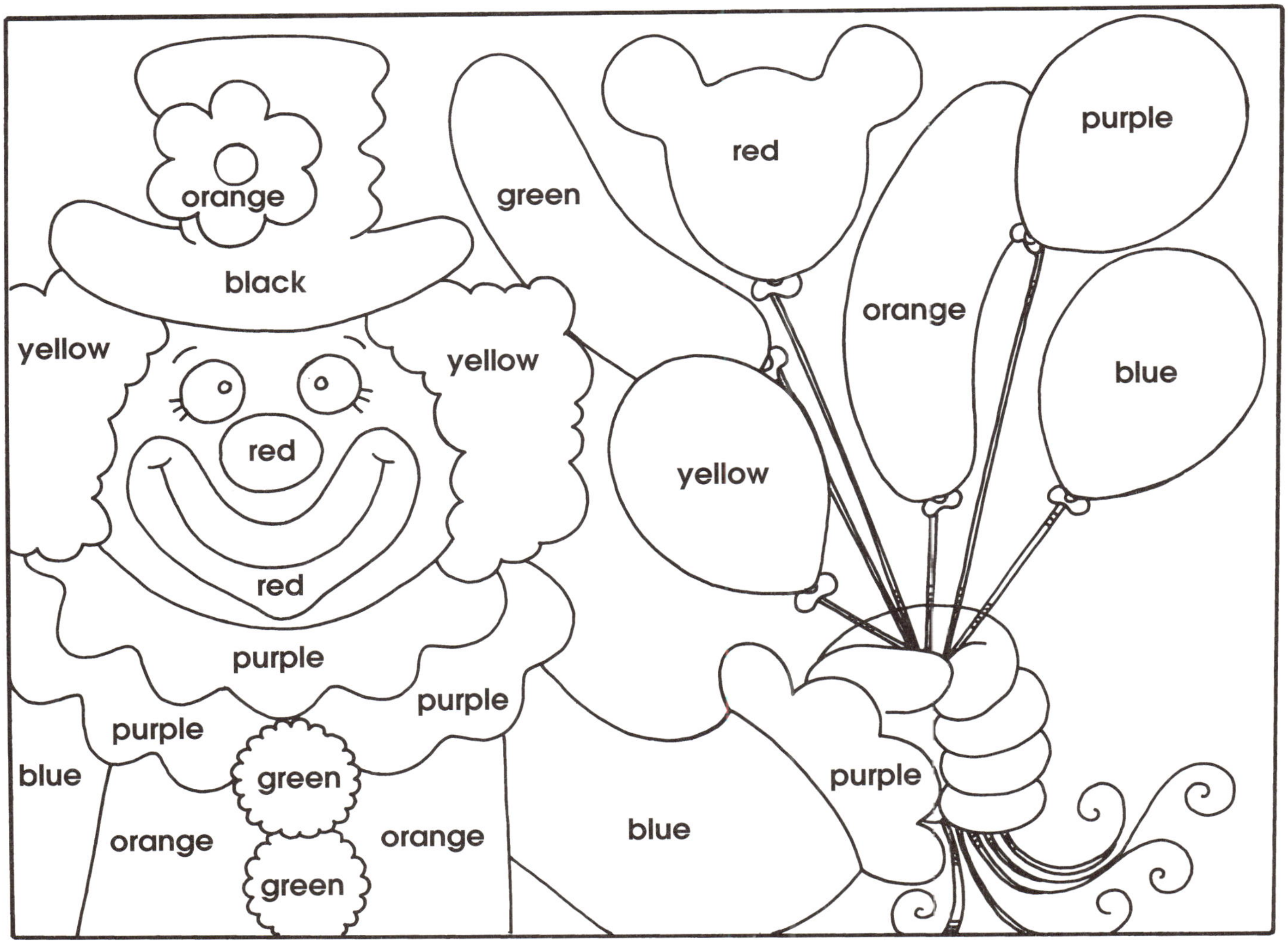

orange
black
green
red
purple
orange
blue
yellow
yellow
yellow
red
red
purple
purple
purple
purple
blue
green
orange
orange
green
blue

Name ______________________________ 

Rolling Through the Hills

Color.

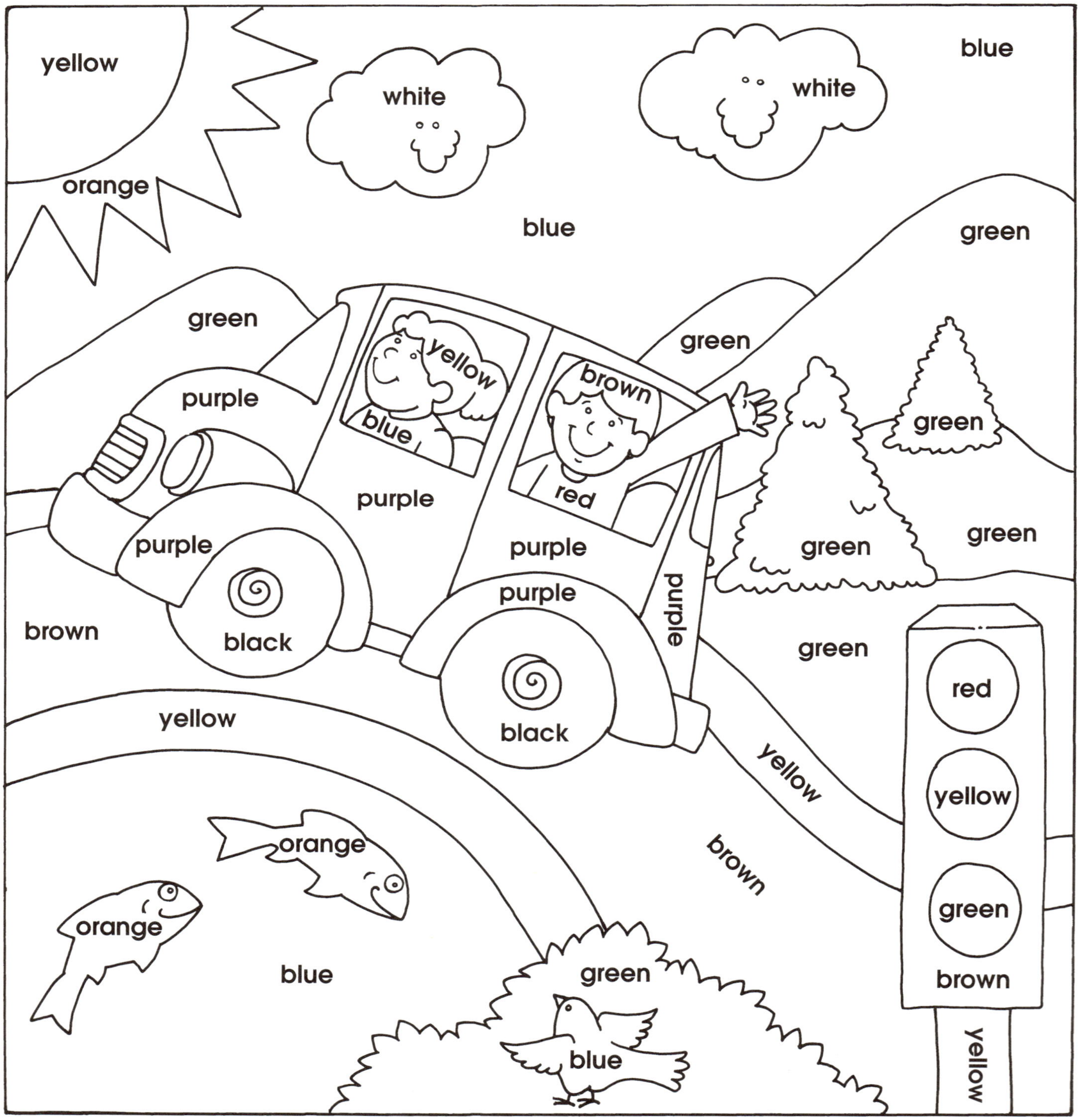

Sorting Shapes

This is a **circle** ◯. This is a **square** □. A square has four sides that are the same length. This is a **rectangle** ▭. A rectangle also has four sides. The opposite sides of a rectangle are the same length. This is a **triangle** △. A triangle has three sides.

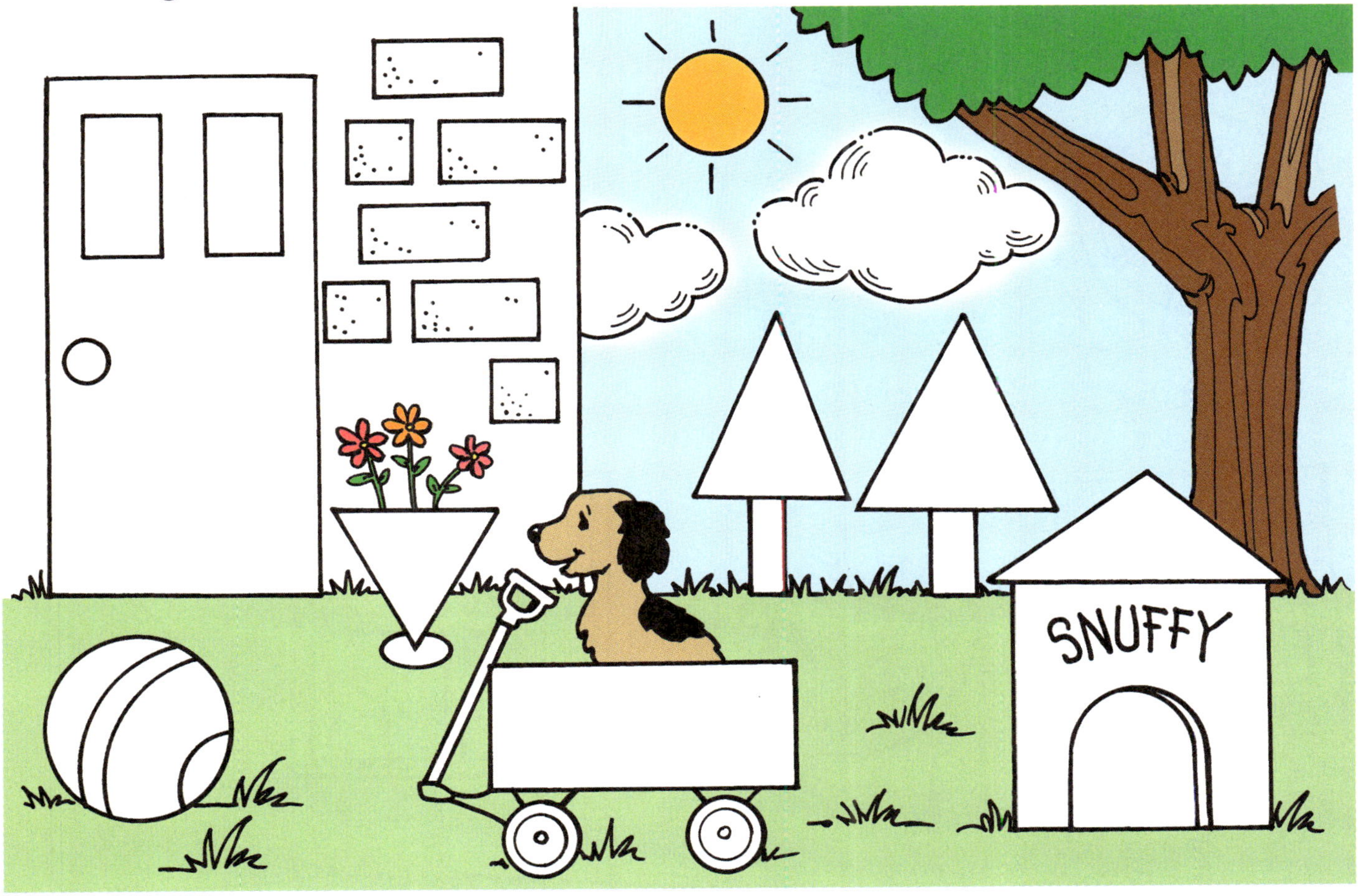

Color the circles yellow.

Color the squares red.

Color the triangles green.

Color the rectangles blue.

Name ______________________________

Circle and Square Search

Color each circle shape.

Color each square shape.

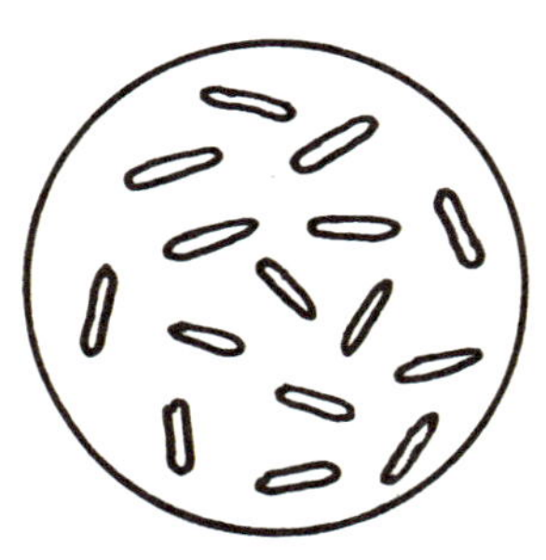

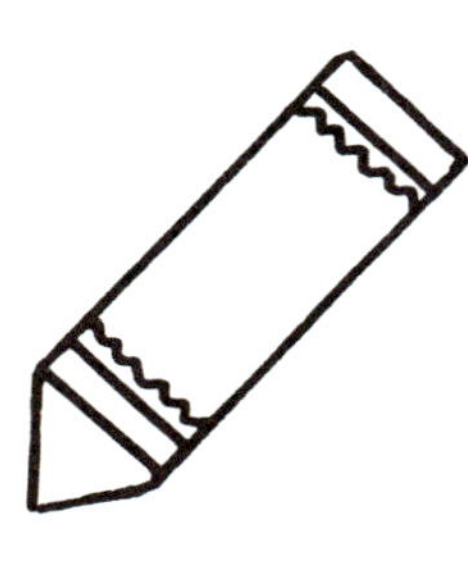

Name ______________________________

Rectangle and Triangle Teasers

Color each rectangle shape.

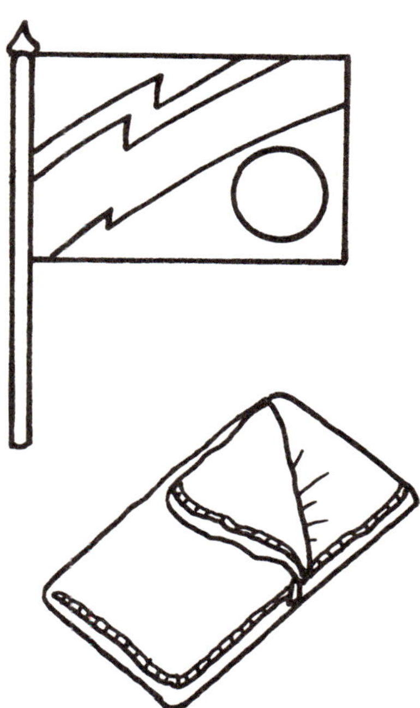

Color each triangle shape.

Name ______________________________

Oval and Diamond Detectives

Color each diamond shape.

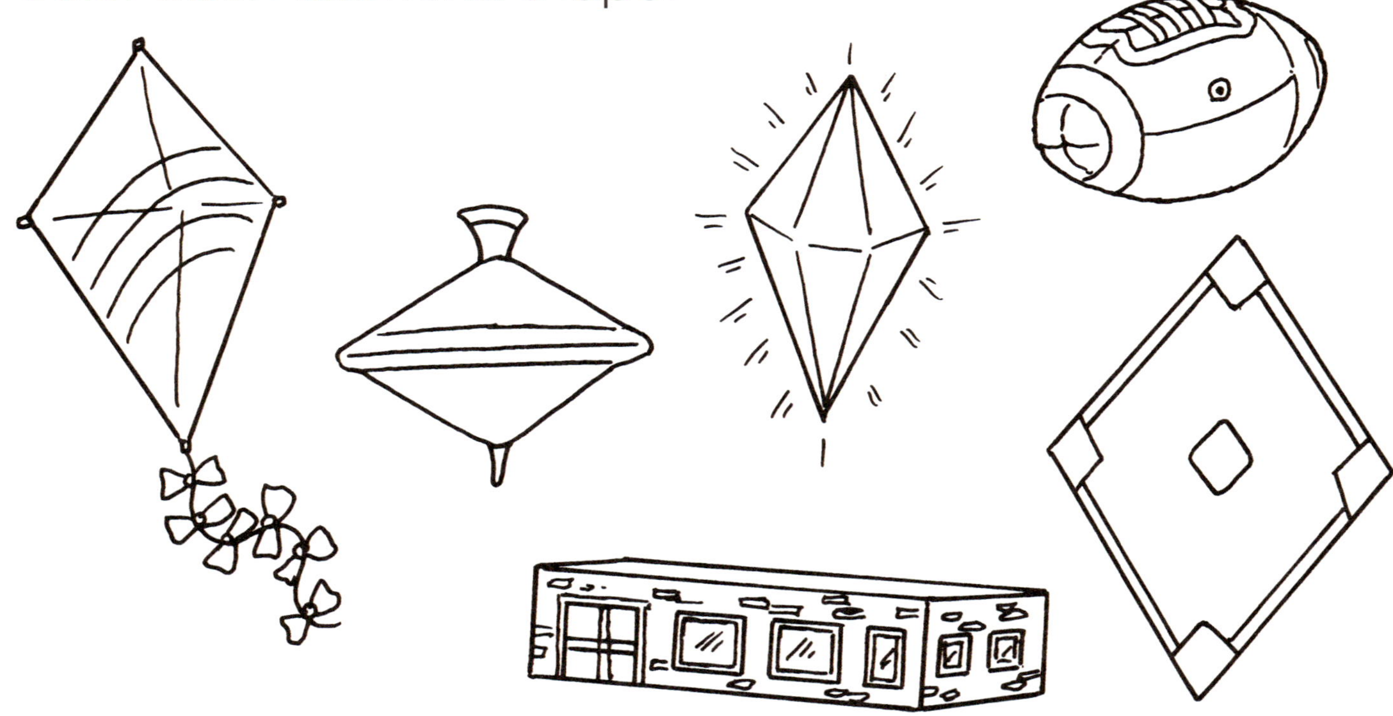

Color each oval shape.

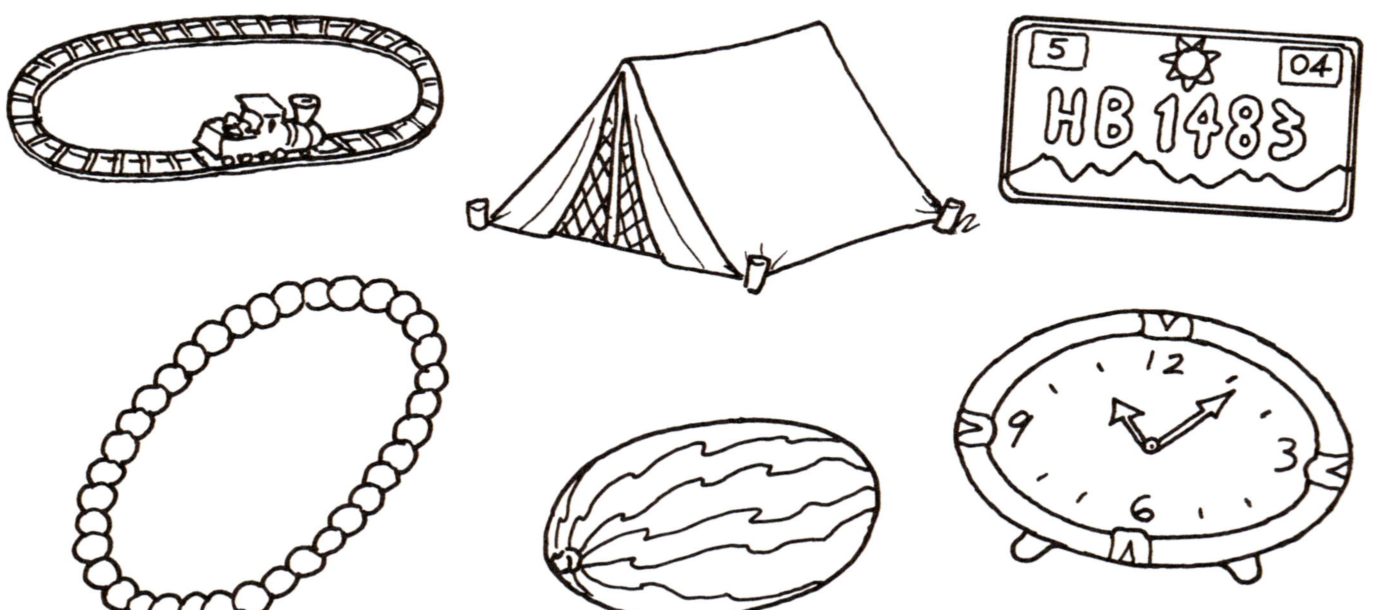

Name ______________________________ 

Shape Match-Up

Trace each shape. Draw a line to match each object to its shape. Color.

square

circle

triangle

rectangle

More Shape Match-Up

Trace each shape. Draw a line to match each object to its shape. Color.

oval

rectangle

diamond

square

Name ______________________________ 

The Mole's Hole

Color each circle ◯ to show the mole's way home.

Shape Teasers

Color each shape using the code.

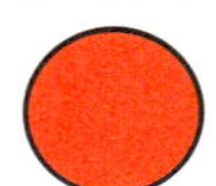 = red  = blue  = green 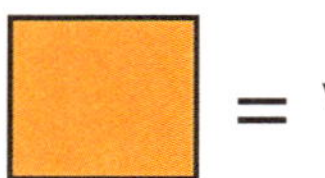 = yellow

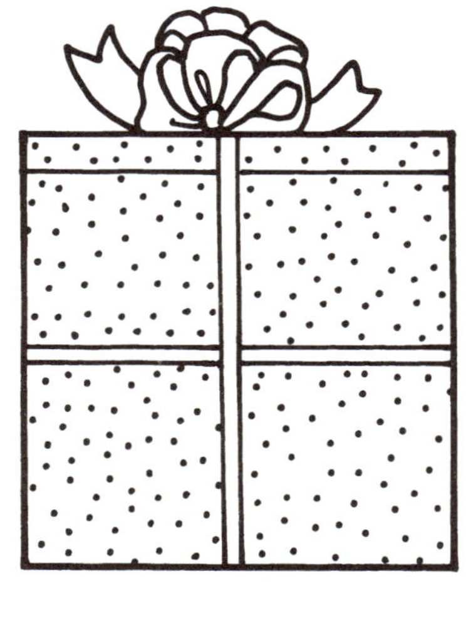

Name something else with each shape.

Name ____________________

Zany Zoo Shapes

Color. 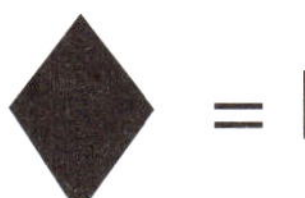 = black  = blue  = red

 = brown  = green  = yellow

Name ___________________________________ 

Flying High With Shapes

Color. ◆ = purple ■ = yellow ▲ = orange

▬ = green ● = blue ⬬ = red

A Shapely Castle

Color.

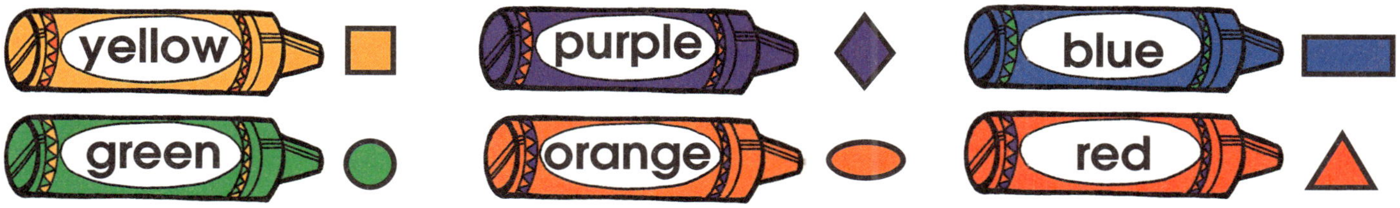

orange

Smiling Shapes

Draw a line to the shape that comes next.

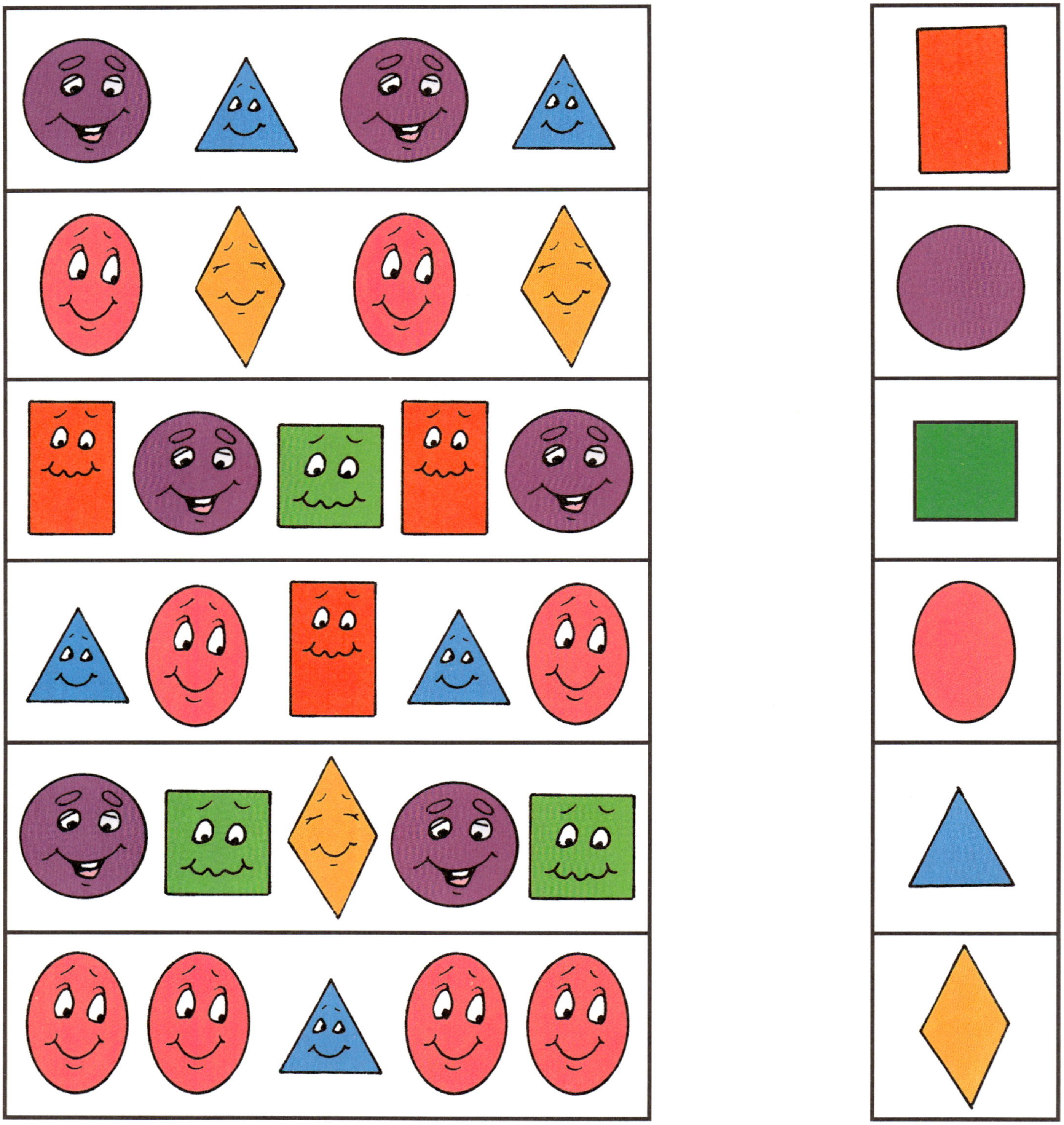

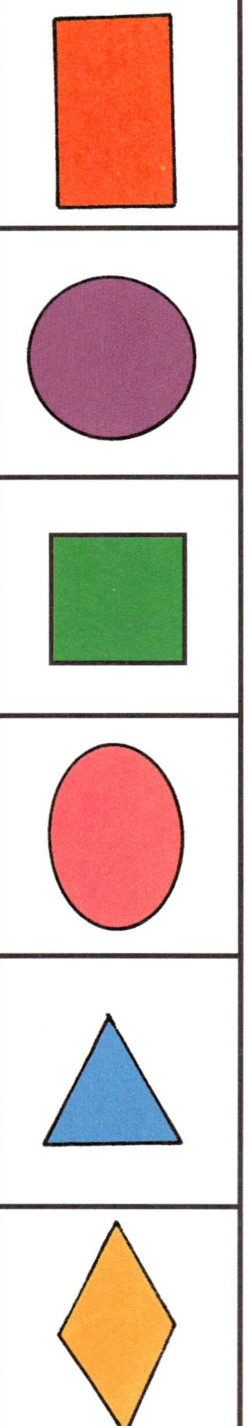

Name ___________________________________

Picking Flowers

Circle what comes next.

Name ______________________________

What Comes Next?

Circle what comes next.

Name ___________________________________

Ordering Outfits

Circle what comes next.

Decorate a Headband

Draw the shapes that finish the patterns. Then color your headband.

Name ______________________

You Can Draw an Apple!

Name ____________________

You Can Draw a Balloon!

Name ___________________________________

You Can Draw a Kite!

1 Draw a diamond.	2 Draw a line from the top to the bottom.	3 Draw a line from left to right.
4 Draw a curvy line for the string.	5 Draw 2 small triangles on the left side of the string.	6 Draw 2 small triangles on the right side of the string.

Name ____

You Can Draw a Dinosaur!

1 Draw a small circle for the head.

2 Draw a large oval for the body.

3 Connect the head and body with two lines.

4 Draw a curved triangle for the tail.

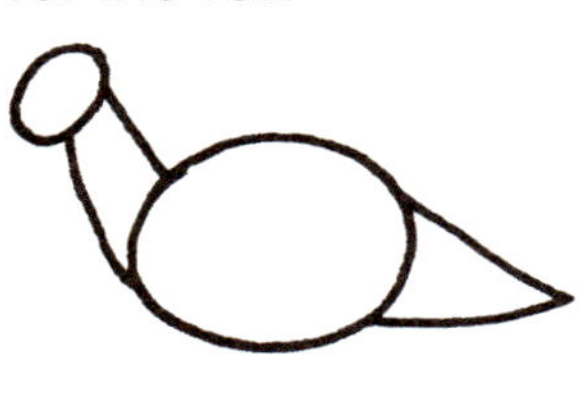

5 Draw four rectangles for legs.

6 Add facial features, spots, and toes.

Name ________________________________

Everything in Order

The **sequence** is the order in which things happen.

Write 1 under the picture that happens first.
Write 2 under the picture that happens second.

________ ________ ________ ________

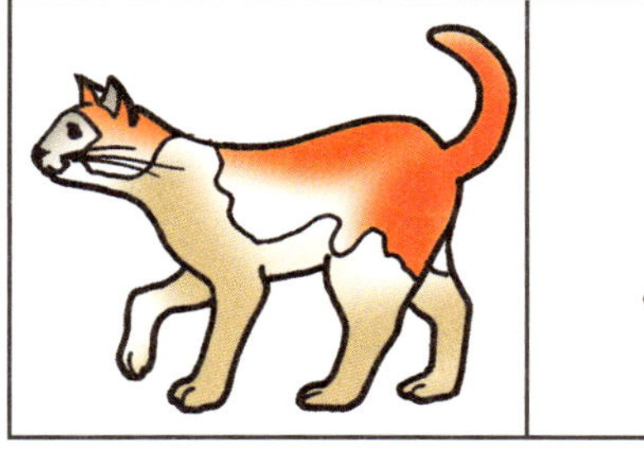

________ ________ ________ ________

________ ________ ________ ________

What do you do first when you wake up?

Name ______________________________

First Things First

Write 1 by what happened first.

Write 2 by what happened second.

Write 3 by what happened third.

Perfect Order

Write 1 by what happened first.

Write 2 by what happened second.

Write 3 by what happened third.

Out of Place

Say the things in the pictures. Circle two things in each picture that do not belong. Color the pictures.

Where Do I Belong?

Draw a line to show where each thing belongs.

On another sheet of paper, draw a picture of something else that might be on a farm.

Name ____

Going to School

Find and color these things in the picture.

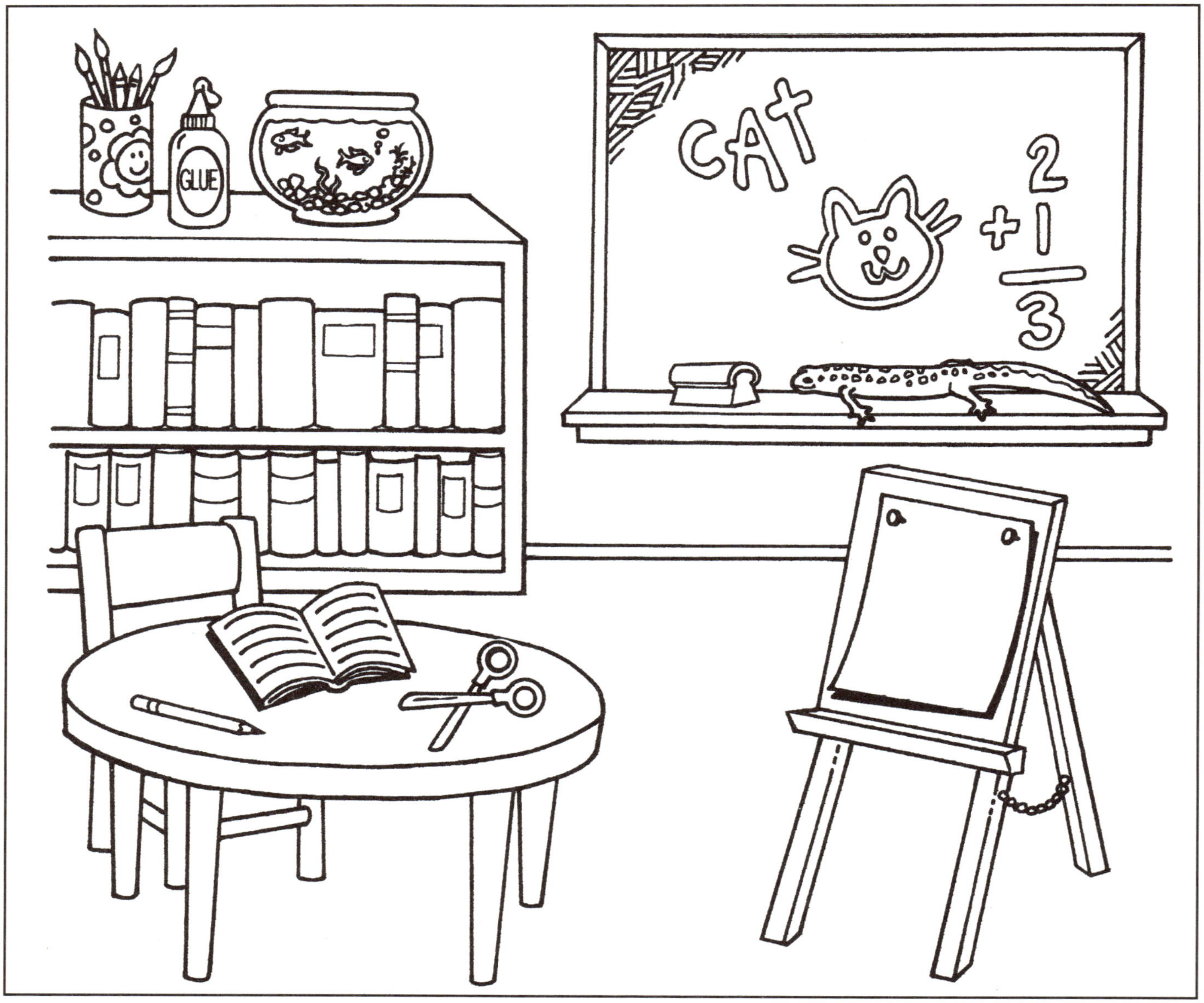

Color one thing in the picture that does not belong.

Name ______________________________ 

Up, Down, and All Around

This mouse is **up**.  This mouse is **down**. 

Color the animals that are up red.
Color the animals that are down blue.

How many animals are up? ________

How many animals are down? ________

Name ______________________________

Pretty Balloons

This is **high**.  This is **low**.

Color the high balloons purple.
Color the low balloons yellow.

Circle the lowest balloon.

Name ______________________________

Up on Top

Draw a ◯ around the  on the **top**.

Draw a ◯ around the  on the **top**.

Draw a ◯ around the  on the **bottom**.

Draw a ◯ around the  on the **bottom**.

Name ____________________ 

Above or Below . . . Sure You Know!

Draw a ☐ around the  **above** the .

Draw a ☐ around the **above** the .

Draw a ☐ around the  **below** the .

Draw a ☐ around the  **below** the .

Name ________________________________ 

Quacky Business

This duck is **over**.  This duck is **under**. 

Circle the correct answer.

Where do you see more ducks?	over	under
Where do you see more frogs?	over	under

 **How many ducks are there altogether in the picture?** ________

In, Out, and All About

Color the animals that are **in** their houses.

Name ______________________________

More In, Out, and All About

This animal is **in**.

This animal is **out**.

Color each animal that is in its home.

Name ______________________________ 

Size It Up

Draw a ◇ around the picture that is **short**.

Draw a ◇ around the picture that is **long**.

Name ____________________ 

Transportation Station

Draw a ▭ around the picture that is **big**.

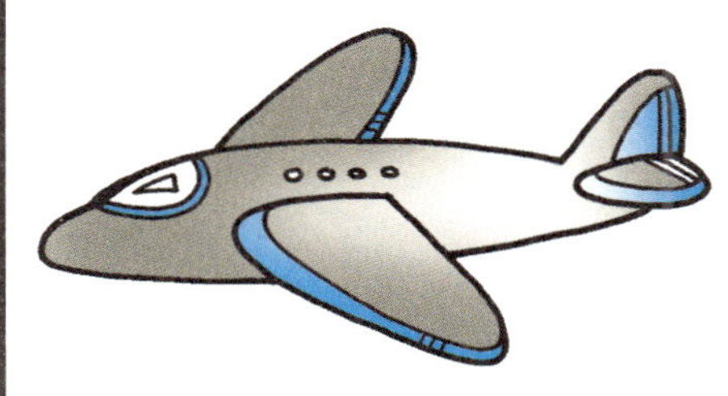

Draw a ▭ around the picture that is **small**.

Just the Right Size

This butterfly is **large**.  This butterfly is **small**. 
Circle the large item on each petal.

Name two things that are larger than you.

Name ____ 

Star Lights

This star is **right** of the moon.

This star is **left** of the moon.

Color each ☆ that is right of the moon yellow.

Color each ☆ that is left of the moon orange.

How many stars do you see in all? ________

Name ______________________________

Mark the Map

Trace a L or R path in each picture.

LEFT

RIGHT

How Do You Feel?

Sometimes you feel **happy**. Sometimes you feel **sad**.

Look at each picture. Draw a line to the happy or sad face to show how the picture makes you feel.

Name ___________________________________ 

Tricks for Treats

Count. Circle the dog with **less** bones.

Name ___________________________________

Time for a Picnic

The rabbit has **more** than the dog.
The dog has **less** than the rabbit.

Write how many. Circle the group that has **more**.

				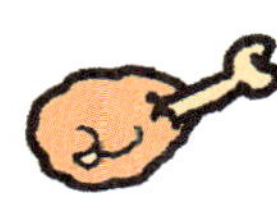	
____	____	____	____	____	____

Write how many. Circle the group that has **less**.

		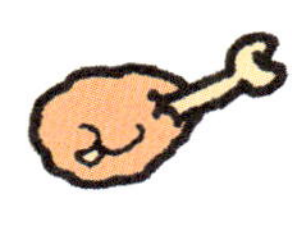			
____	____	____	____	____	____

Name ______________________________ 

What Is Really Real?

Things that are **pretend** are not **real**.

Color the real pictures.
Do not color the pretend pictures.

GUM

Make up a story about a pretend trip to the moon. Tell your story to a grown-up.

Name ______________________________________ 

A Silly City

Circle 5 pretend things in the picture.

Searching for Opposites

An elephant is big. A mouse is little.
Big and little are **opposites**.

Circle the picture that shows the opposite.

 happy	 sad 
 up	 down 
 boy	 girl 
 fast	 slow 

Name something you can do fast. Name something you can do slow.

Name ______________________________ 

Searching for More Opposites

Circle the picture that shows the **opposite**.

 big	  little
 in	  out
 hot	 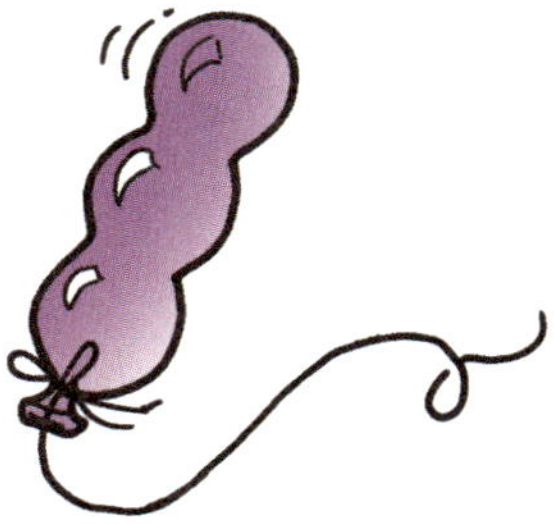 cold
 full	 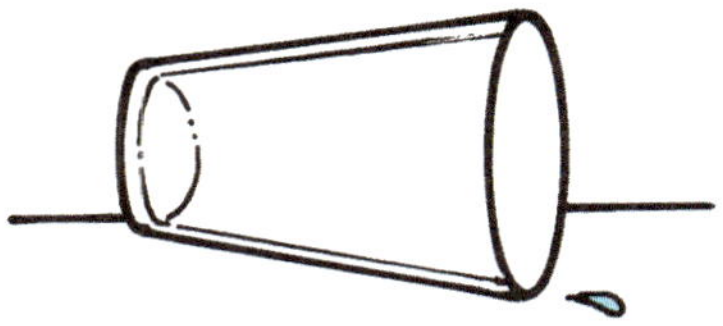 empty

On another sheet of paper, draw a picture of a something that might be larger than an elephant.

Rounding Up Opposites

Circle the picture that shows the opposite.

 full	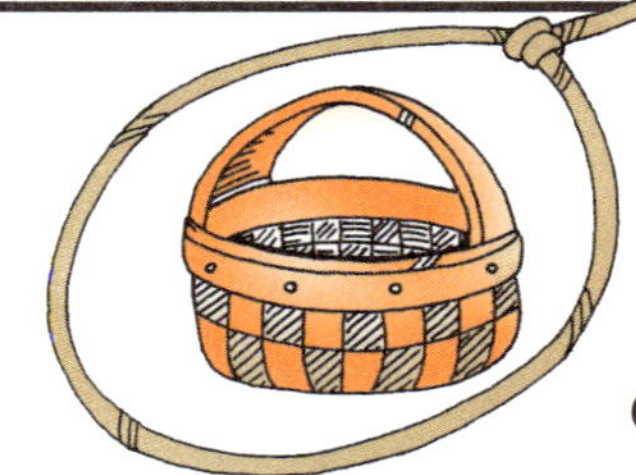 empty 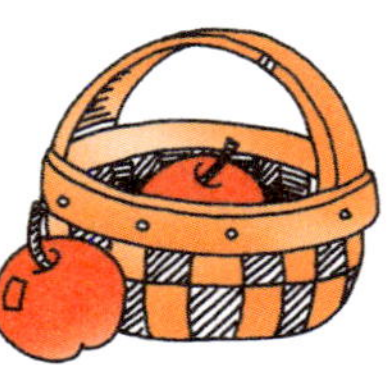
 loud	 quiet 
slow	 fast 
 over	 under 
wet	 dry 

Name ______________________________ 

Different as Can Be

Follow the maze to match the pictures that show the opposite.

A Perfect Match

 and  are the **same**.

Connect the cars that are the same.

Name one way you and a friend are the same.

Name ______________________________ 

A Ride in the Clouds

 and  are **different**.

Circle the plane that is different in each row.

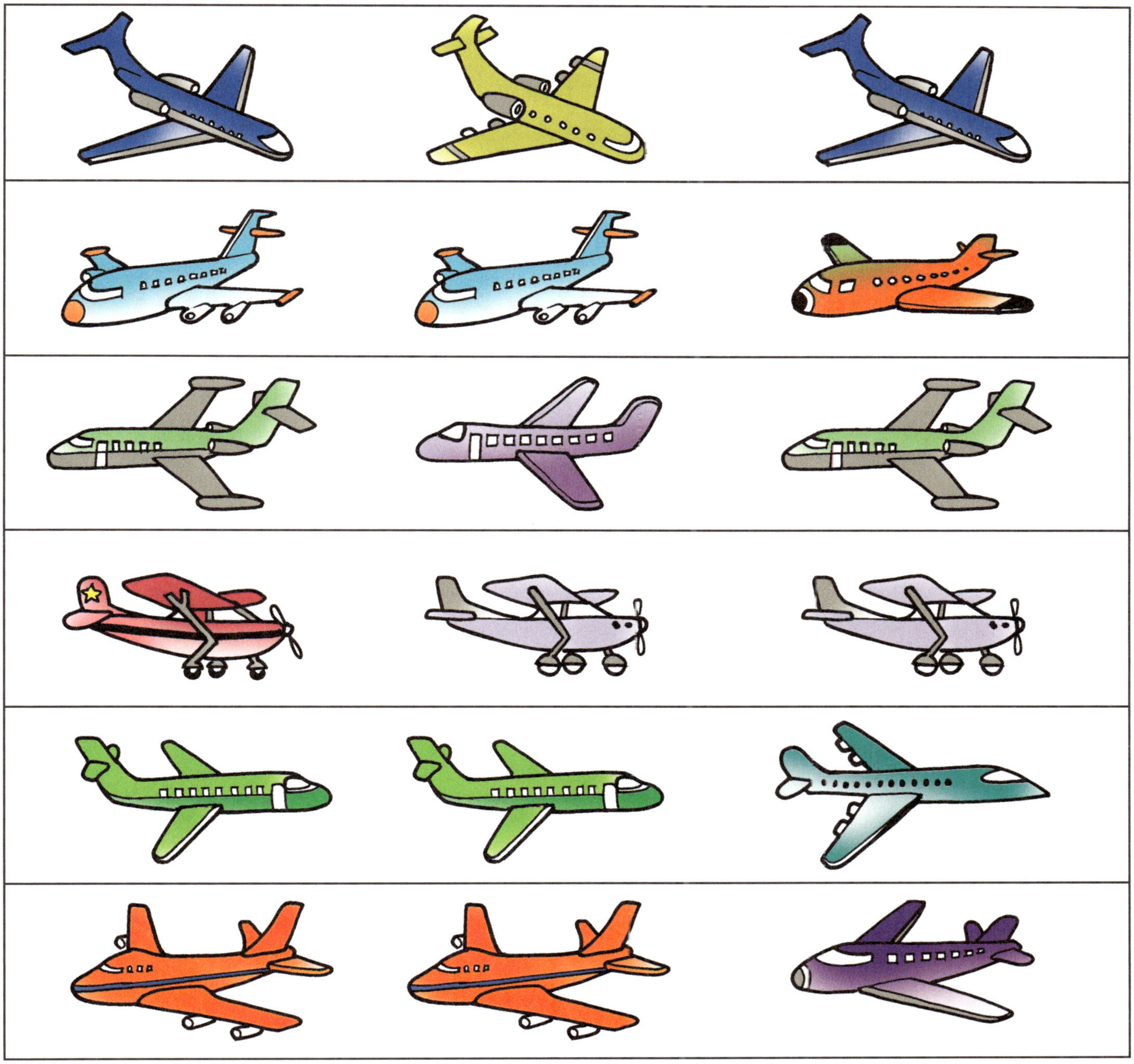

 **Name one way you and a friend are different.**

Name ____________________ 

Triangle Teasers

Draw a △ around the picture that is **different**.

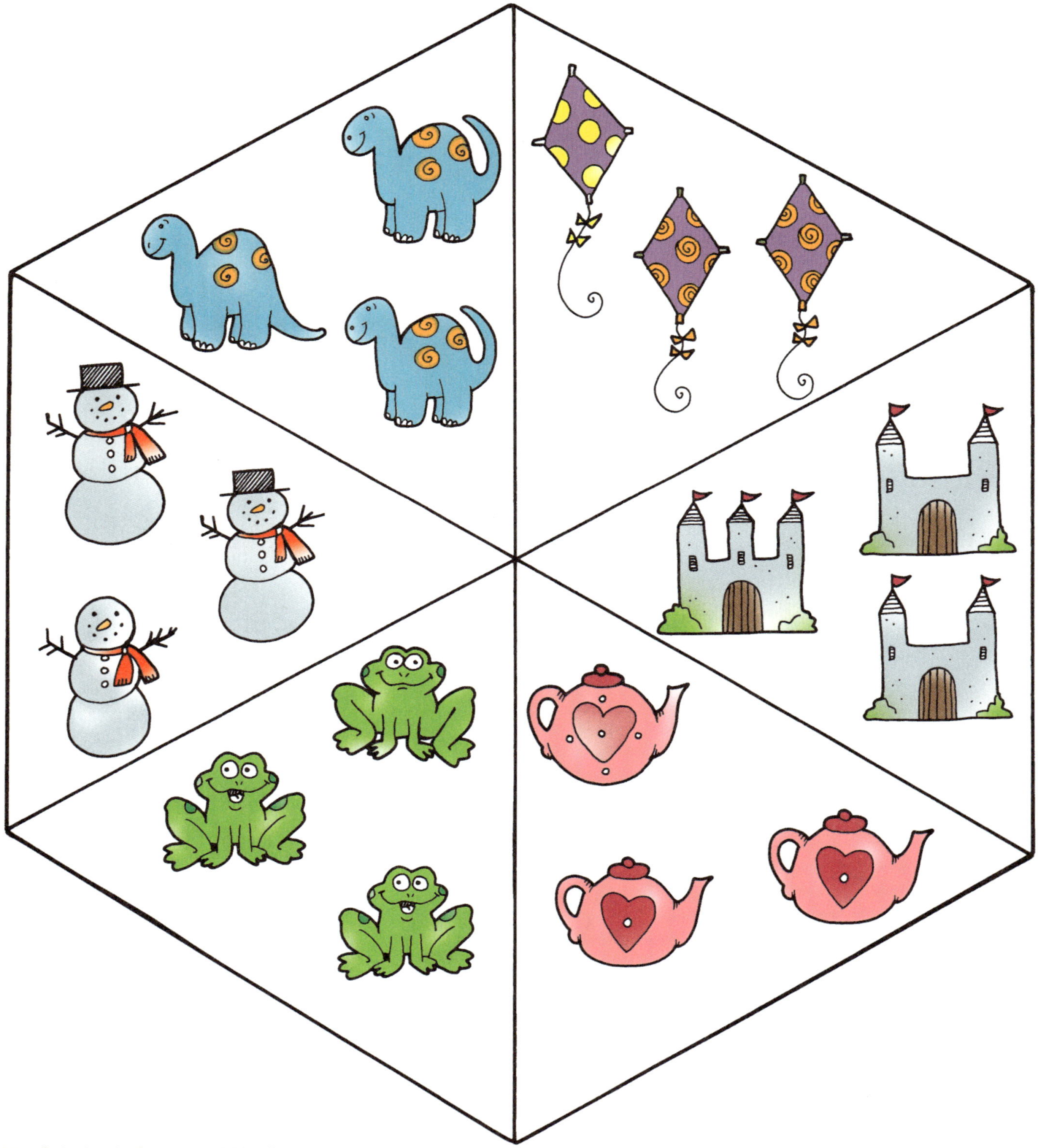

Small but Strong

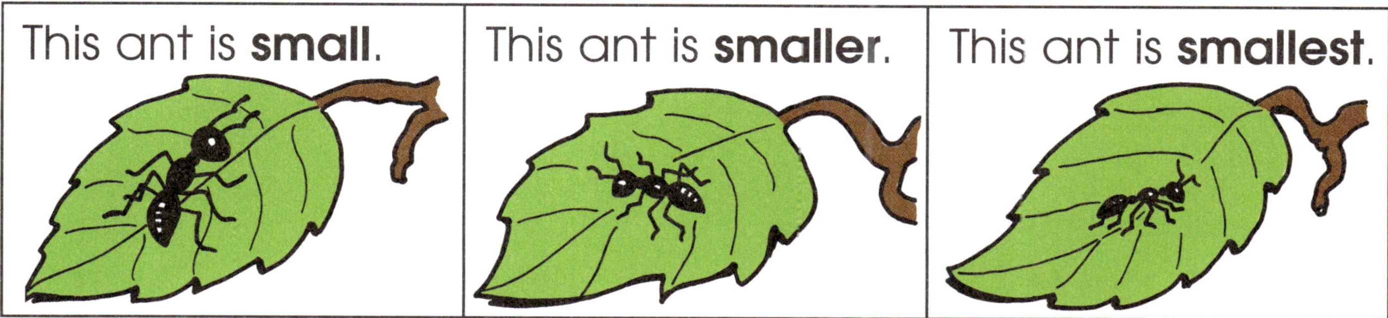

Put an **X** on the smallest animal in each row.

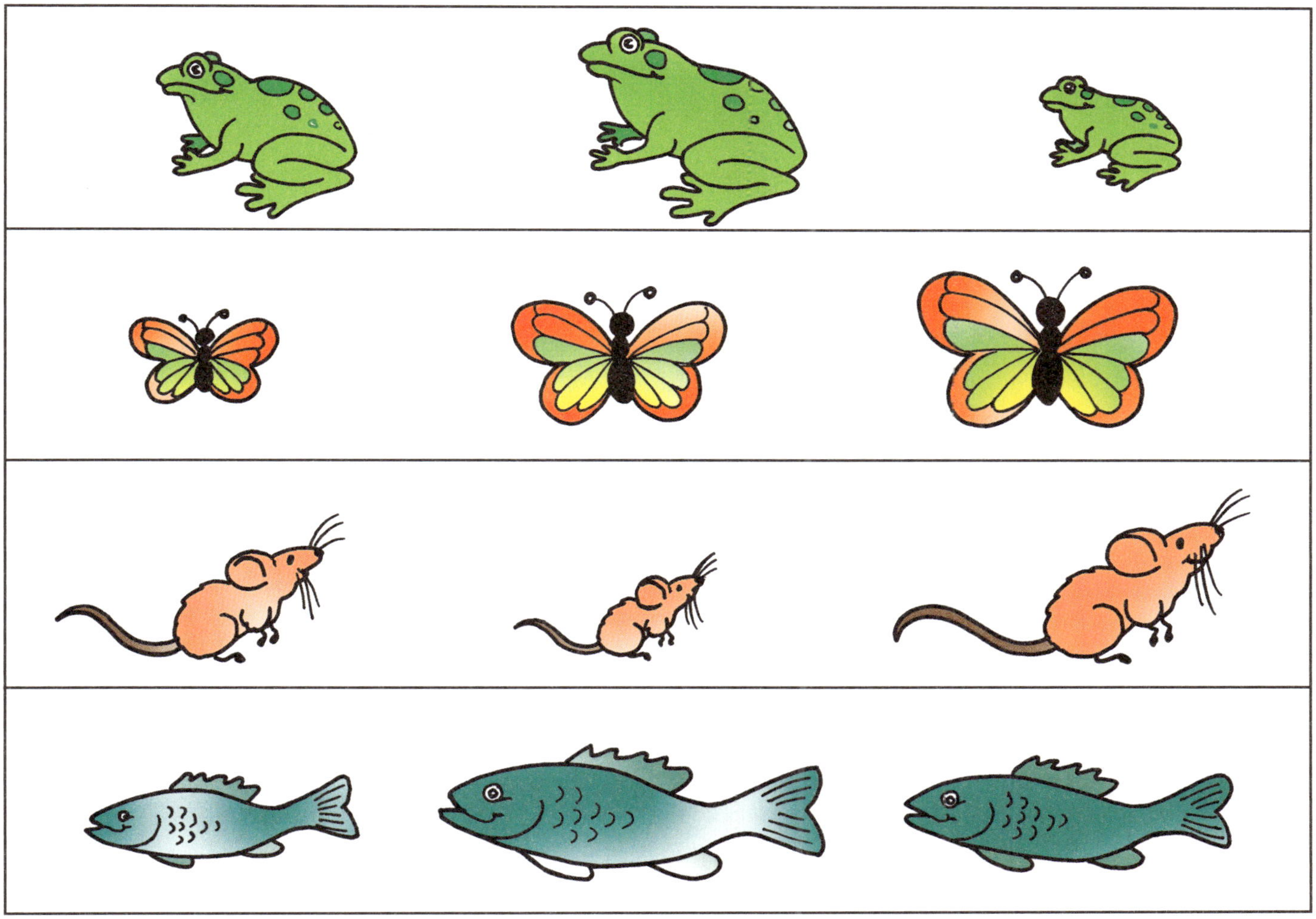

On another sheet of paper, draw something smaller than a watermelon.

Name ______________________________

Bigger and Better

This bear is **big**.	This bear is **bigger**.	This bear is **biggest**.

Draw a rectangle around the biggest animal in each row.

On another sheet of paper, draw a picture of something bigger than a bear.

Side by Side

Draw a line to match the pictures that go together.

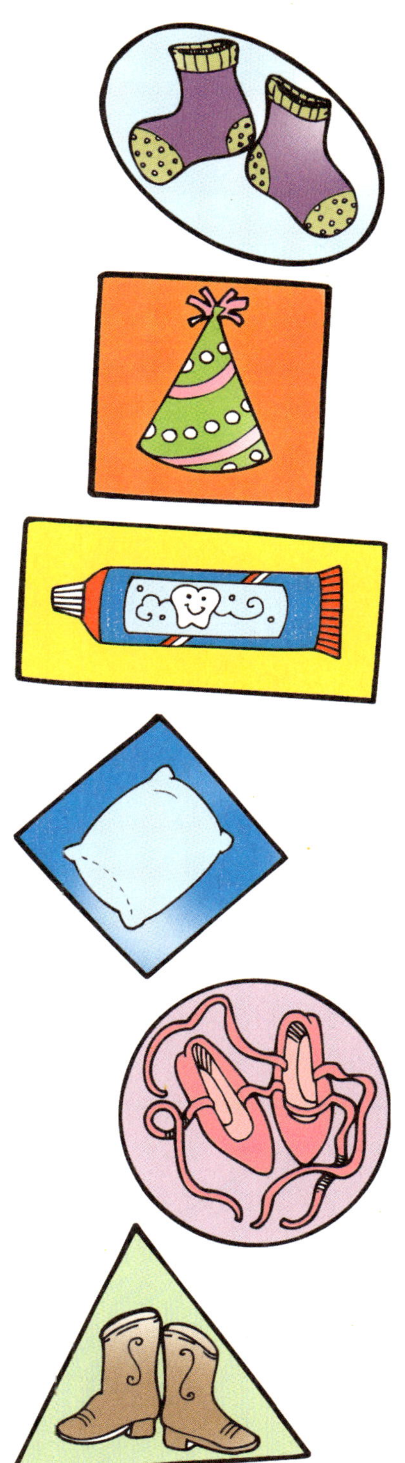

Name ____________________

Out of Place

Put an **X** on the picture that does not belong.

Name ______________________________

Together Is Better

Color the picture that goes with the first picture in each row.

Name ________________________________ 

Special Helpers

Draw a line to match the workers to their tools.

Name ____

I Want My Mommy!

Draw a line from each animal **baby** to its **mother**.

Circle the baby that hatches from an egg.

Name ________________________________

How Is the Weather?

What we can do outside each day depends on the **weather**.

Draw a line from each weather word to its picture.

sunny

windy

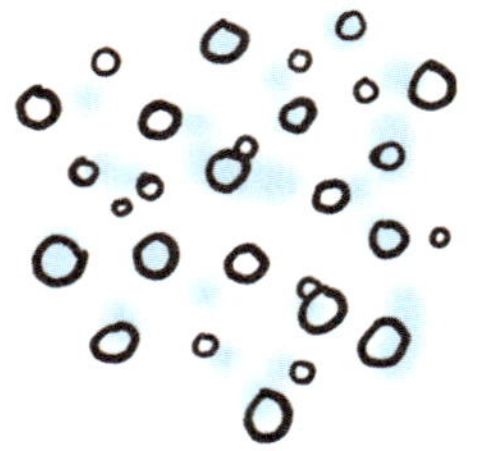

snowy

rainy

All Dressed Up

We wear **clothes** to go with the weather.

Connect the top, bottom, and shoes that go together.

On another sheet of paper, draw a picture of you in your favorite clothes.

Special Helpers

Special people **work** each day to help others.

Match each worker to something the worker uses to help others.

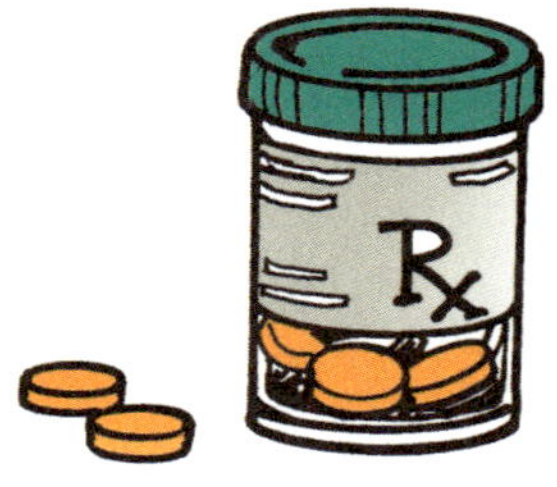

Think of three things you can do to help your family.

Name ______________________________ 

Time to Work

People use **tools** to do work.

Color the tool in each row that the worker needs.

Talk about what you want to be when you grow up.

Time to Travel

Transportation is how we get from one place to another.

Color the transportation for land green.
Color the transportation for water blue.
Color the transportation for air purple.

Name all the kinds of transportation you have used.

Name ____________________

Totally Amazing

The **body** is made up of many parts.
Draw a line to each body part.

eyes

hair

nose

leg

arm

foot

hand

chest

Name three other body parts.

Sensational Senses

We use our **senses** to learn about new things.

We **see** with our .

We **hear** with our .

We **smell** with our 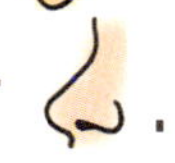.

We **taste** with our .

We **touch** with our .

Look at each picture. Circle the sense you would use.

Name ______________________________

A Place to Call Home

Find the children's houses on the map. Then use the color words on their shirts to color the houses.

OUR NEIGHBORHOOD

7

15

River Road

19

Elm Street

25

30

Oak Lane

I live at 25 Oak Lane.

blue

I live at 7 River Road.

yellow

I live at 30 Oak Lane.

red

I live at 19 Elm Street.

green

I live at 15 River Road.

purple

Say your address.

Ring-a-Ling

Say the numbers for each **phone number**. Push the buttons and pretend to call each one.

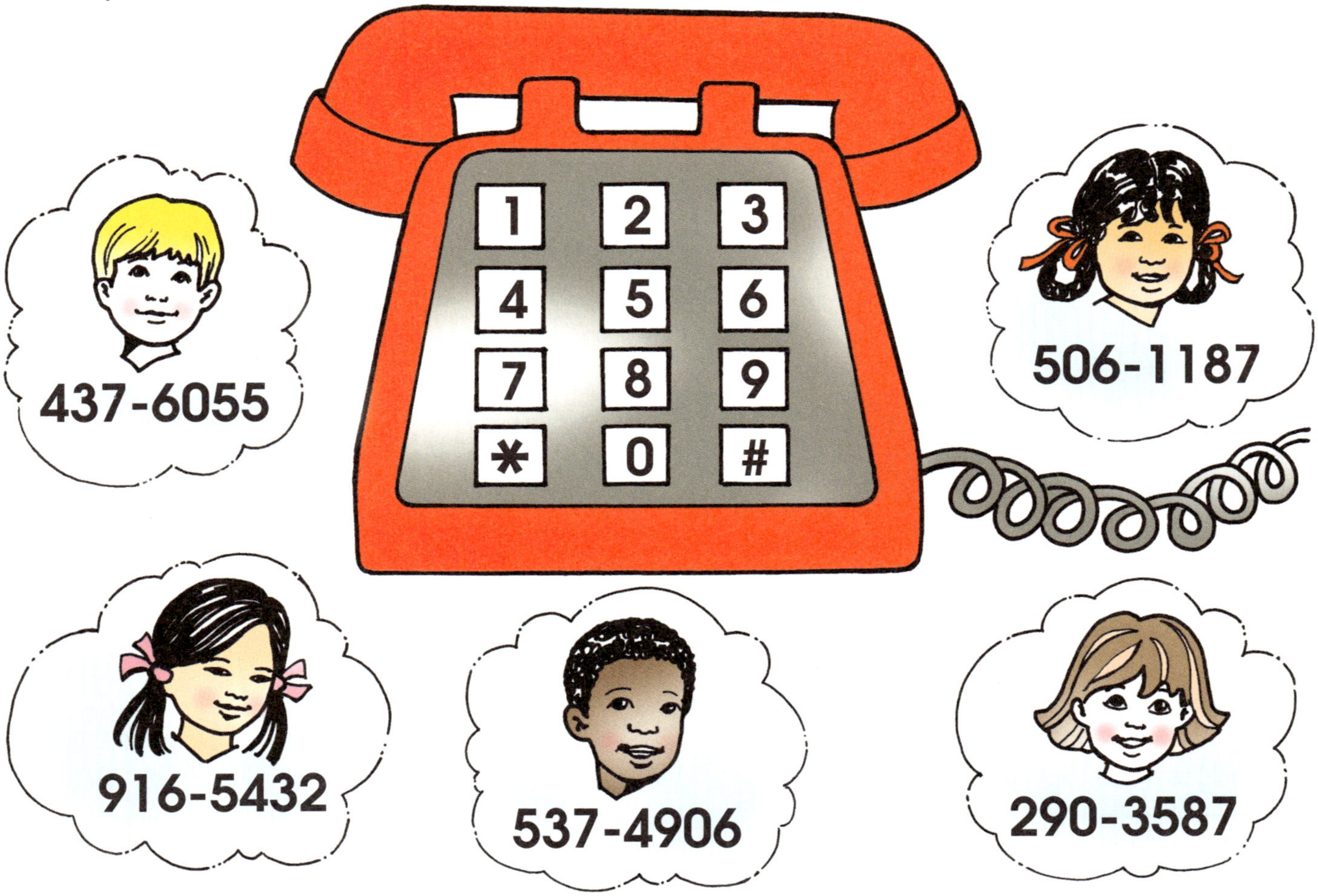

437-6055

506-1187

916-5432

537-4906

290-3587

Write your phone number in the boxes.

Color the numbers in your phone number on the phone above.

Do you know to dial 9-1-1 for an emergency?

Scholastic Success With

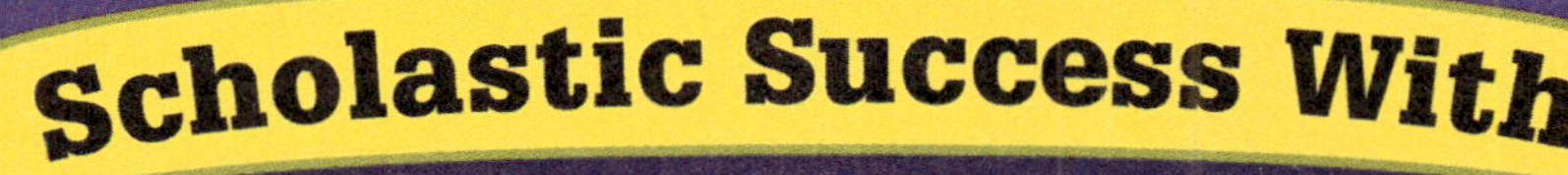

PHONICS

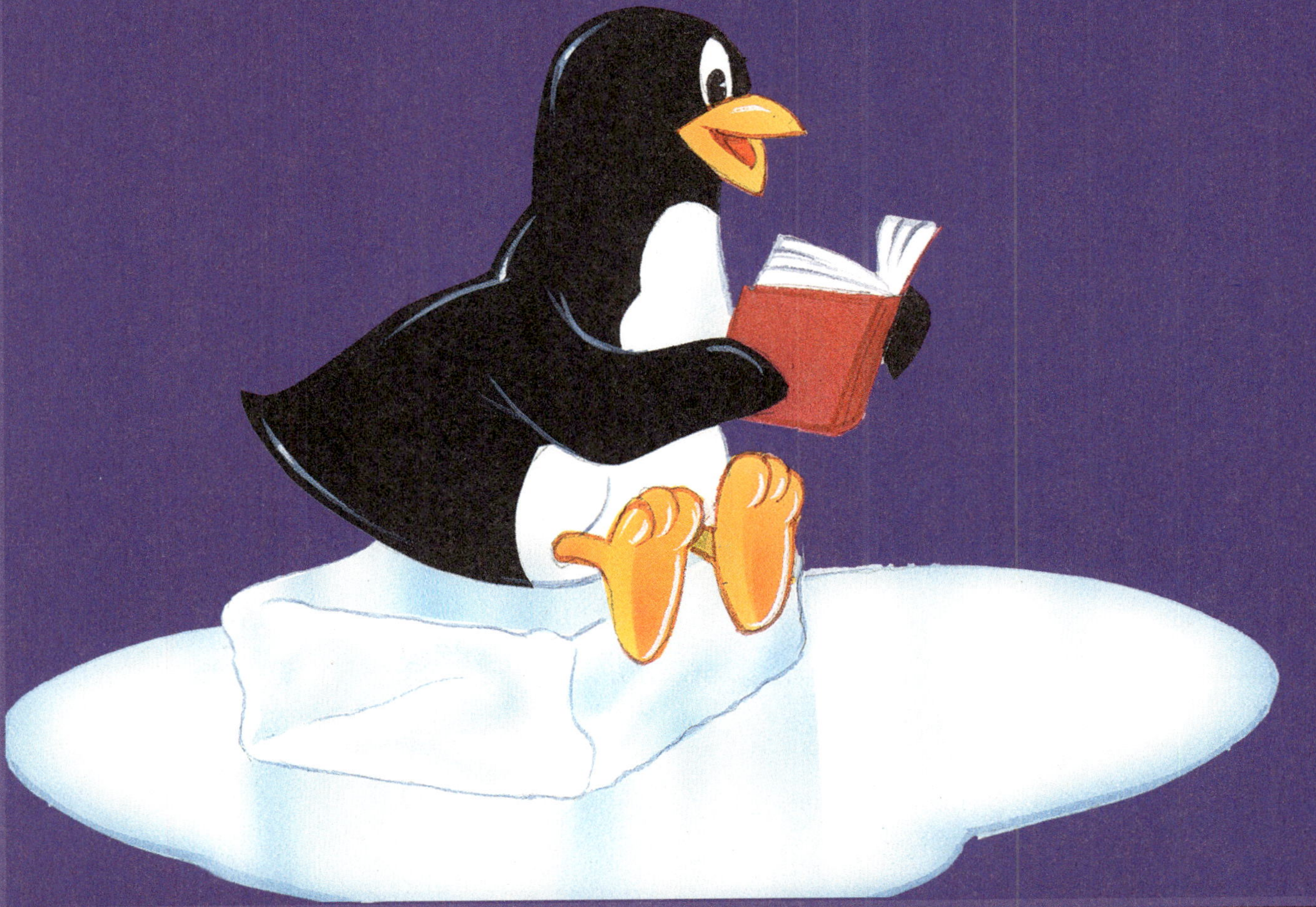

Name ____________________ 

Hop to It!

Color the lily pad with the letter that matches the frog in each row. Then circle the picture that begins with that letter.

Frog	Lily pads			Pictures
A	D	A	E	
B	B	D	H	
C	G	A	C	
D	F	D	B	
E	E	F	H	
F	C	E	F	

Name ______________________________________ 

Hop to It!

Color the lily pad with the letter that matches the frog in each row. Then circle the picture that begins with that letter.

G	A	C	G	
H	H	G	B	
I	J	L	I	
J	J	O	M	
K	L	I	K	
L	I	L	P	
M	M	N	K	

Name ____________________

Letter Flags

Color the carrot with the letter that matches the flag in each row. Then circle the picture that begins with that letter.

Flag				
N	P	N	M 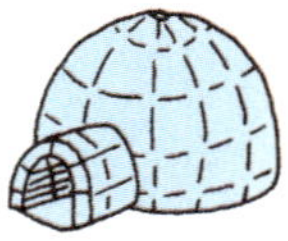 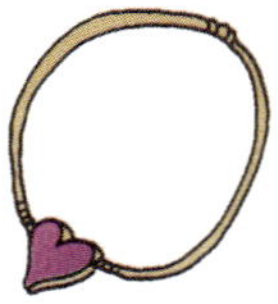	
O	J	K	O 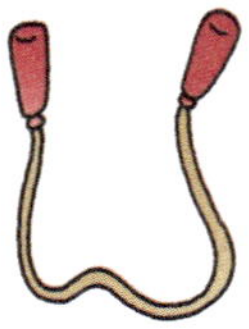 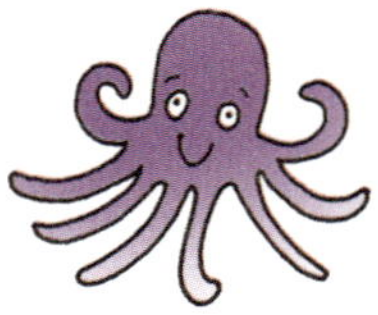	
P	O	P	N 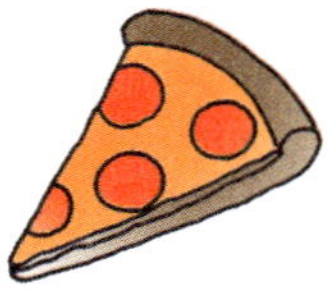 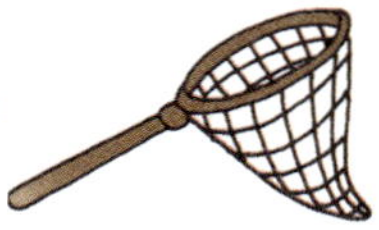	
Q	Q	U	X 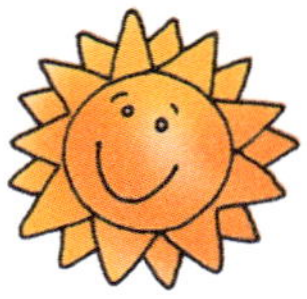 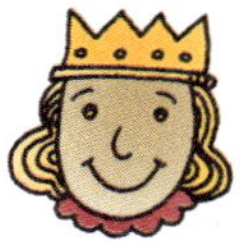	
R	V	T	R 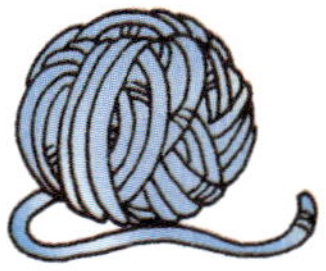 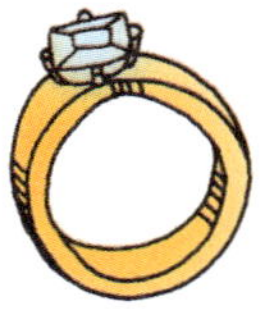	
S	S	Z	W 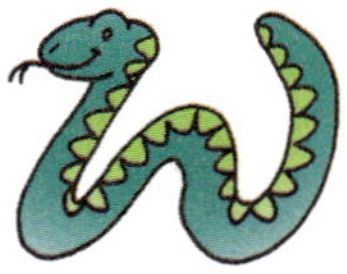 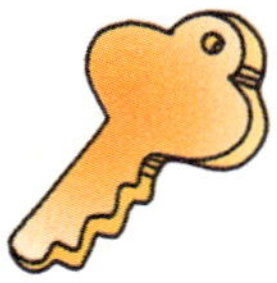	

Name ___________________________________ 

Letter Flags

Color the carrot with the letter that matches the flag in each row. Then circle the picture that begins with that letter.

Flag				
T	X	T	R	
U	U	Q	W	
V	Y	S	V	
W	W	V	R	
X	Q	X	Z	
Y	R	U	Y	
Z	Z	T	S	

Name ______________________________ 

What Is a Consonant?

Can you say the alphabet? There are 26 letters in the alphabet. Five of the letters are vowels: *A, E, I, O,* and *U.*

All the rest are consonants.

Look at the alphabet below. Mark an **X** through the five vowels: *A, E, I, O,* and *U.* Now say the names of all the consonants.

A B C D E F G H I

J K L M N O P Q

R S T U V W X Y Z

How many consonants are there? ______

Color each balloon that has a consonant in it.

F M A B

Name ___________________________________ 

Bobby the Bear

 **B** *makes the sound you hear at the beginning of the words* **Bobby** *and* **bear***.*

Bobby the bear is going shopping for things that begin with **b**. Help Bobby find ten things in this store that begin with **b**. Draw a circle around each one.

 **What insect buzzes around flowers and makes honey? Draw it on another sheet of paper. Tell a friend what you know about this insect.**

Doctor Dave

D *makes the sound you hear at the beginning of the words* **doctor** *and* **Dave***.*

Look in Doctor Dave's bag. Color only the pictures that begin with **d**. Put an **X** on the pictures that do not begin with **d**.

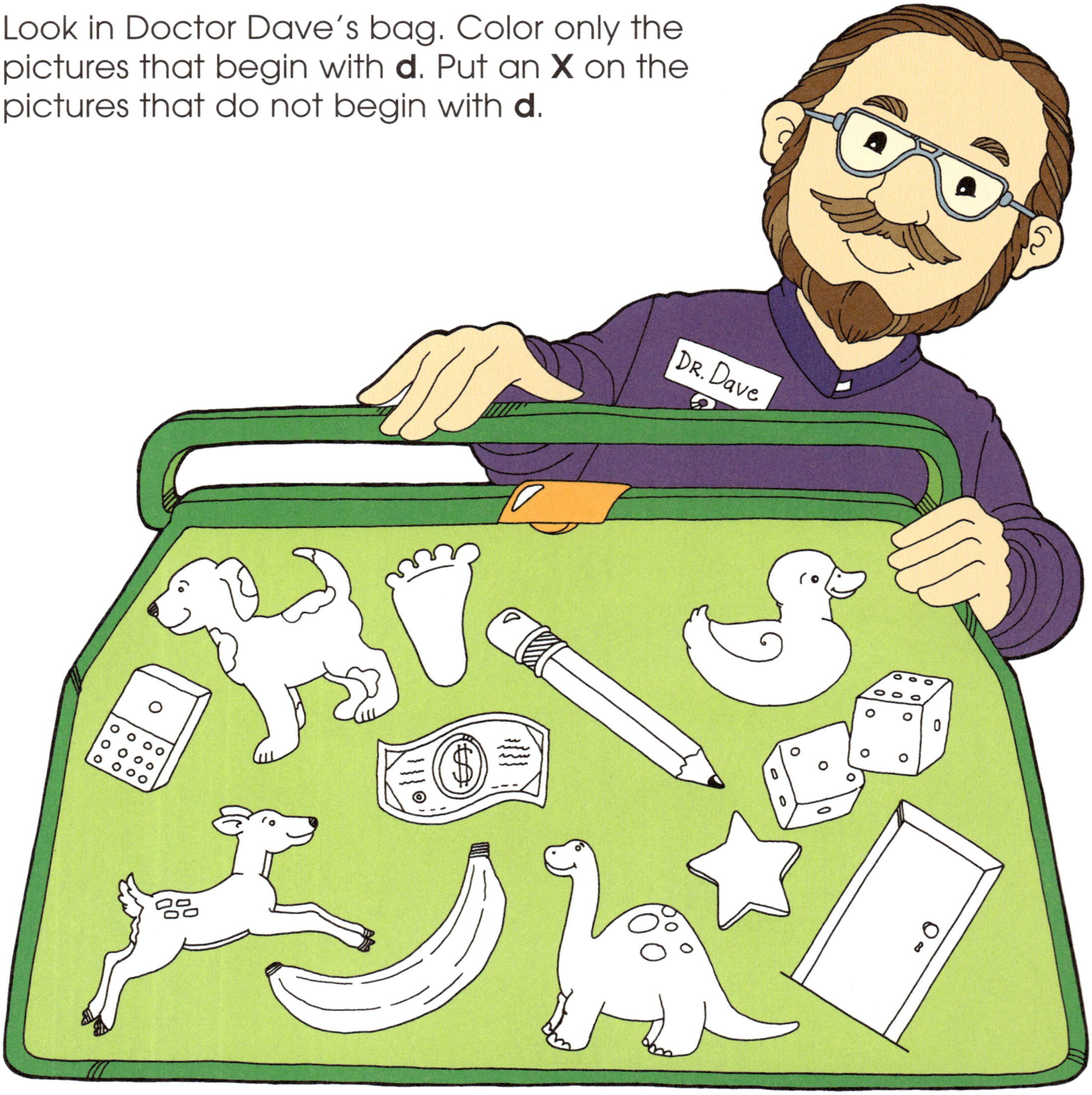

She is another kind of doctor. She works on your teeth. Her job begins with *d*. Who is she? On another sheet of paper, draw yourself at her office.

Name ______________________________

Fancy the Fish

F *makes the sound you hear at the beginning of the words* **fancy** *and* **fish**.

Fancy the fish is blowing bubbles. Draw a bubble around the pictures that begin with **f**. Put an **X** on the pictures that do not begin with **f**.

This word begins with *f*. It names a brave person who saves people when their houses are burning. Who is this person? On another sheet of paper, draw a picture of this person's truck.

Name ____

Happy the Hippo

H *makes the sound you hear at the beginning of the words* **happy** *and* **hippo.**

Help Happy the hippo find the **h** words. Say the picture in each box. Color only the pictures that begin with **h**.

This game begins with *h*. One child counts to ten and then tries to find the other children. Do you know what it is? At playtime, play this game with your friends.

Joe the Janitor

***J** makes the sound you hear at the beginning of the words **Joe** and **janitor**.*

Help Joe the janitor find the **j** words. In each trash can, draw a box around two pictures that begin with **j**.

What kind of candy begins with *j*, looks like beans, and comes in lots of different colors? Say the answer. On another sheet of paper, draw a glass jar with 21 of these in it. Count carefully! Color them.

Name ______________________________

Katie the Kangaroo

K *makes the sound you hear at the beginning of the words* **Katie** *and* **kangaroo***.*

Help Katie the kangaroo find the pictures that begin with **k**. Color them in.

This word begins with *k*. It can mean a young goat, or it can mean a young person. It rhymes with *lid*. What is it?

Lazy the Lion

L *makes the sound you hear at the beginning of the words* **lazy** *and* **lion**.

Help Lazy the lion find a word that begins with **l** to match each picture. Circle the correct word.

lamp clock	zipper lace	tree leaf	ladder hoe
ladybug bee	lake town	dog lamb	hand leg
lightning snow	apple lemon	book letter	lettuce corn
nose lips	lizard goat	worm lobster	log rock

This word begins with an ***l*****. It is a good feeling that you have about the people you like the most. It makes you want to hug someone! What is it? On another sheet of paper, draw or write a list of all the people you feel this way about.**

Name ___________________________ 

Mike the Mailman

 **M** *makes the sound you hear at the beginning of the words* **Mike** *and* **mailman**.

Help Mike the mailman sort the mail. Find the pieces of mail that have a picture that begins with **m**. Draw a line from the picture to the bag marked with an **m**.

I am a woman in your family. I cook for you. I wash your clothes. I take care of you when you are sick. I love you. You call me a name that begins with *m*. Who am I? On another sheet of paper, draw a picture of this person and tell something nice about her.

Nancy the Nurse

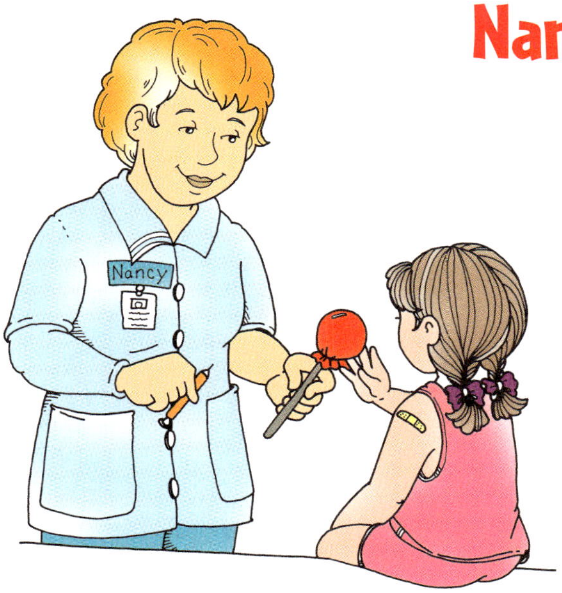

N *makes the sound you hear at the beginning of the words* **Nancy** *and* **nurse**.

After Nancy the nurse gives a shot, she also gives a lollipop to help her young patients feel better. Color the lollipops below that have pictures beginning with **n**.

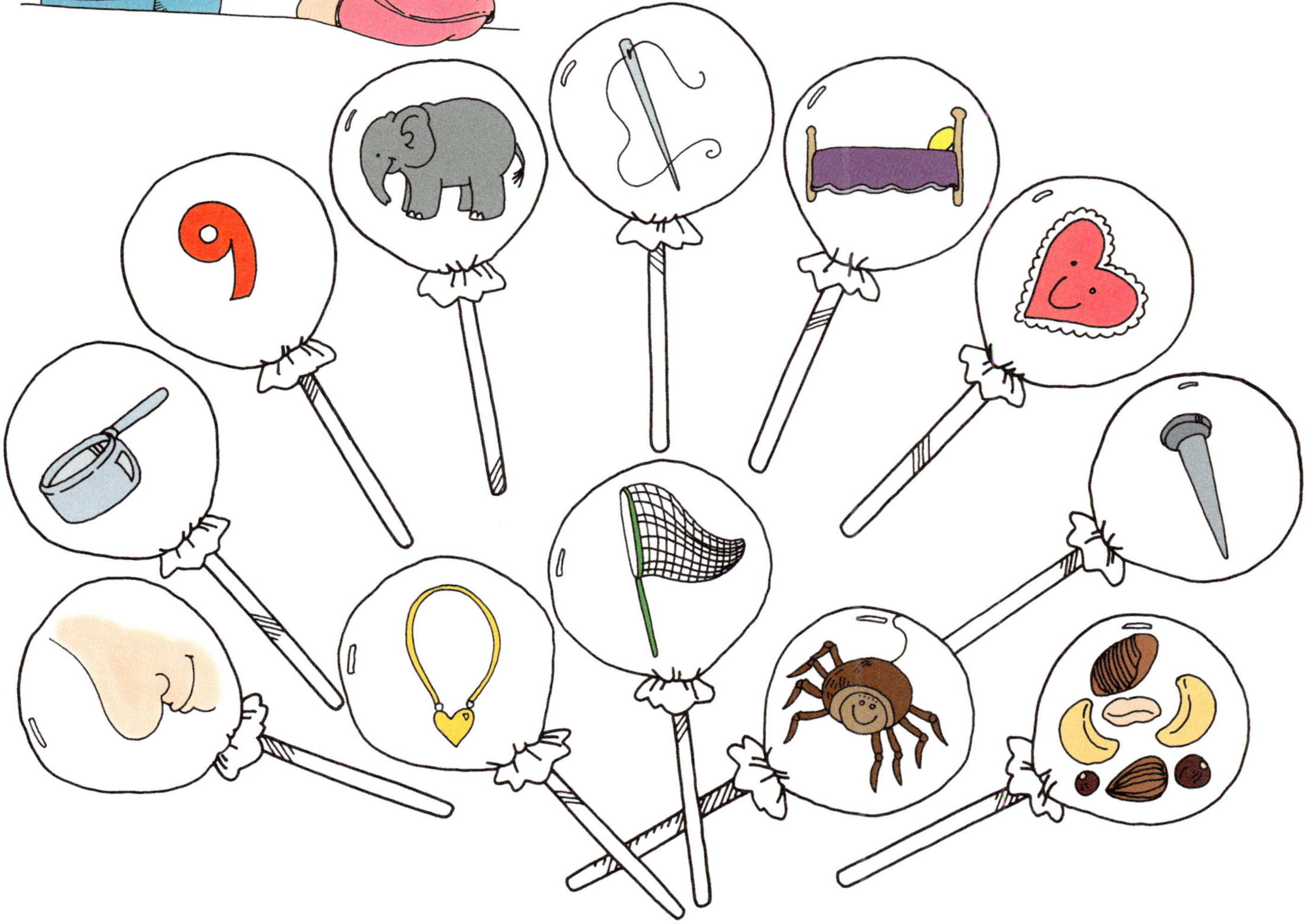

This item begins with *n*. It is made of big sheets of paper. It has lots of pictures and words on it. It tells what is happening in the world. Grown-ups like to read it. What is it? Find one of these and look at one page of it. Find words you know. Circle them with a marker. Show a grown-up what you can read!

Name ______________________________________

Patsy the Pig

P *makes the sound you hear at the beginning of the words* **Patsy** *and* **pig***.*

Help Patsy the pig find the words that begin with **p**. Use a purple crayon to write the letter **p** on top of each picture below that begins with **p**.

This item begins with *p*. It has a head and a tail, but it is not an animal. It is a copper-colored coin. What is it? Draw it on another sheet of paper, or put one under the paper and rub over it with a crayon.

Name ______________________________________

Ricky the Rabbit

R *makes the sound you hear at the beginning of the words* **Ricky** *and* **rabbit**.

Look at all the fun things that Ricky the rabbit can do. Circle the **r** word that tells what Ricky is doing in each picture.

 rest play	 swim run	 ride hug
 rock look	 climb rake	 stand roll
 read sing	 rope feed	 rip talk
 row eat	 race walk	 sleep rush

This word begins with *r*. It blasts off into outer space. It orbits Earth. What is it? On another sheet of paper, draw a picture of one that has landed on the moon. Pretend you are an astronaut. Make up a story about your picture.

Silly Sally

***S** makes the sound you hear at the beginning of the words **silly** and **Sally**.*

Silly Sally is looking for something that starts with **s**. You can help her find it hidden in the puzzle below. Color each space orange that has a picture in it that begins with **s**. If the picture does not begin with **s**, do not color that space.

If you take two pieces of bread and put peanut butter on one and jelly on the other, then stick them together, what have you made? It begins with *s*. Pretend you are making one by acting it out.

Name ________________________________

Tammy the Teacher

T *makes the sound you hear at the beginning of the words* **Tammy** *and* **teacher***.*

1. Trace over the letter in each row.
2. Color the pictures in each row that begin with *t*.

t

t

t

t

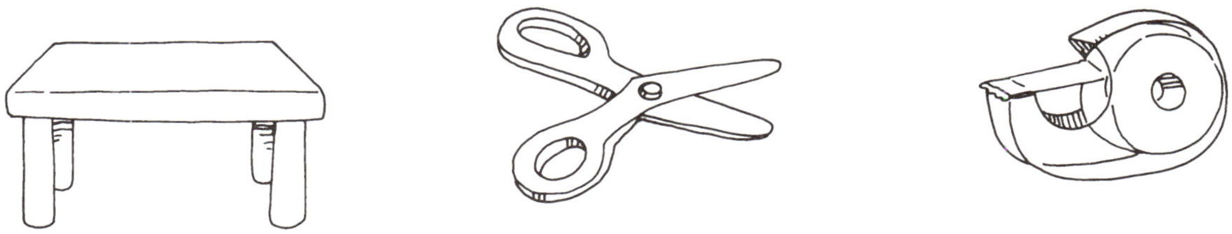

This item begins with *t*. Campers sleep in it. What is it?

Vicki's Vacation

V *makes the sound you hear at the beginning of the words* **Vicki** *and* **vacation***.*

Vicki is going on a vacation. Help Vicki load her van with things that start with **v**. Draw a line from the **v** words to the van.

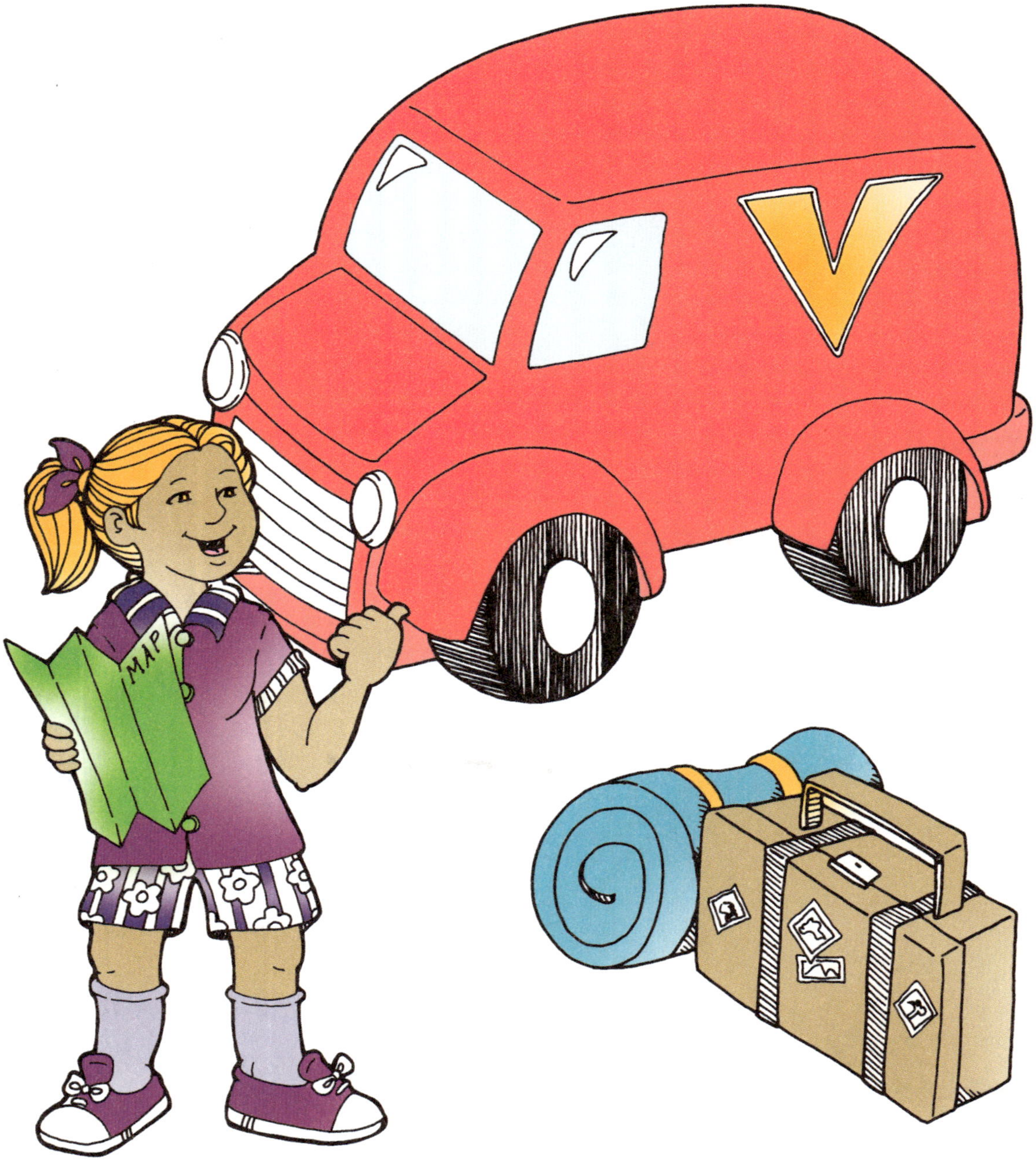

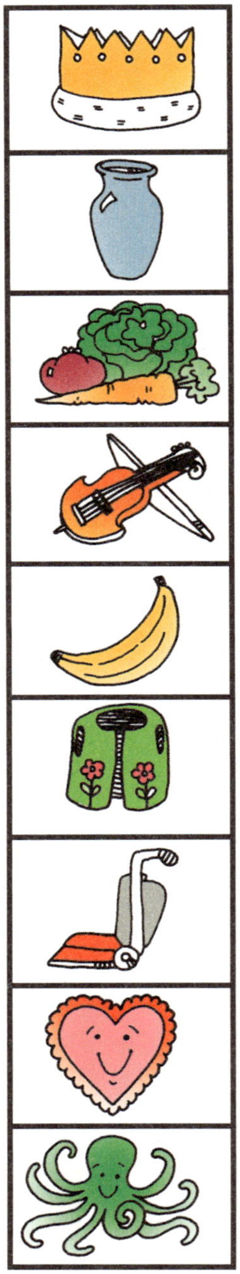

This kind of mountain has lava inside. Sometimes the lava comes out of the top and runs down the sides. What do you call this kind of mountain? Hint: It begins with the letter *v*. On another sheet of paper, draw one and color it.

Willy the Worm

***W** makes the sound you hear at the beginning of the words **Willy** and **worm**.*

In the story below, there are 11 words that begin with **w**. Draw a wiggly line under each one.

Willy the worm felt hungry. He wanted something to eat. He saw a watermelon in the window. He climbed up on the wagon. He wiggled up the wall. Then he took a bite. Wow! It was wonderful!

Now, circle each word that you underlined in the puzzle. The words go across and down.

x	w	i	g	g	l	e	d	v	t
w	a	t	e	r	m	e	l	o	n
o	g	e	k	p	r	s	b	y	w
w	o	r	m	h	f	l	x	z	i
k	n	c	w	i	n	d	o	w	l
g	v	w	a	n	t	e	d	a	l
u	w	h	s	r	z	q	g	l	y
w	o	n	d	e	r	f	u	l	a

This begins with *w*. You cannot see it, but you can feel it. Sometimes you can hear it blowing. It makes the trees sway. What is it? Now, roll up a very small piece of paper and put it on your desk. Blow on it. What happens? Why?

Name ______________________________________ 

Yolanda's Yearbook

 **Y** *makes the sound you hear at the beginning of the words* **Yolanda** *and* **yearbook**.

Yolanda got a yearbook at school today. It has funny pictures in it. Which pictures go together? Draw lines to match the pictures in Yolanda's yearbook. The words in each picture begin with **y**. Can you say them?

 **This word begins with *y*. It is one way to answer a question. When you say it, you nod your head up and down. What word is it? Now play this game. Take turns acting out these words without saying anything:** *No. I don't know. Who, me? Stop! Come here. Be quiet. Too loud!*

Name ______________________________ 

Zachary the Zebra

 **Z** *makes the sound you hear at the beginning of the words* **Zachary** *and* **zebra**.

Zachary the zebra is lost! Help him find his way back to the zoo. Circle only the things that begin with **z**. Connect them to the **z**'s you find along the way.

 **What word begins with *z* and sounds like a car speeding by very fast? (Hint: It rhymes with *broom*.) On another sheet of paper, draw a race car. Think of a story to tell with your picture.**

Name James

Hidden Picture

Say the pictures in the puzzle.

Color words that begin with *t* red

Color words that begin with *b* yellow

Color words that begin with *s*

Color words that begin with *d*

This vessel begins with *s*. It floats on the water. The wind blows it along. It is in the puzzle above. What is it? On another sheet of paper, draw a beautiful island where this could take you.

Name ____________________

What Is a Vowel?

There are 26 letters in the alphabet. Five of the letters are **vowels**. *They are* a, e, i, o, *and* u.

Look at the alphabet train.

Color the *a* car red.
Color the *e* car blue.
Color the *i* car orange.
Color the *o* car purple.
Color the *u* car green.

Sometimes the letter y *can be a vowel.*

Color the *y* car yellow.

Look at each store sign. Circle each vowel you can find. There are 13 of them.

Name ____ 

Abby's Apples

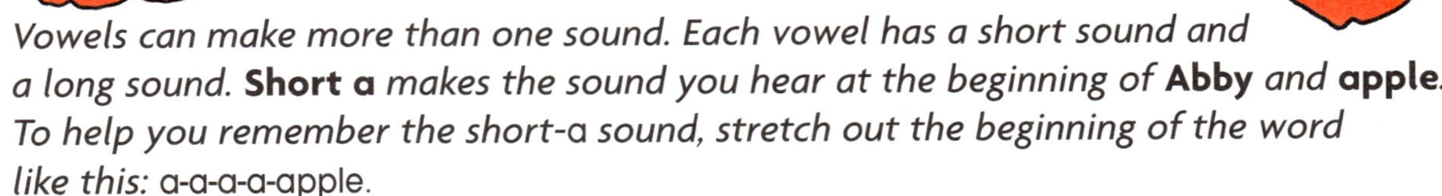

Vowels can make more than one sound. Each vowel has a short sound and a long sound. **Short a** *makes the sound you hear at the beginning of* **Abby** *and* **apple**. *To help you remember the short-*a *sound, stretch out the beginning of the word like this:* a-a-a-a-apple.

Abby loves to eat red apples. Help Abby find the apples that have pictures with the short-*a* sound. Color these apples red. If the picture does not have a short-*a* sound, color the apple green.

This reptile looks like a crocodile, only smaller. It swims in the water. It begins with the short-*a* sound. What is it? On another sheet of paper, draw one in a zoo.

Find the Rhyme

Color the things in the picture that rhyme with **rat**  .

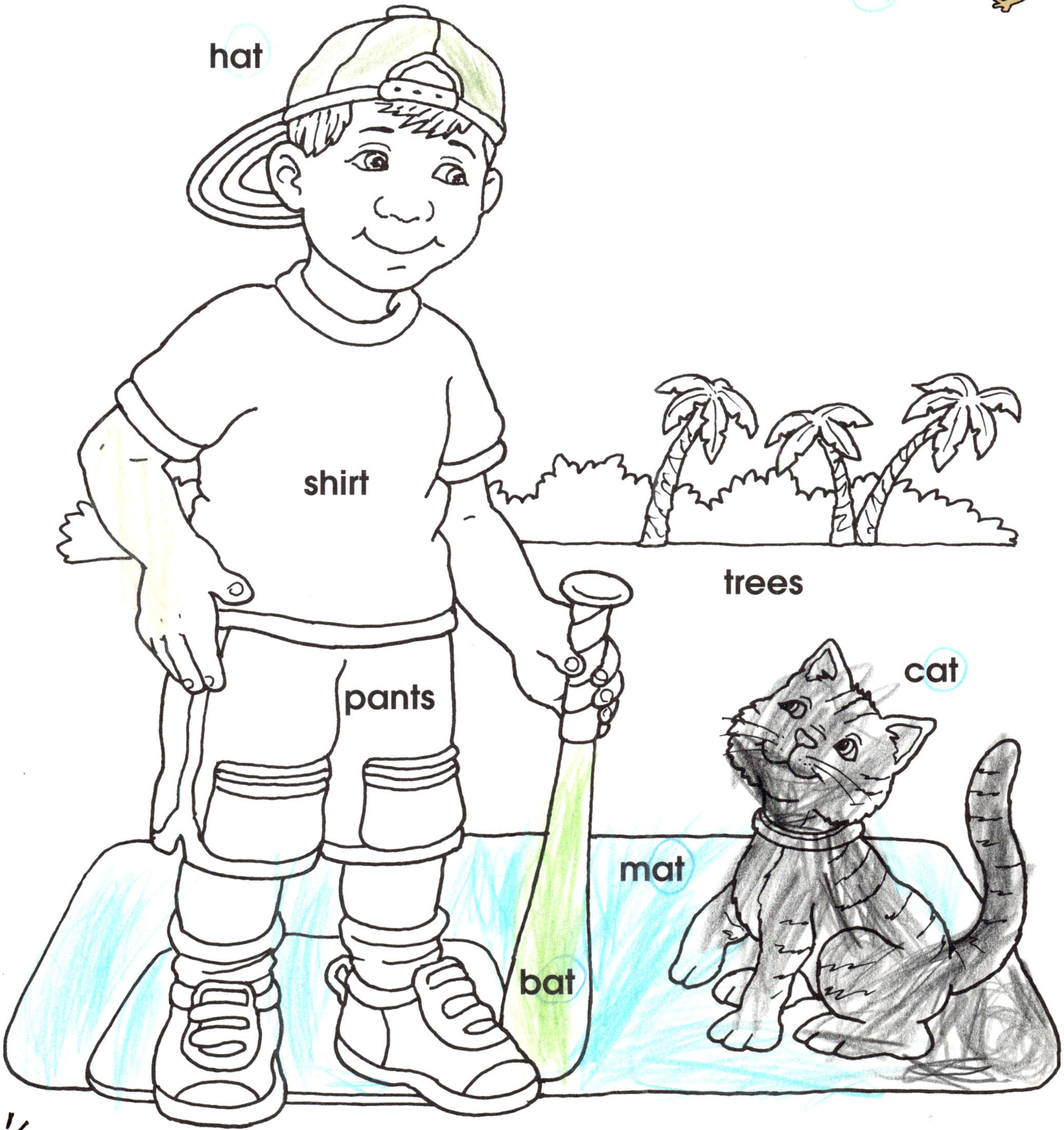

hat

shirt

trees

pants

cat

mat

bat

Think of two words that rhyme with *rat* that are not in the picture.

Hop Along

Help Tad Frog find his way across the pond. Color the pictures green that rhyme with **pad** .

dad

fan

van

mad

sad

cat

glad

Color the other pictures red.

Name ______________________________  *-an* **word family**

Special Delivery

Help make the delivery. Follow the pictures that rhyme with **van** .

rat

bag

man

hat

can

fan

bat

pan

Count how many cans of soup you have at home.

Name ______________________________  *-ack* **word family**

Don't Step on the Tack!

Find and color the pictures that rhyme with **back** .

sack

tack

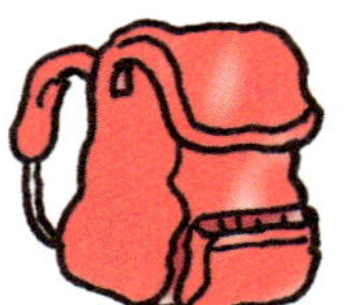

backpack

crack

Think of two more words that rhyme with *back*. On another sheet of paper, draw a picture of one of them.

Name ____________________

Picture This!

Color the picture in each row that rhymes with the first picture.

fan	hat	pan	glad
bat	man	sad	cat
sad	mad	rat	fan
sack	can	van	backpack

Name ______________________________

Rhyming Tic-Tac-Toe

Say each picture name. Find and color three pictures in a row that rhyme.

Ed's Eggs

Short e *makes the sound you hear at the beginning of* **Ed** *and* **egg***. To help you remember the short-*e *sound, stretch out the beginning of the word like this:* e-e-e-egg.

It is time for Ed to gather the eggs. Help Ed find the eggs that have pictures with the short-*e* sound. Color these eggs brown. If the picture does not have the short-*e* sound, leave the egg white.

When you say this word you nod your head up and down. It means the opposite of *no*. It has the short-*e* sound. What word is it? Think of three questions that you would answer with this word.

Name ______________________________

Farmer Ben

Color things in the picture that rhyme with **den** .

hat

cat

10

ten

pail

hen

dog

pen

men

Find two other things that rhyme in the picture.

Name ___________________________________ 

Watch Out!

Help Ted find his way down the hill without hitting the shed. Follow the pictures that rhyme with **shed**.

Taking the Pet to the Vet

Say the names of the pictures. Color the pictures that rhyme with **met** .

jet	pet	hen
sled	net	wet
bed	pen	vet

Show and Tell

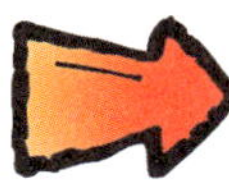

Read the story with a grown-up. Find and color the picture words in the story that rhyme with **tell***.*

bell

shell

yell

well

It was time for Show and Tell. Bobby was so excited, he began to . Maria told about her bell. Leigh had brought her favorite . Ted showed a picture of a wishing .

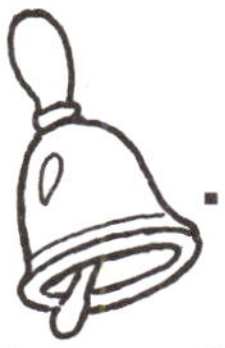

Name ______________________________  **Review**

Flower Power

Color the pictures red that rhyme with **sled** .

Color the pictures yellow that rhyme with **ten** .

Color the pictures 

that rhyme with **yell** .

Color the pictures 

that rhyme with **net** 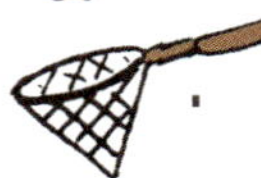.

bed

bell

pen

vet

jet

hen

shell

shed

On another sheet of paper, draw a flower with four petals. On each petal, draw something with a short-*e* sound.

Name ____

Igloo Inn

Short i *makes the sound you hear at the beginning of* **igloo** *and* **inn**. *To help you remember the short-*i *sound, stretch out the beginning of the word like this:* i-i-i-igloo.

Welcome to the Igloo Inn. Color the space around the pictures with the short-*i* sound blue. If the picture does not have a short-*i* sound, draw an **X** on it.

IGLOO INN

This is part of a baseball game. There are nine of them. The word has two short-*i* sounds. When you play baseball, someone throws a ball to a batter. This word also has a short-*i* sound. What are the two words?

Name ___________________________________

Strike!

See how many bowling pins you can knock down.
Mark an **X** on the ones that rhyme with **pin**.

kick

chin

wing

grin

lick

fin

twig

Name two more words that rhyme with *pin*.

Name ____________________  *-ig* **word family**

Going to the Pig Shindig

 *Read the story with a grown-up. Find and color the picture words in the story that rhyme with* **big**.

 pig  wig  twig  big

Once there was a  who wanted to go to the  shindig. She put on her pretty pink . The  was way too 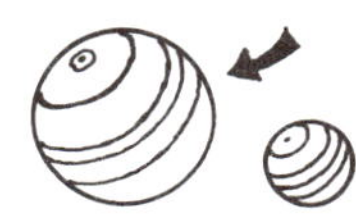. On the way to the shindig, the wig got stuck on a . The  lost her wig.

Fit for a King

Color the pictures that rhyme with **king** on the crown.

wing

wig

sing

pig

ring

fin

string

Tell a story about a king and other things that have the *-ing* sound.

Name ____________________

Where's the Rhyme?

Say the name of the pictures.
Color the pictures that rhyme with **lick**  .

pig	king	kick
ring	sick	wig
grin	sing	brick
chick	chin	twig

Name ____________________

Oliver's Olives

Short o *makes the sound you hear at the beginning of* **Oliver** *and* **olive***. To help you remember the short-*o *sound, stretch out the beginning of the word like this:* o-o-o-olive.

Oliver likes to put green olives in his salad. Help Oliver find the olives that have pictures with the short-*o* sound. Color these olives green. If the picture does not have the short-*o* sound, color the olive black.

This creature lives in the sea. It has eight arms. Its head looks like a balloon. It begins with the short-*o* sound. What is it? Tell what you could do if you had eight arms!

Freddy the Frog

Read the story with a grown-up. Find and color the picture words in the story that rhyme with **jog**.

frog

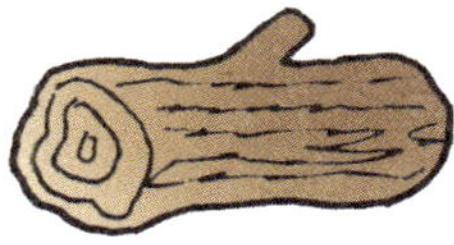

log

dog

hog

Freddy is a very large bull . He is as big as a 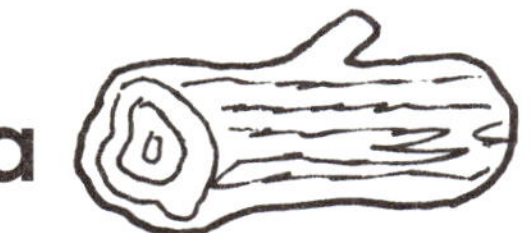 **. His best friends are a bull**  **and a . Together they play leap**  **. See them jump over the**  **.**

Name ______________________________  *-op* **word family**

Under the Big Top

Say the names of the pictures in the balls.
Color the pictures that rhyme with **pop** .

mop

hop

dog

pot

STOP

stop

top

lock

 **On another sheet of paper, draw a picture about this sentence: Mop up the soda pop.**

Name ______________________________

Dot the Robot

Circle the things in the picture that rhyme with **knot** .

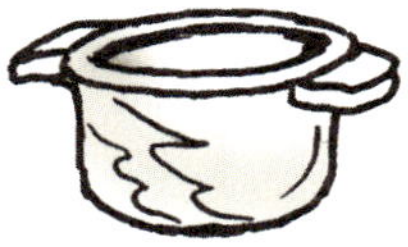

pot **spot** 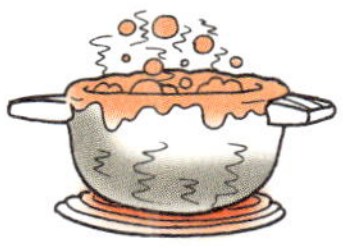 **hot** **dot**

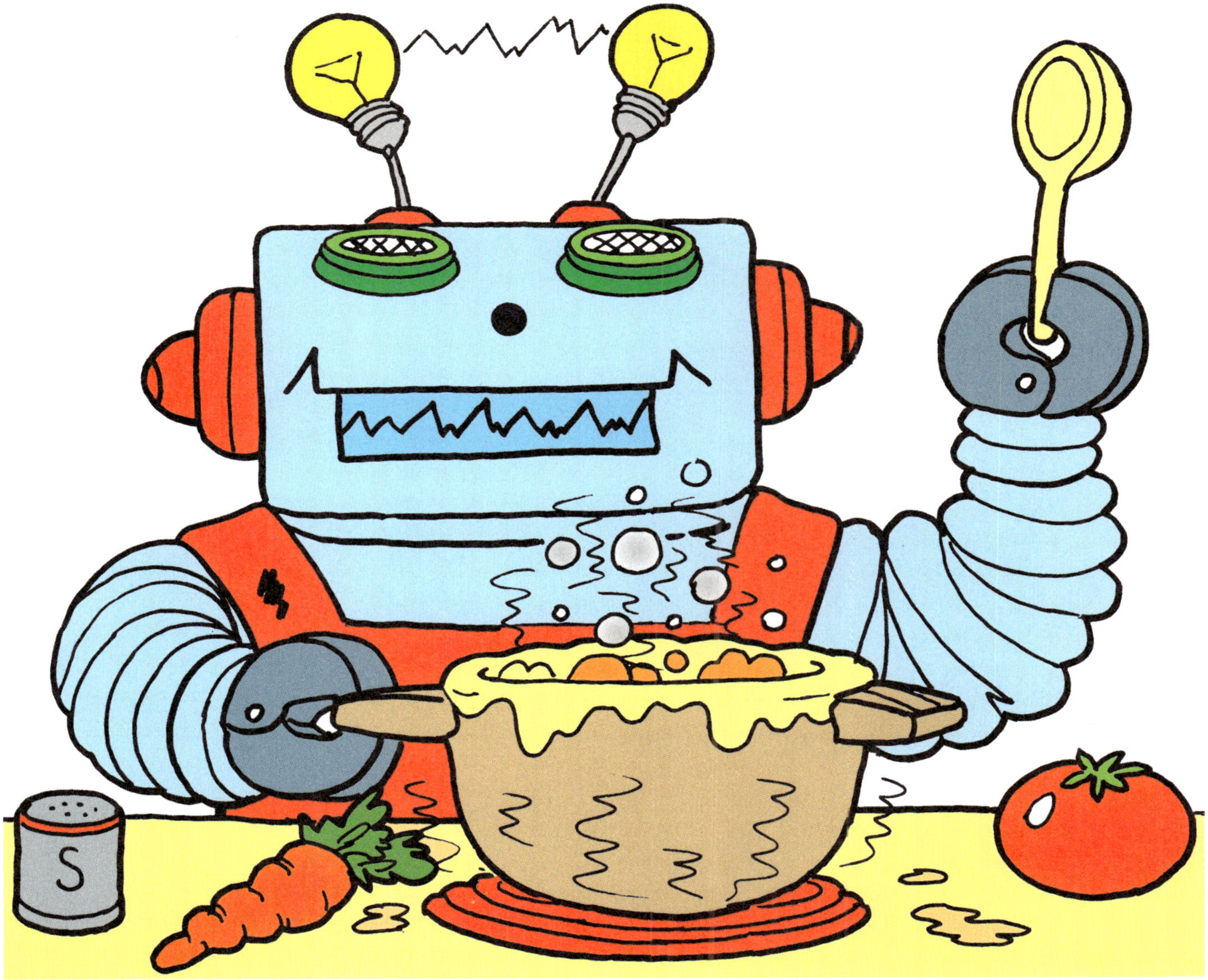

Think of one more word that rhymes with *knot*.

Name ______________________________

Sherlock's Clues

Help Sherlock find the way to the missing lock. Color the pictures that rhyme with **clock** .

clock	sock	log	dog
mop	rock	knock	hog
pot	spot	block	lock

Name ____ 

My Uncle's Umbrella

Short u *makes the sound you hear at the beginning of* **uncle** *and* **umbrella**. *To help you remember the short-*u *sound, stretch out the beginning of the word like this:* u-u-u-umbrella.

My uncle needs to buy a new umbrella! Help him find the umbrellas that have pictures with the short-*u* sound. Color these umbrellas with red and blue stripes. If the picture does not have the short-*u* sound, write *NO* on the umbrella.

Name ______________________  *-ug* **word family**

Let's Dance!

 *Read the story with a grown-up. Find and color the picture words in the story that rhyme with* ***dug****.*

 **rug**  **bug**  **mug**  **hug**

Once there was was a lady . **She liked to dance on a** 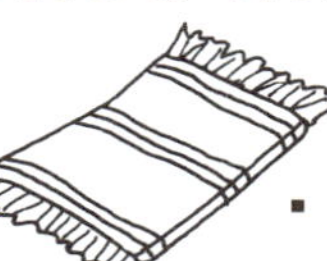 . **Her favorite dance was the jitter**  . **She won a first-place**  . **Everyone gave her a**  **for being the best dancing lady** .

Name ______________________________________ *-un* **word family**

Hit a Home Run!

Randy hit a home run. Start at home plate and color the bases that rhyme with **fun** .

The Stuck Duck

Help the duck across the pond. Color the pictures that rhyme with **duck**.

sun

truck

bun

puck

hug

rug

duck

bug

mug

yuck

run

Name ____

Review

Rhyme and Color

Color the pictures yellow that rhyme with **luck**.

Color the pictures blue that rhyme with **rug**.

Color the pictures orange that rhyme with **run**.

bird

sun

hug

boy

ball

shell

duck

bun

bug

truck

shoes

mug

Name ______________________________

Short Vowel Crosswords

Use the picture clues to add a short vowel to each puzzle.

1.

2.

3.

4.

5.

F

B T

N

Name ______________________________ **Review**

Short Vowel Tic-Tac-Toe

Say the picture names.
Find and color 3 pictures in a row with the same short vowel sound.

1. Short-*a* Sound as in 

2. Short-*i* Sound as in 

3. Short-*e* Sound as in 

Name ______________________________

City C and Country C

*C can make two sounds. If the vowels **e** or **i** come after the **c**, then **c** will have the **s** sound. If one of the other vowels (**a**, **o**, **u**) comes after the **c**, then **c** will have the **k** sound.*

Look at the pictures and words on this page. If it begins with an **s** sound, as in *city*, circle **s**. If it begins with a **k** sound, as in *country*, circle **k**.

couch	centipede	cow	cinnamon roll
k s	k s	k s	k s
corn	**cent**	**cereal**	**coat**
k s	k s	k s	k s
cake	**ceiling**	**cobra**	**cat**
k s	k s	k s	k s
celery	**coconut**	**circles**	**comb**
k s	k s	k s	k s

Name ______________________________

Use the words on page 354. Write each word that begins with the same sound as *city*.

______________ ______________ ______________

______________ ______________ ______________

____

Write each word that begins with the same sound as *country*.

______________ ______________ ______________

______________ ______________ ______________

______________ ______________ ______________

This word has two *c*'s in it. The first *c* sounds like an *s*. The other one sounds like a *k*. It is a fun place to see a show. There are clowns and elephants in a big tent. People do amazing tricks. What is it? On another sheet of paper, draw a picture of yourself doing a trick there.

Name ____

Gary the Goat and George the Giraffe

G can make two sounds. Usually, words that begin with g *make the same sound that you hear in* **Gary** *and* **goat**. *But sometimes a* g *can sound like a* j, *as in* **George** *and* **giraffe**. *This usually happens when the vowels* e *or* i *come after the* g, *but not always. The best way to figure out which* g *sound to use is to try both sounds and see which one makes sense. For example, try saying* goat *with both* g *sounds. See? One of them does not make sense!*

Look at each picture below. If the picture begins like *goat,* circle **g**. If the picture begins like *giraffe,* circle **j**.

Use the words on page 356. Write each word that begins with the same sound as *Gary* on the goat.

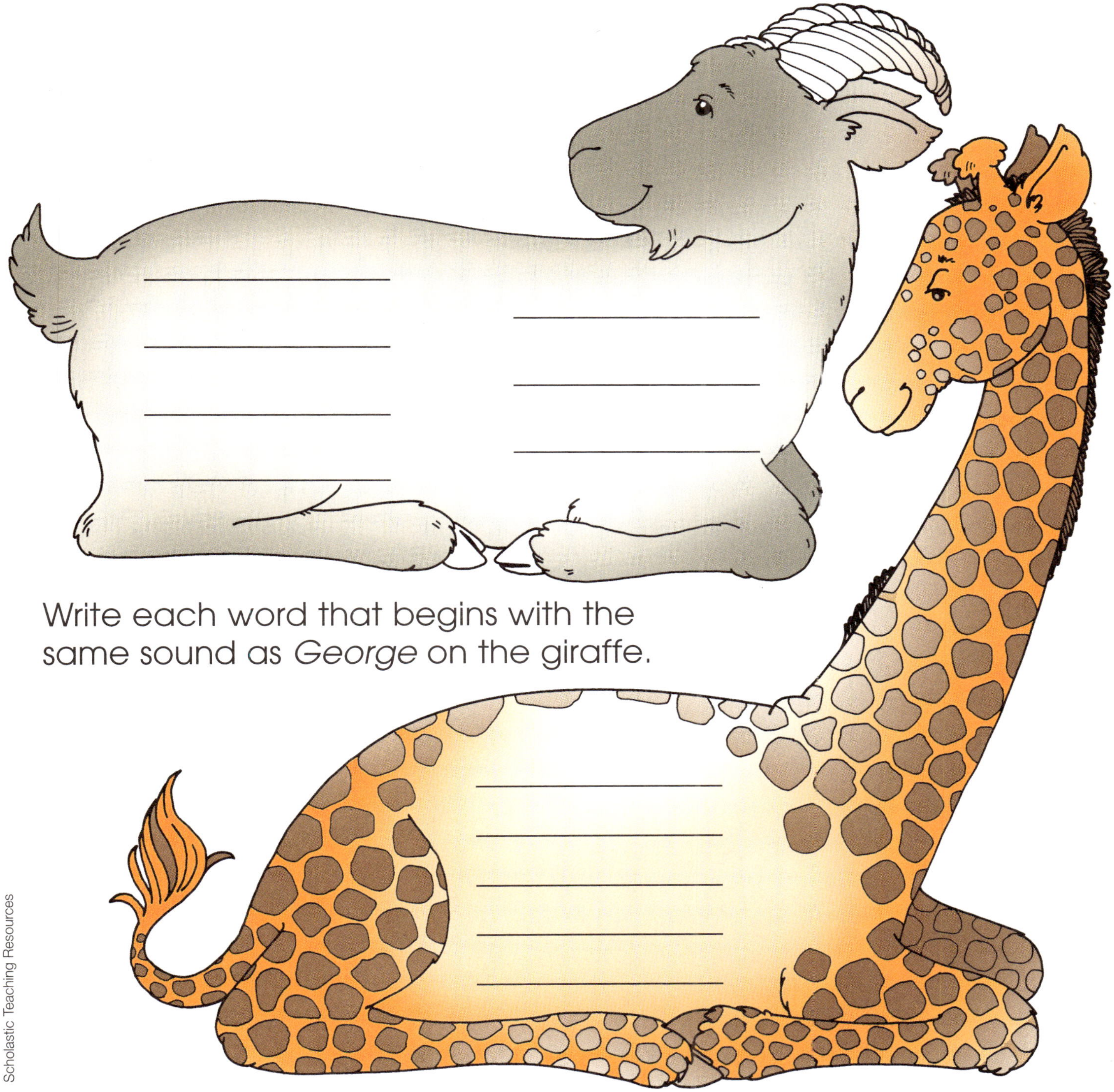

Write each word that begins with the same sound as *George* on the giraffe.

This word begins with a *g* that sounds like a *j*. It is a huge room. You can sit in the bleachers and watch a basketball game there. Most high schools have one. What is it? Think of another game that can be played there. On another sheet of paper, draw a picture of it.

Queen Q and Her Maidservant U

 **Q** *makes the sound you hear at the beginning of the word* **queen**.

Queen **Q** is very special. She has a maidservant named **U**. When Queen **Q** and Maidservant **U** work together, they make a sound that sounds like *kw*.

In each crown, write the word from the Word Box that matches the picture. (Hint: Do the easy ones first!)

Word Box

question quiet quarrel
quarter quack quail quilt

 **This word begins with *q*. Sometimes a teacher gives one to see if the students know their spelling words. It is another word for *test*. It rhymes with *Liz*. What is it? At playtime, pretend to be a teacher. Ask someone to be your student. Ask them questions. Then change places.**

Superhero X to the Rescue

X *makes the sound of* ks. *(Hint: Say the word* kiss *very fast!) Most of the time, an* **x** *is in the middle or at the end of a word.*

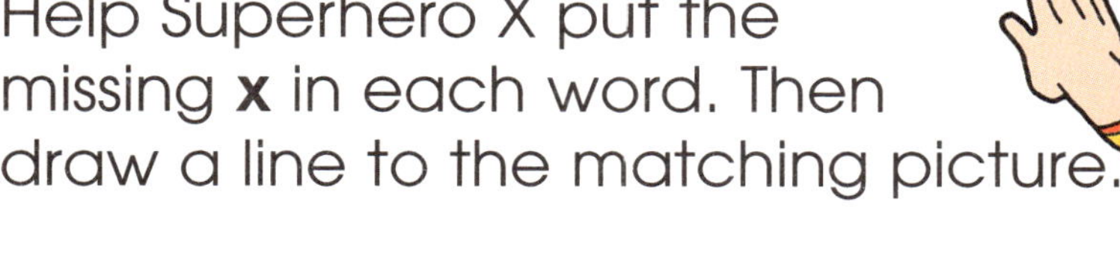

Help Superhero X put the missing **x** in each word. Then draw a line to the matching picture.

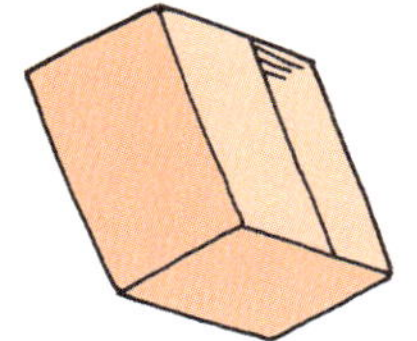

fo___

mi___er

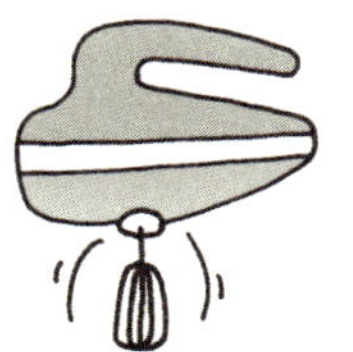

ta___i

e___it

a___

si___

o___

bo___

e___ercise

tu___edo

It begins with *x*. It is a special kind of picture that a doctor takes so that she can see your bones. What is it? See if you can feel the bones in your fingers and hands. Make them wiggle!

Animal Tails

Consonants can come at the beginning, middle, or end of a word. To help you hear the ending sound, say the word and stretch out the last sound. For example, when you see the picture of the bear, say "bear-r-r-r-r-r."

Say the name of each animal. Write the ending sound in the box by its tail.

This creature lives in the sea. It does not have a tail. It has eight arms. Its head looks like a balloon. It ends with *s*. What is it? On another sheet of paper, draw one eating eight candy canes.

Name ____

Larry Last

Help Larry Last find the last sound that each word makes. Circle the correct letter under each lunchbox.

k n s

r g l

s f r

n d z

b m n

t k p

k f d

m x r

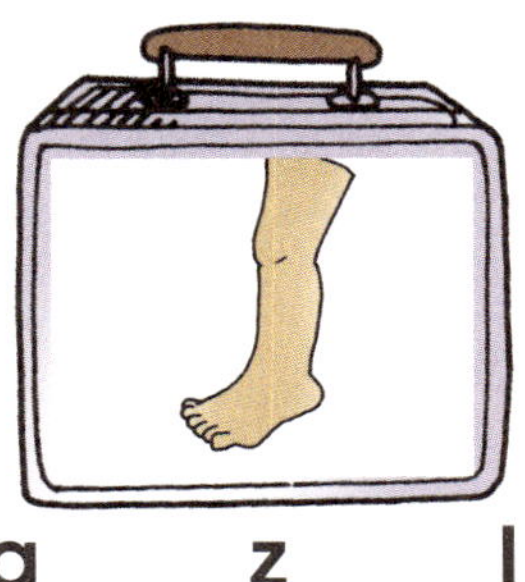

g z l

d v r

l k d

g t f

You do this while you are asleep. It is like watching a movie in your head. It ends with *m*. What is it? On another sheet of paper, draw a picture about one that you have had. Tell about it.

Name ______________________________ 

Consonant Caboose

Find two words on each train that end with the same sound. Color them. Then write the letter of the ending sound in the caboose.

1\.

2\.

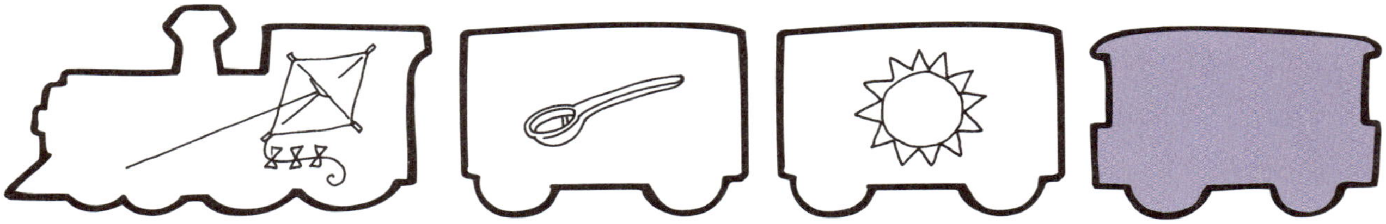

3\.

4\.

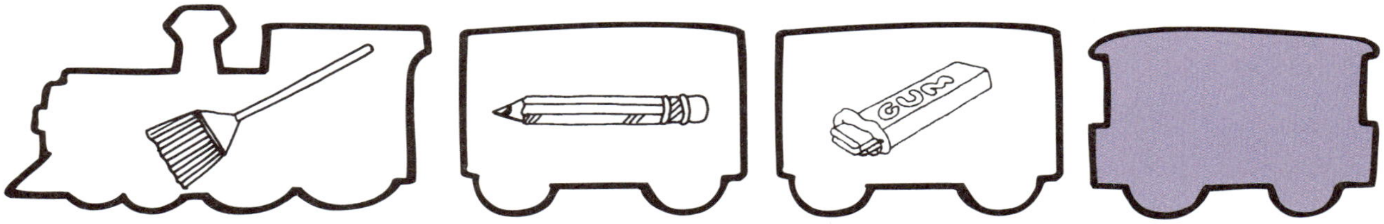

5\.

6\.

7\.

Name ____

What Do You See?

Say the words.
Listen for the ending sounds.
Use the Ending Sounds Color Code to make a picture.

Ending Sounds Color Code

blue = s	green = t	black = d	red = l	white = m

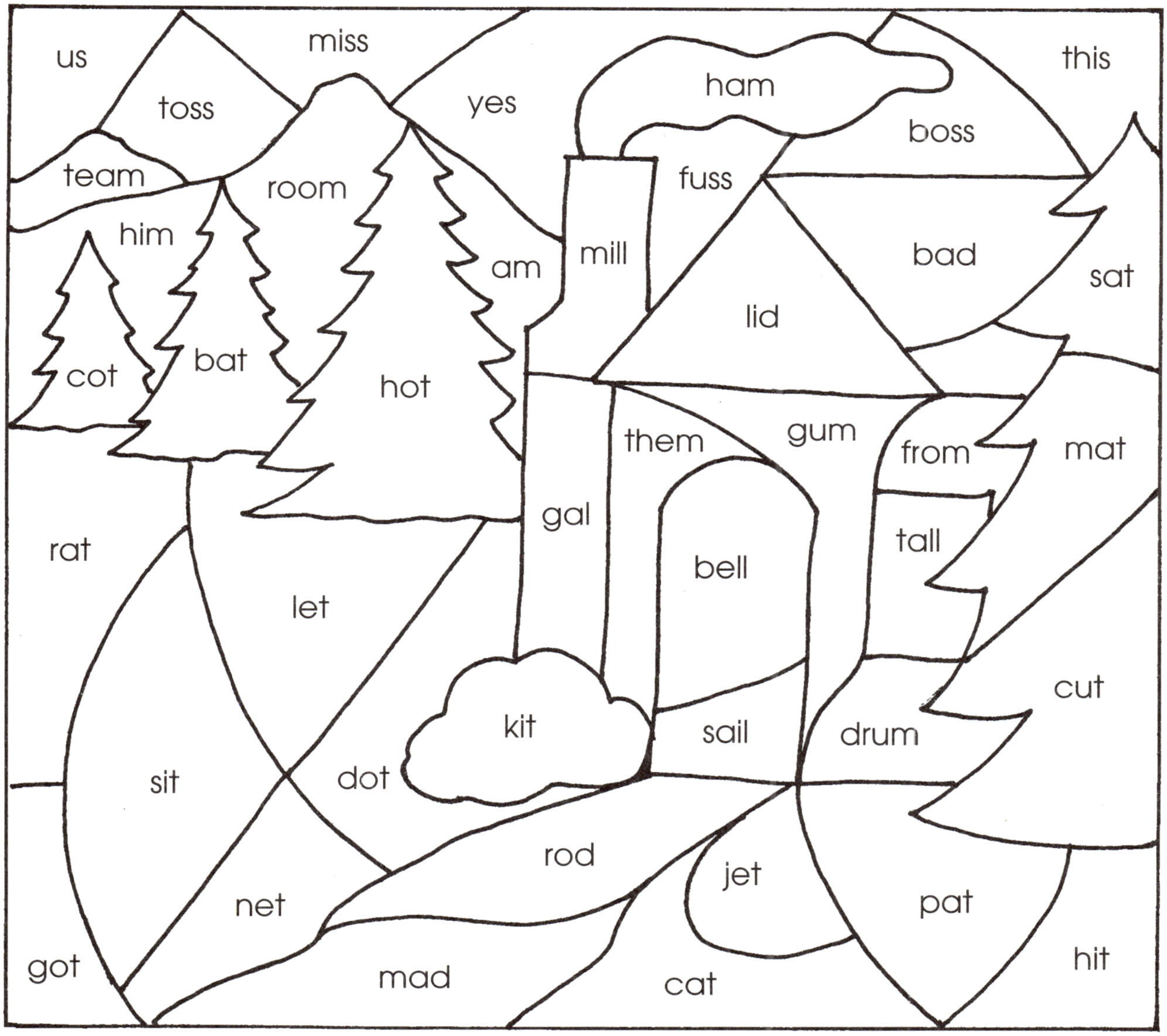

Name ____

Amy's Aprons

Every vowel has a long sound and a short sound. **Long a** *makes the sound you hear at the beginning of* **Amy** *and* **apron**. *To help remember the long-*a *sound, stretch out the beginning of the word like this:* a-a-a-a-apron.

Amy needs a new apron. Help Amy find the aprons that have pictures with the long-*a* sound. Color these aprons pink. If the picture on an apron does not have a long-*a* sound, color it purple.

RED

There is a first one, a second one, and a third one. When you hit the baseball, you run and step on them. The word has the long-*a* sound. What is it? On another sheet of paper, draw a baseball field. Draw arrows that point to your answer.

Don't Forget Your Skates!

Find and color the things that rhyme with **ate**  .

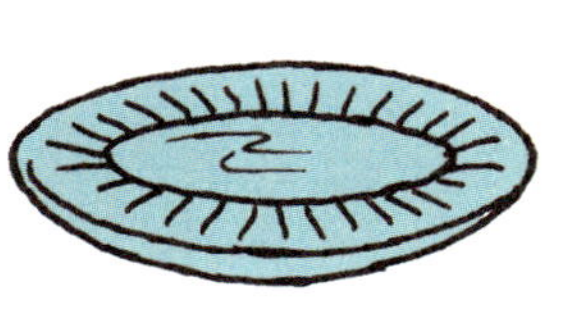

plate

skate

gate

Say a girl's name that rhymes with *ate*.

Jake the Snake

Color the pictures below that rhyme with **snake** .

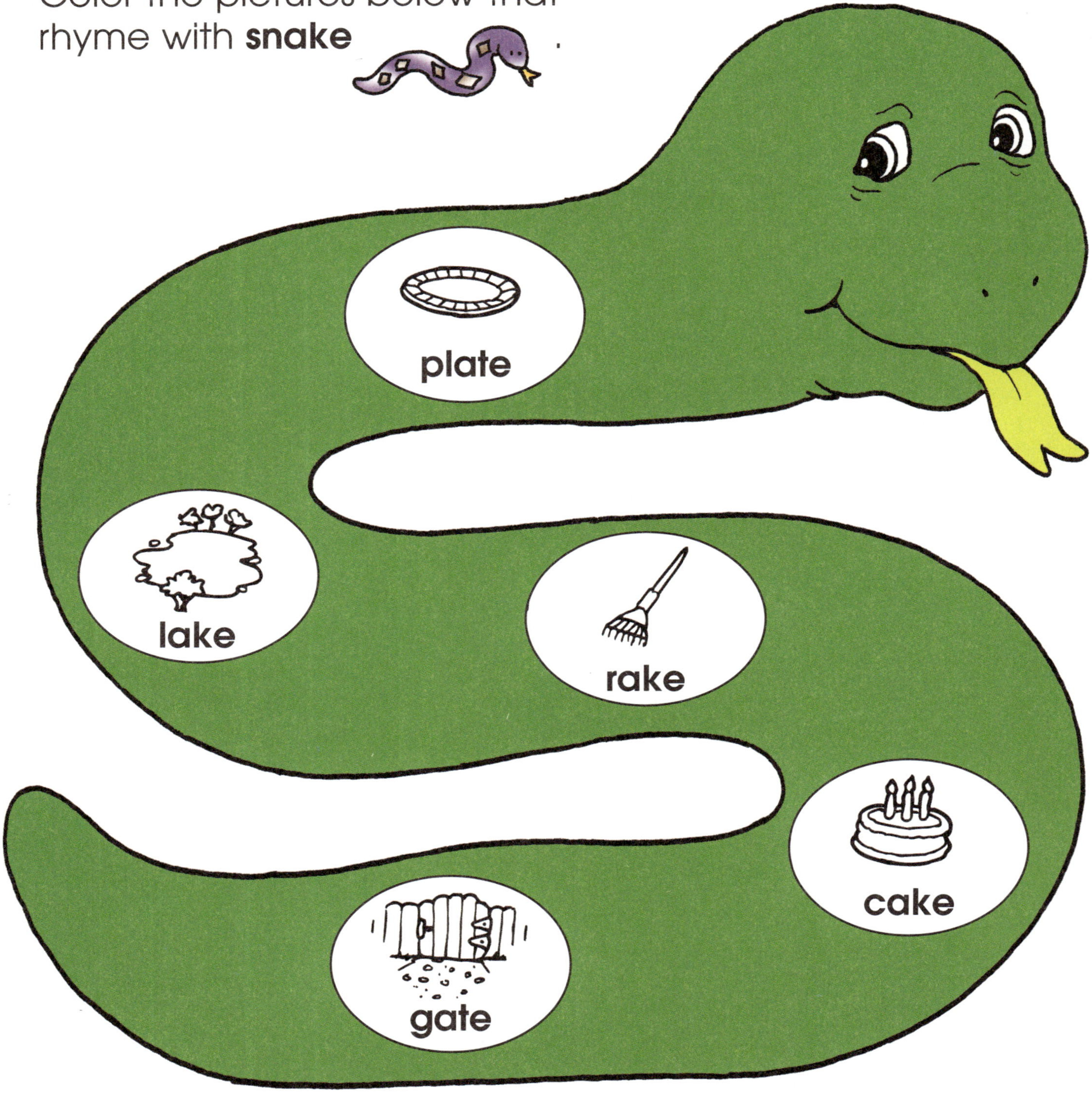

plate

lake

rake

cake

gate

A Day at the Beach

 *Read the story with a grown-up. Find and color the picture words in the story that rhyme with* ***nail****.*

 pail

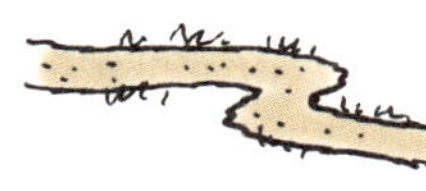 trail

 snail

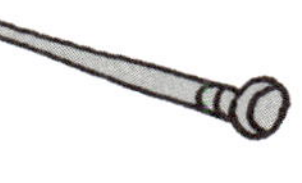 nail

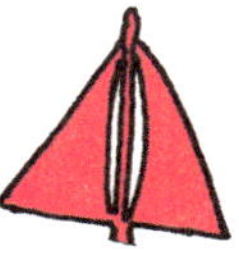 sail

Sam was walking down the (trail). He was looking for things to put in his . The first thing Sam saw was a . He picked up the  and put it in his . Farther down the  Sam saw a 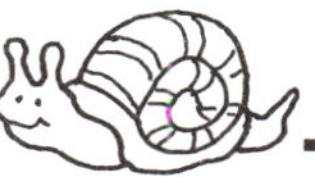. He put the  in the . Sam had room for one more thing in his . Lying on the   was a boat with a broken (sail).

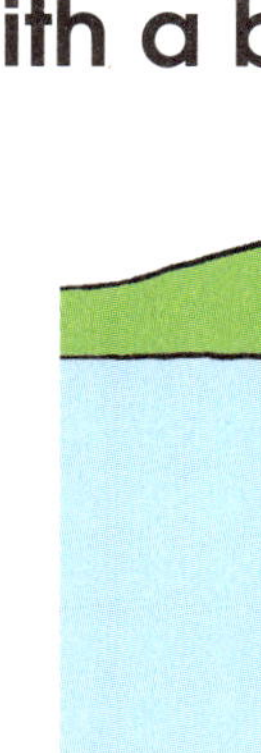

Name ______________________________________ **Review**

Color the Rhyme

Color the pictures **red** that rhyme with **lake** .

Color the pictures **yellow** that rhyme with **ate** .

Color the pictures 

that rhyme with **sail** 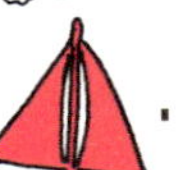.

snail

gate

pail

snake

cake

nail

plate

rake

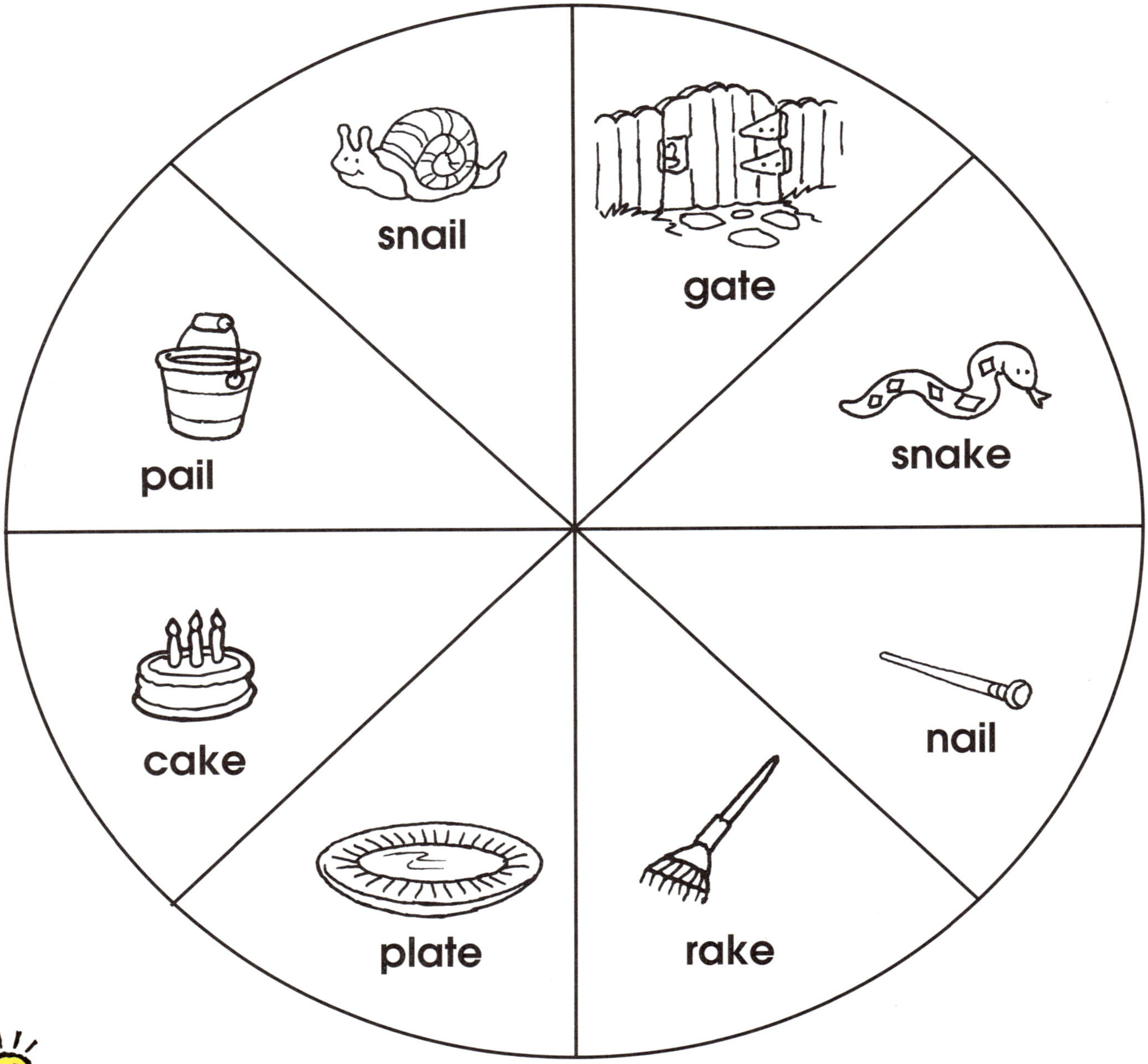

On another sheet of paper, draw a picture of something else that rhymes with *snail*.

Name ____________________

Ethan's Eagle

Long e *makes the sound you hear at the beginning of* **Ethan** *and* **eagle**. *To help you remember the long-*e *sound, stretch out the beginning of the word like this:* e-e-e-eagle.

Ethan's eagle is lonely. He needs a friend. Help Ethan find the eagles that have pictures with the long-*e* sound. Color these eagles brown. If the picture on an eagle does not have a long-*e* sound, write *NO* on it.

You have one of these on the end of your pencil. It is made of rubber. You need it when you make a mistake! It begins with the long-*e* sound. What is it? Write your name with a pencil. Now rub it off with the answer to the riddle.

Name ______________________________

What Do You See at the Park?

Color the things in the picture that rhyme with **see**.

bee 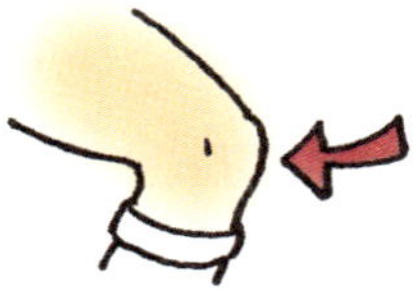 **knee**  **three**  **tree**

On another sheet of paper, draw a picture of something that makes you shout with glee.

Name ______________________________

Beep, Beep

In each row, cross out the pictures that do not rhyme with **beep**.

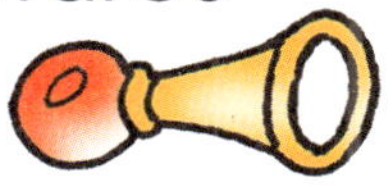

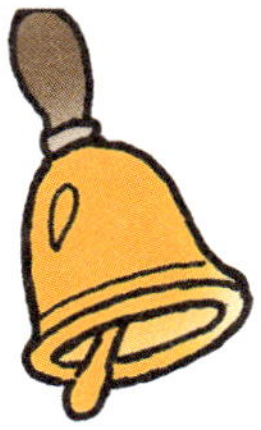 bell	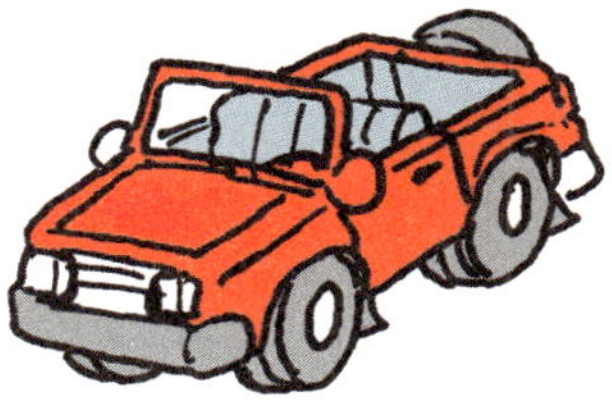 jeep	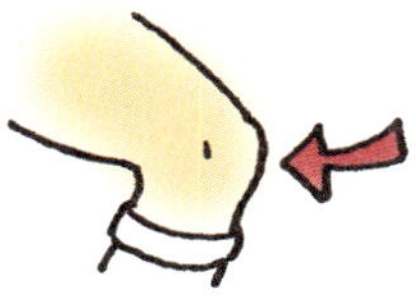 knee
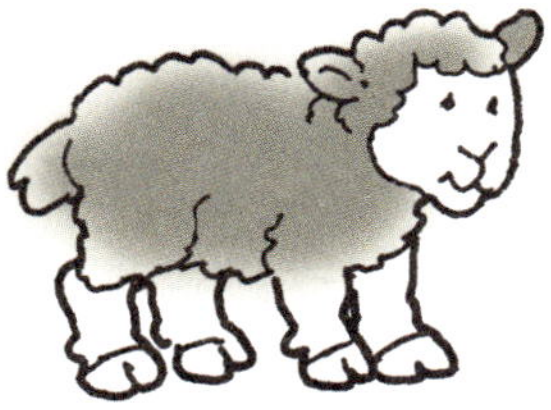 sheep	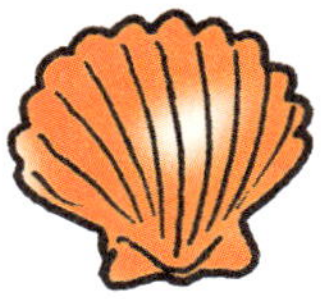 shell	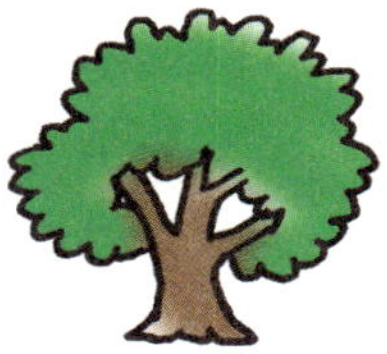 tree
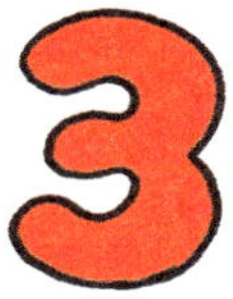 three	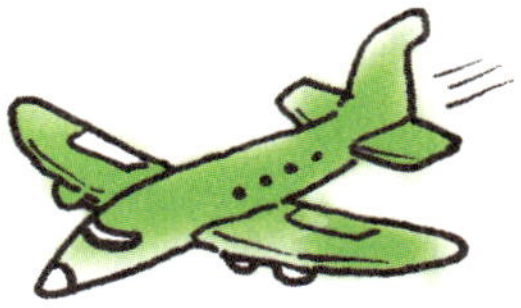 jet	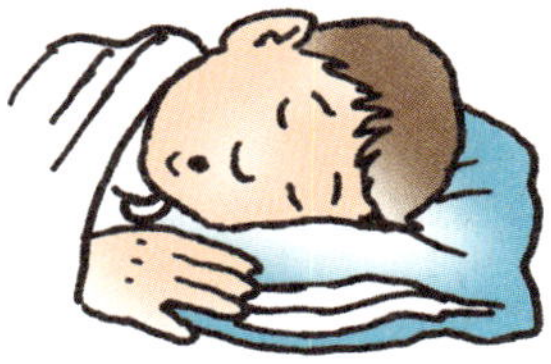 sleep
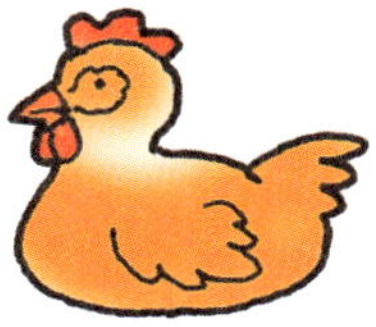 hen	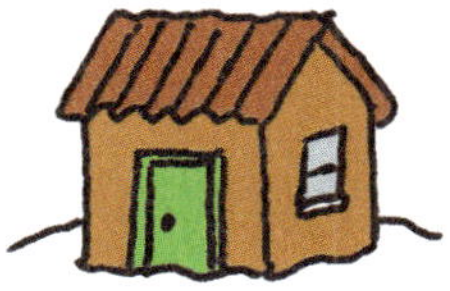 shed	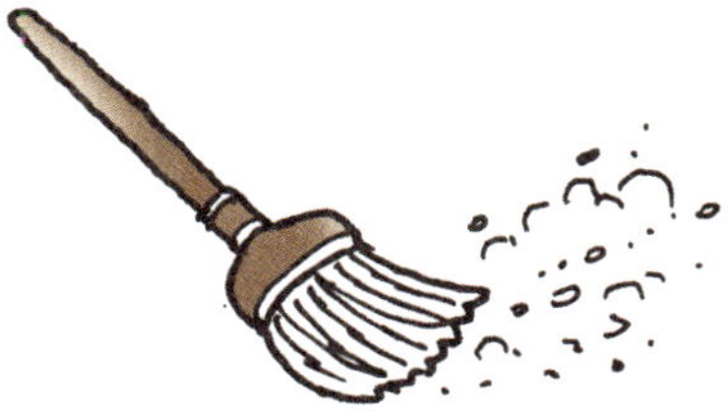 sweep

Name the nursery rhyme that tells about a girl who lost her sheep.

Ivan's Ice

Long i *makes the sound you hear at the beginning of* **ice**. *To help you remember the long-*i *sound, stretch out the beginning of the word like this:* i-i-i-ice.

It is so hot today! Ivan needs some ice in his drink. Help Ivan find the ice cubes that have pictures with the long-*i* sound. Outline these ice cubes in blue. If the picture on an ice cube does not have a long-*i* sound, draw a puddle of water around it to make it look like it is melting.

This is something your lips do when you are happy. It is another word for *grin*. It has the long-*i* sound. What is it? On another sheet of paper, draw a picture of your face with one of these on it.

Be Mine!

Color the hearts with pictures that rhyme with **valentine** .

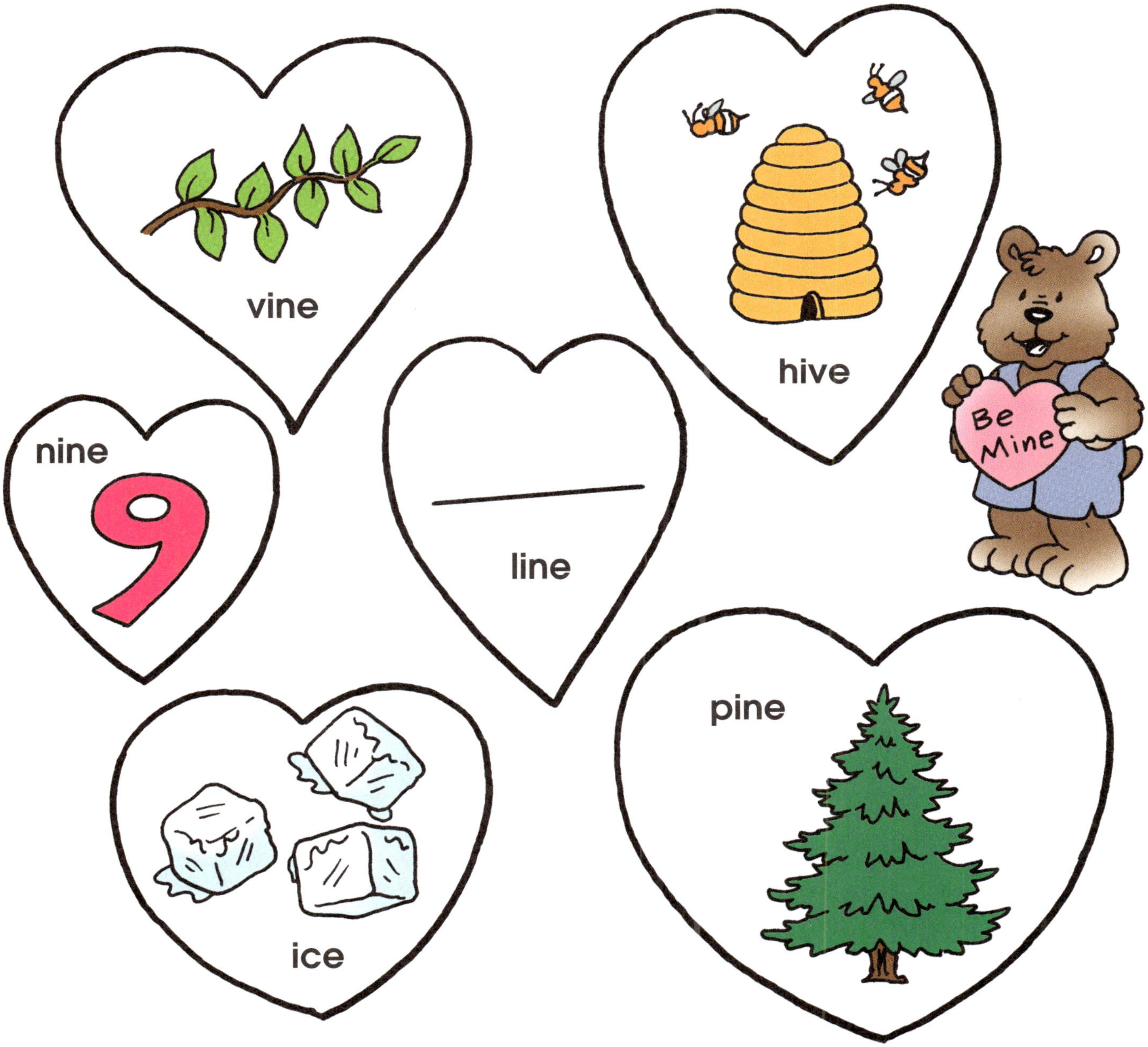

vine

hive

nine

line

ice

pine

 **Make a valentine that says *Be mine*, and give it to somebody special .**

Name ____________________________________  *-ice* **word family**

For the Right Price

Find and color the things that rhyme with **price**  .

mice

ice

rice

string

button

vine

dice

cheese

Name ______________________________  *-ive* **word family**

Buzzy Bees

Help the bees find the way back home. Follow the pictures that rhyme with **hive**.

five

line

mice

ice

dive

vine

nine

drive

Rhyme Time

Draw lines to connect the pictures that rhyme.

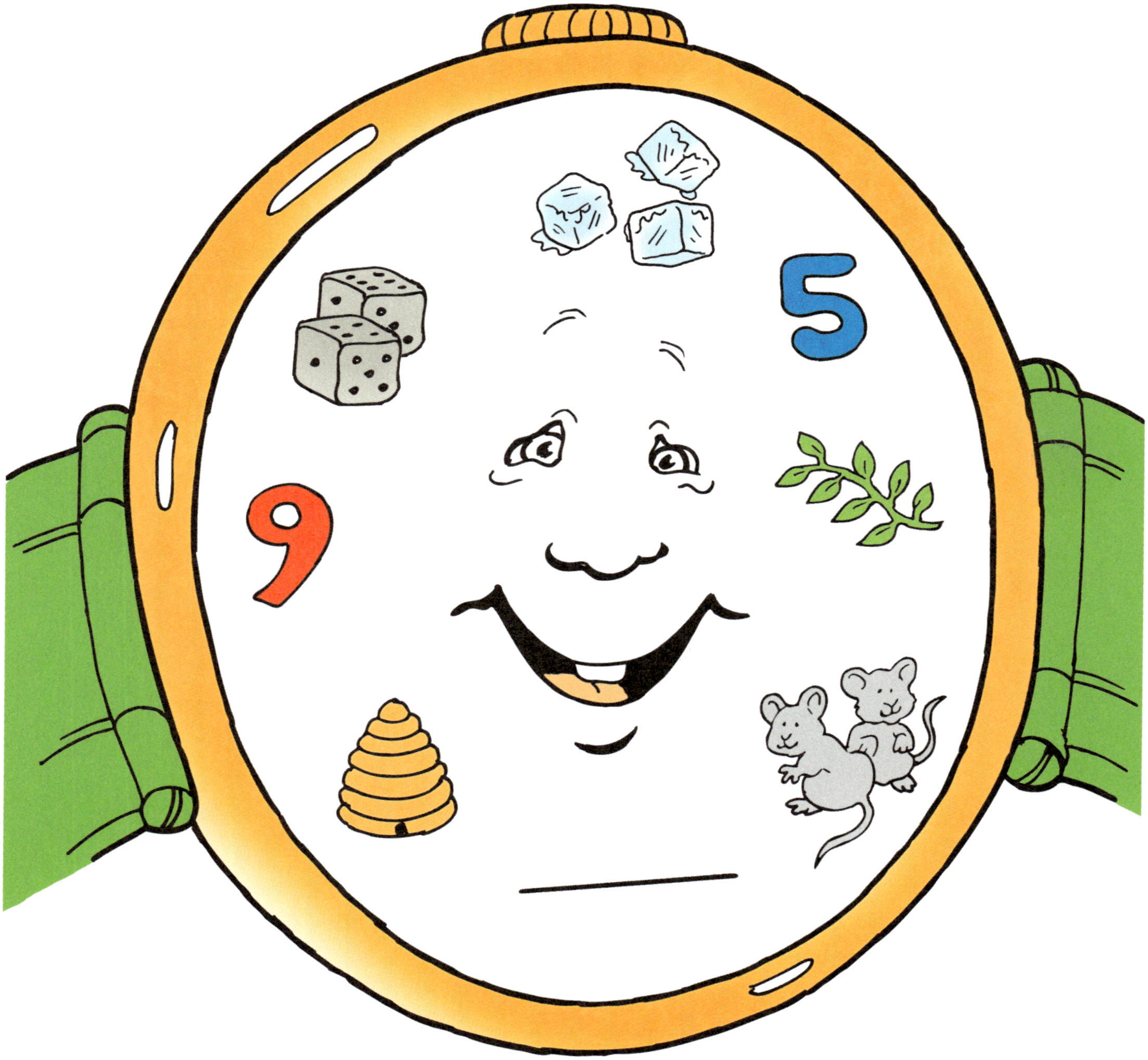

Make your own rhyming clock. Think of three new sets of rhyming pictures. On another sheet of paper, draw them in a clock.

Name ____

Miss Ova's Ovals

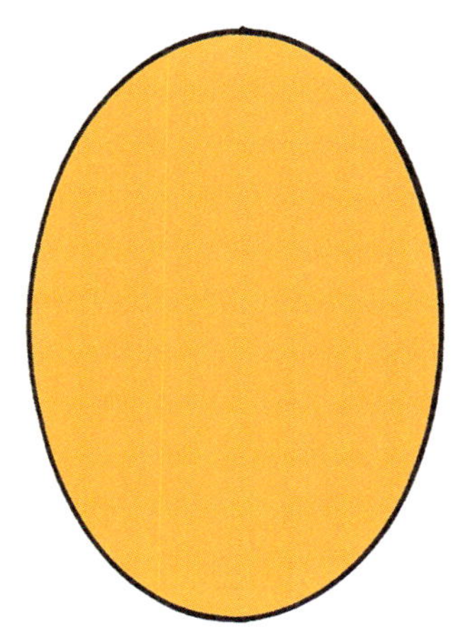

Long o *makes the sound you hear at the beginning of* **Ova** *and* **oval**. *To help you remember the long-*o *sound, stretch out the beginning of the word like this:* o-o-o-oval.

Miss Ova is teaching her class about shapes. Today they learned about ovals. Draw an oval around the pictures that have the long-*o* sound. If the picture does not have a long-*o* sound, draw a square around it.

You might see this word on a sign in the window of a store. It lets you know you can go inside. It is the opposite of *closed*. It begins with a long-*o* sound. What is the word? On another sheet of paper, make one of these signs and decorate it.

Name ______________________________________

Construction Zone

Help the digger fill the right dump trucks. Color the trucks that have pictures that rhyme with **stone** .

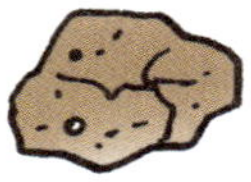

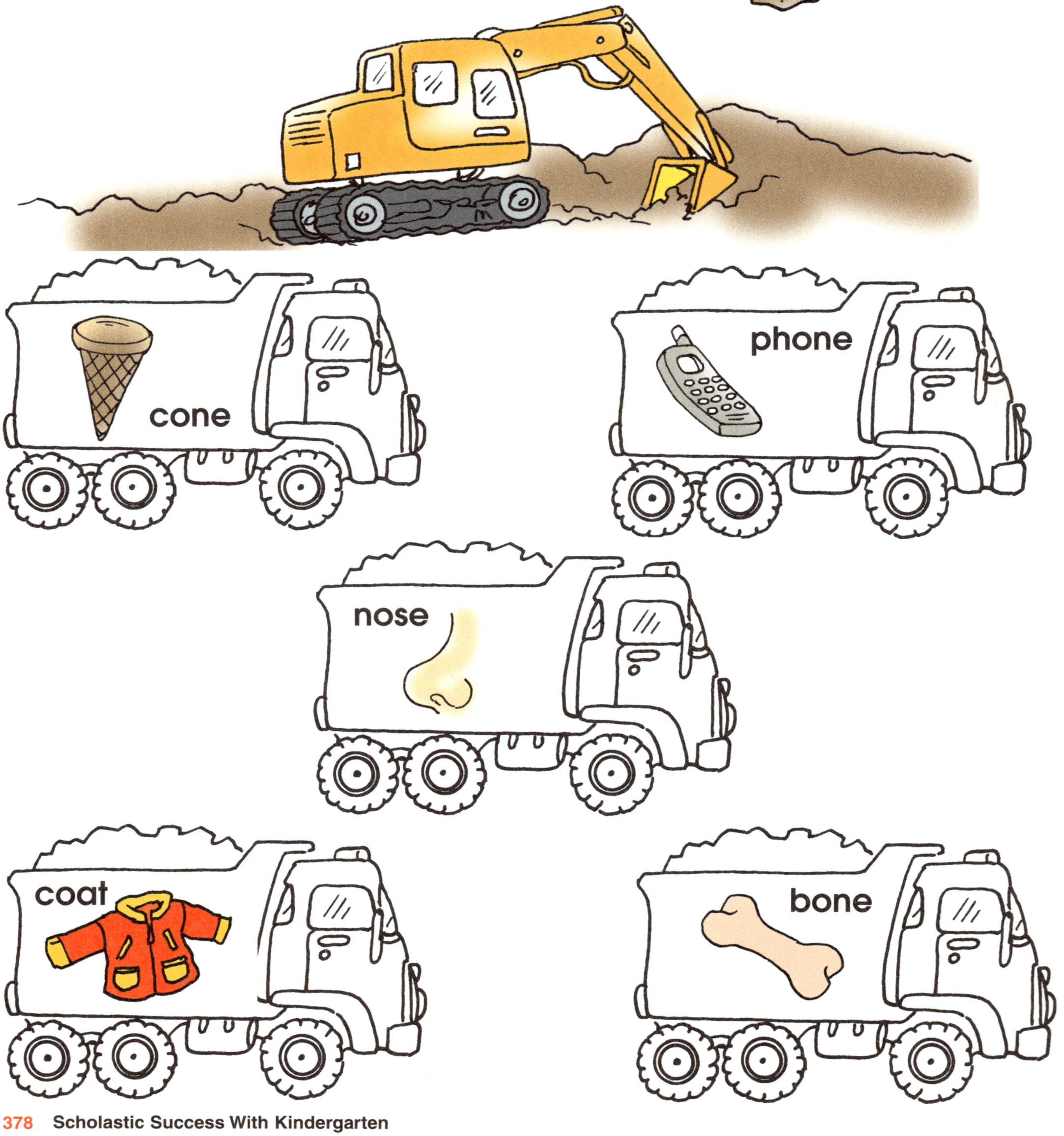

cone

phone

nose

coat

bone

Name ______________________________  *-oat* **word family**

Row, Row, Row Your Boat

Help the rowboat find the shore. Color the pictures that rhyme with **float**.

coat

goat

cone

phone

throat

nose

Name ____ 

Mighty Firefighter

Help the firefighter put out the fire. Color the pictures in the windows that rhyme with **hose** 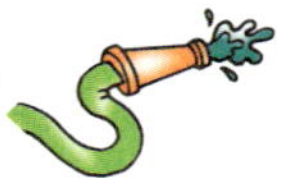 blue. Color the other windows red.

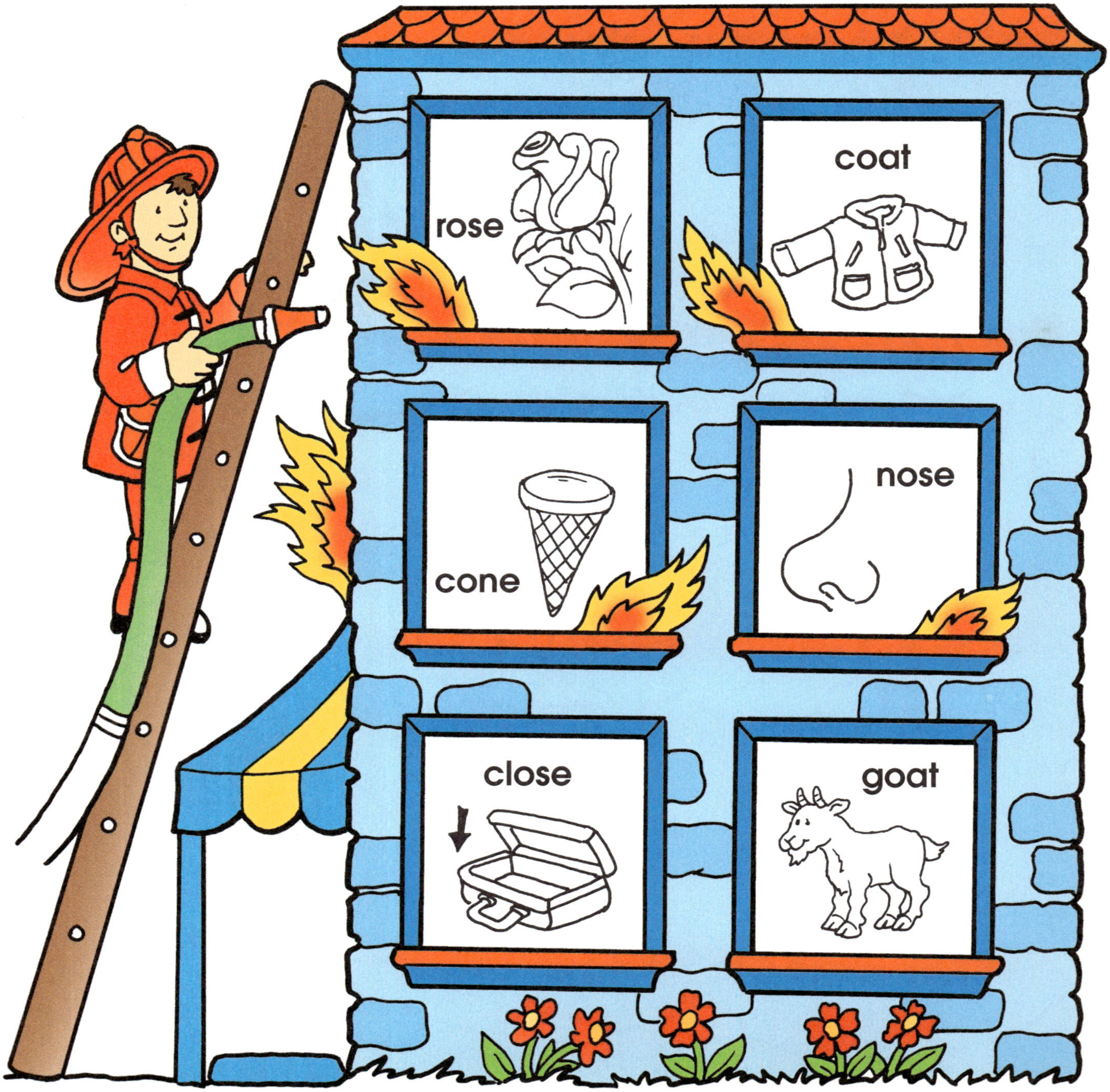

rose

coat

cone

nose

close

goat

Name ____ 

Unicorn University

Long u *makes the sound you hear at the beginning of* **unicorn**. *To help you remember the long-*u *sound, stretch out the beginning of the word like this:* u-u-u-unicorn.

This unicorn is smart! He goes to Unicorn University. Find every book that has a picture with the long-*u* sound. Color these books blue. If the picture does not have a long-*u* sound, draw an **X** on it.

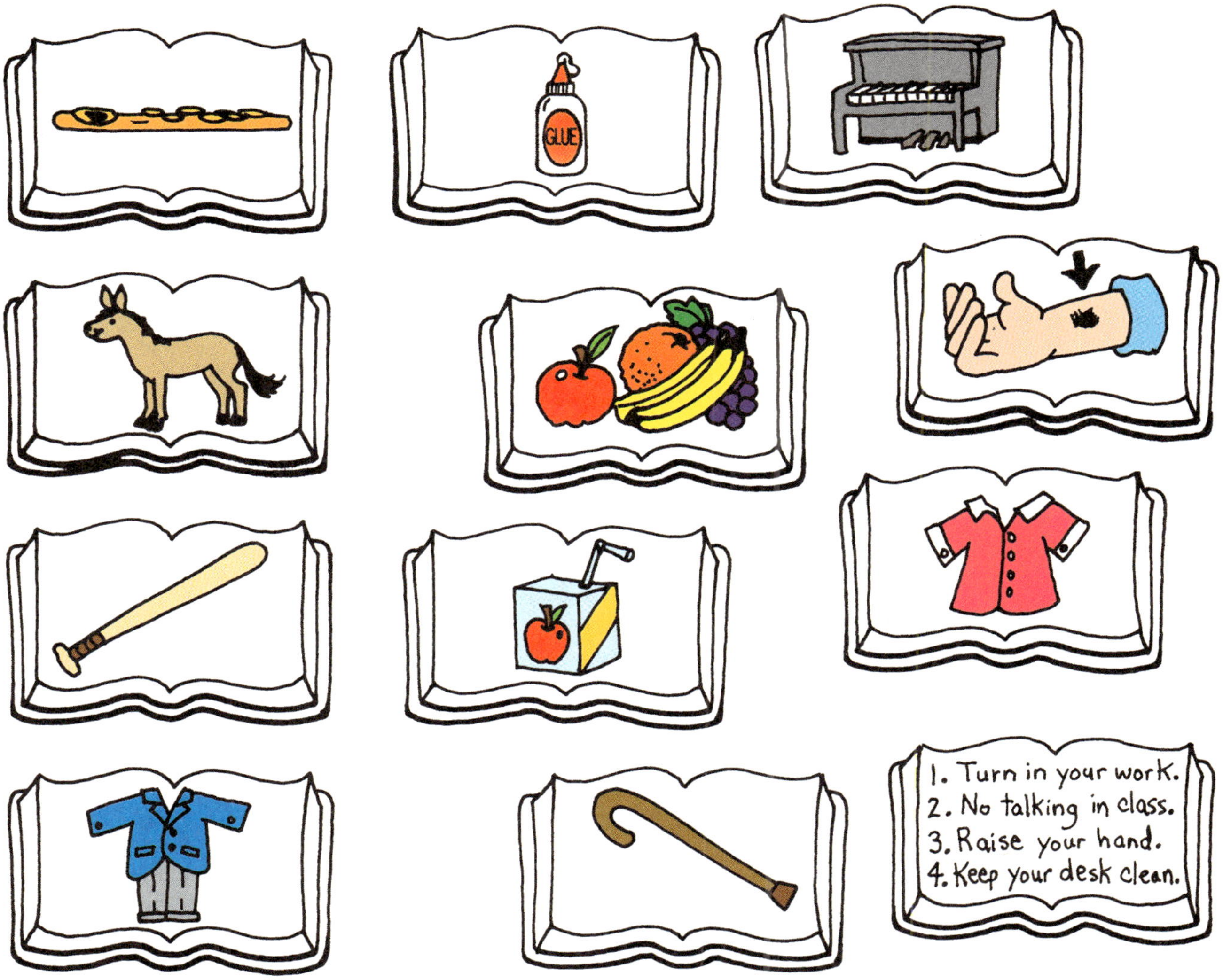

GLUE

1. Turn in your work.
2. No talking in class.
3. Raise your hand.
4. Keep your desk clean.

This is the name of a country. It is made up of 50 states. Its president lives in Washington, D.C. The first word begins with a long-*u* sound. What country is it? On another sheet of paper, draw the flag of this country.

Long-u Word Fruit

Look at the word on each piece of fruit. Fill in the blank to make a rhyming word. Read your words to a friend.

suit fr______ dude r______ Luke d______

tube c______ cute fl______ blue cl______

mule r______ tune J______ glue tr______

This is the color of the sky and the sea. It has a long-*u* sound. What is it? Think of something else that is this color. On another sheet of paper, draw and color it.

Name ____________________  Review

Long Vowel Tic-Tac-Toe

Say the picture names.
Find and color 3 pictures in a row with the same long vowel sound.

1. Long-*e* sound

2. Long-*i* sound

3. Long-*o* sound

Name ______________________________ 

Time for Rhymes

Say the name of each picture. Circle the two pictures that rhyme in each group.

Name ______________________________ 

Check the Signs

Say the name of each picture. Circle the animal with the picture that rhymes with the first picture in each row.

Name ______________________________

Be a Word Builder!

Make your own rhyming words. Look at the picture and say the word. Copy the word. Then change the first letter using each of the letters on the hammer to make new words.

s l b

hand

h c m t w f

ball

f j l h

dog

p s r m f h b

cat

This word rhymes with *fish*. It rhymes with *dish*. It is what you make when you blow out the candles on your birthday cake! What is it? Draw yours on another sheet of paper.

Scholastic Success With

ITTY-BITTY WORD BOOKS

How to Assemble the Word Books

1. Tear out each page along the perforation.

2. Cut along the dashed lines; fold along the solid lines.

3. Place the pages in order and staple along the spine.

I live in

____

16

My Little Neighborhood Book

1

traffic light

14

house

3

post office

12

firehouse

5

car

10

police officer

7

school

2

school bus

15

store

4

stop sign

13

police station

6

mail carrier

11

firefighter

8

flag

9

scarecrow

16

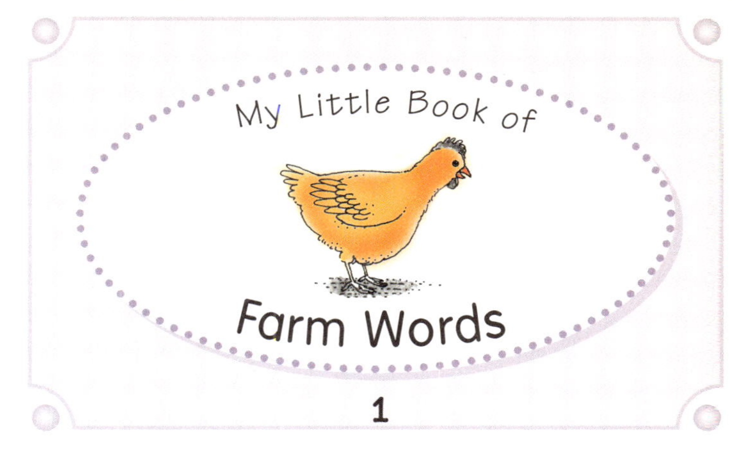

My Little Book of

Farm Words

1

goat

14

cow

3

grain

12

sheep

5

tractor

10

horse

7

barn

2

farmer

rooster

4

chicken

13

milk

6

egg

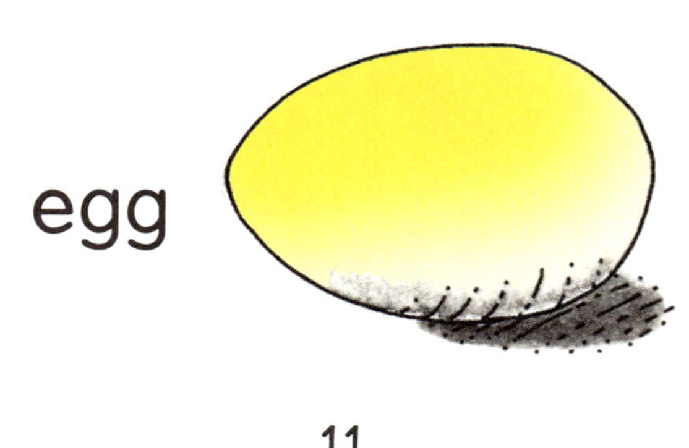

11

duck

8

pig

9

My favorite kind of weather is

____

16

1

tornado

14

wind

3

lightning

12

snow

5

umbrella

10

hail

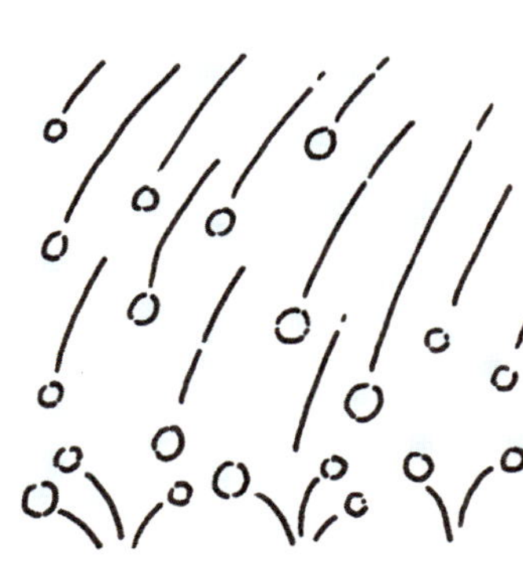

7

sun

2

snowballs

15

rain

4

blizzard

13

fog

6

thermometer

11

hot

8

cold

9

I made this mini-book
in the month of

____

16

1

New Year 

14

February 

3

 November

12

April

5

September

10

June 

7

January

2

seasons

15

March

4

December

13

May

6

October

11

July

8

August

9

Me in my favorite outfit:

16

Clothes for All Seasons

1

dress

14

pants

3

raincoat

12

mittens

5

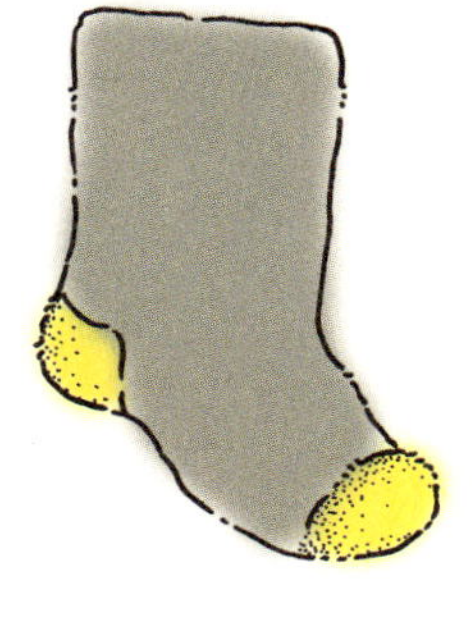

socks

10

vest

7

shirt

2

sweater

15

hat

4

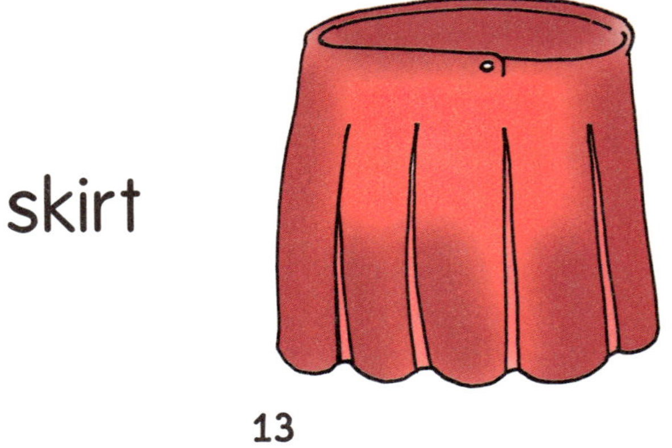

skirt

13

scarf

6

t-shirt

11

shorts

8

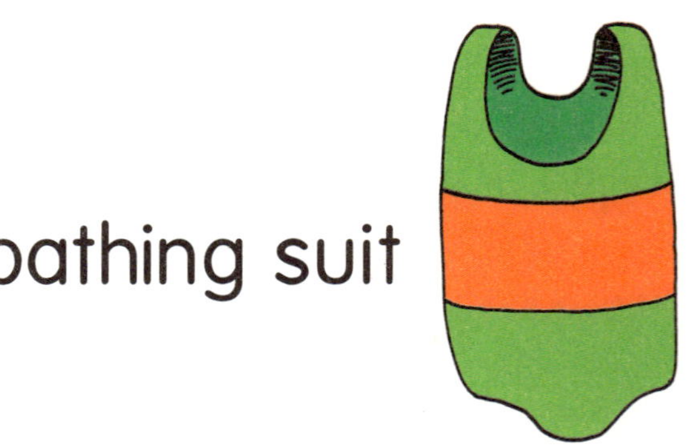

bathing suit

9

My favorite fruit:

____

My favorite vegetable:

____

16

1

corn

14

oranges

3

broccoli

12

banana

5

pears

10

watermelon

7

apples

2

lemons

4

strawberries

6

pineapple

8

celery

15

peas

13

carrot

11

grapes

9

My favorite way to travel is by

____

16

wagon

14

truck

12

running

10

LET'S GO!

Transportation Words

1

bus

3

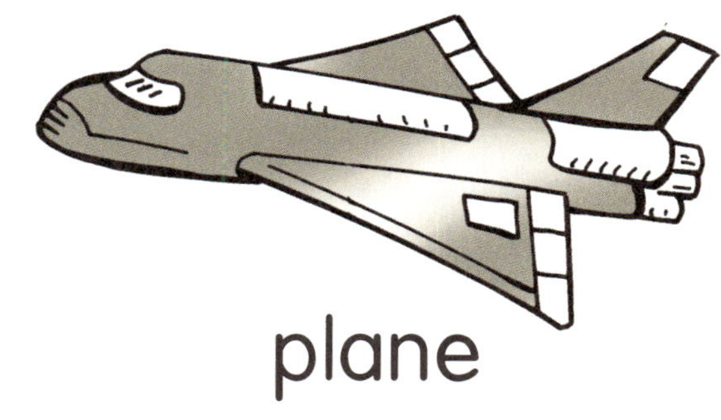

plane

5

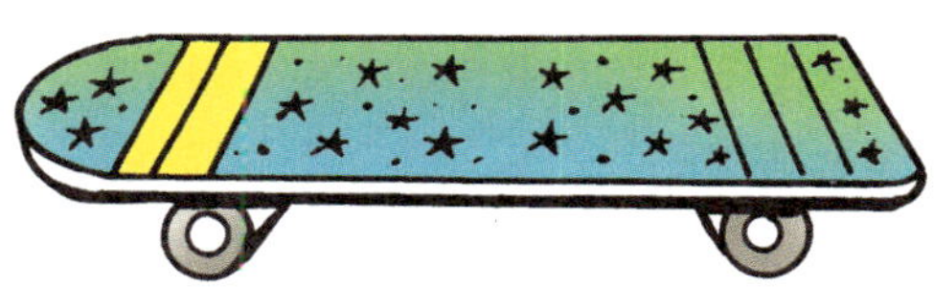

skateboard

7

car

2

train

4

bike

6

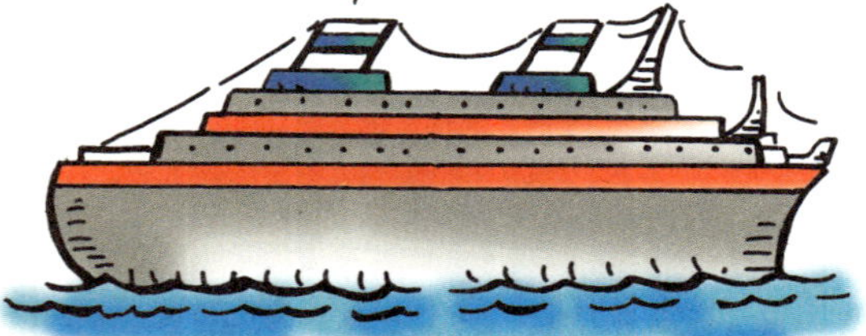

ship

8

rocket

15

van

13

scooter

11

walking

9

I would like to take care of a baby

____

16

gosling

14

piglet

12

lamb

10

My Book of Baby Animals

1

cub

3

puppy

5

calf

7

duckling

2

owlet

15

kitten

4

tadpole

13

seal pup

6

joey

11

chick

pony

9

My favorite big animal is:

____

16

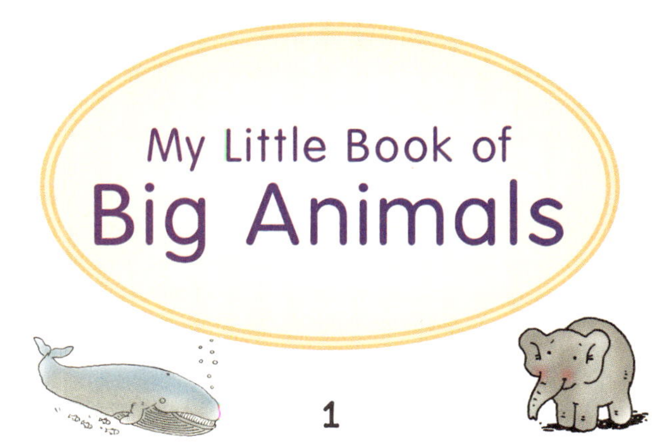

My Little Book of Big Animals

1

ostrich

14

polar bear

3

dinosaur

12

whale

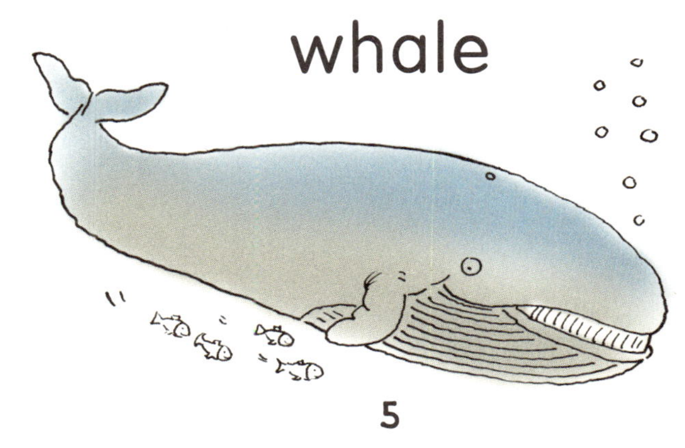

5

tiger

10

jaguar

7

elephant

2

camel

15

rhinoceros

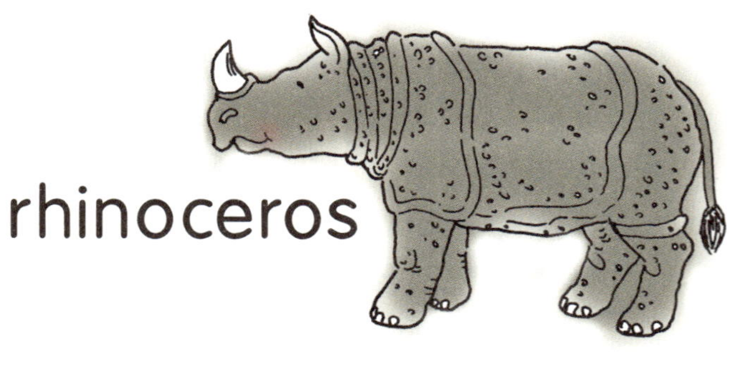

4

panda

horse

6

zebra

11

buffalo

8

moose

9

I would like a

____

for a pet.

16

My Mini-Book of Pets

1

iguana

14

dog

3

snake

12

gerbil

5

parakeet

10

mouse

7

cat

2

frog

4

hamster

6

fish

8

an imaginary pet!

15

rabbit

13

parrot

11

turtle

9

Right now I feel

____

16

Feelings & Faces

1

angry

14

sad

3

silly

12

mad

5

sleepy

10

worried

7

frustrated

2

funny face!

15

happy

4

calm

13

content

6

nervous

11

surprised

8

excited

9

My favorite shape is

____

16

A Small Book of Shapes

1

box

14

square

3

ball

12

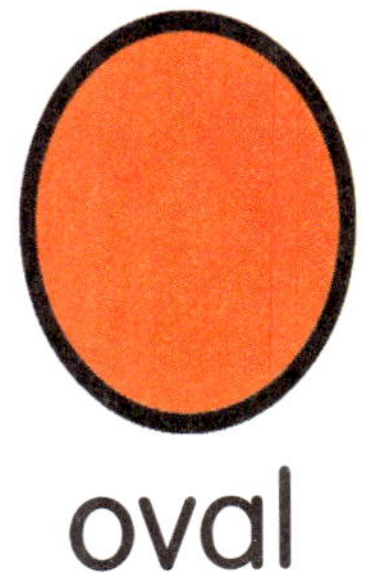

oval

5

cube

10

octagon

7

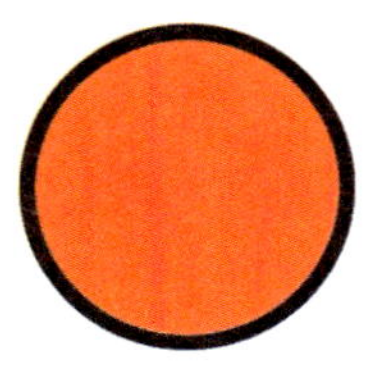

circle

2

cylinder

15

rectangle

4

pentagon

13

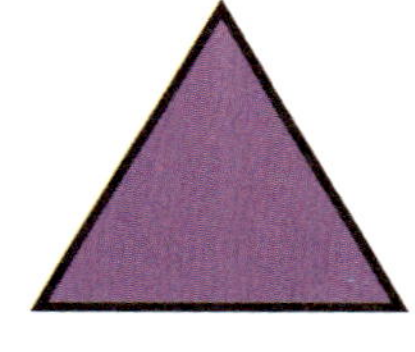

triangle

6

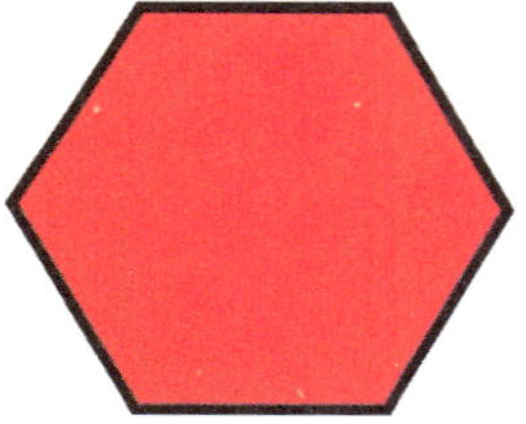

hexagon

11

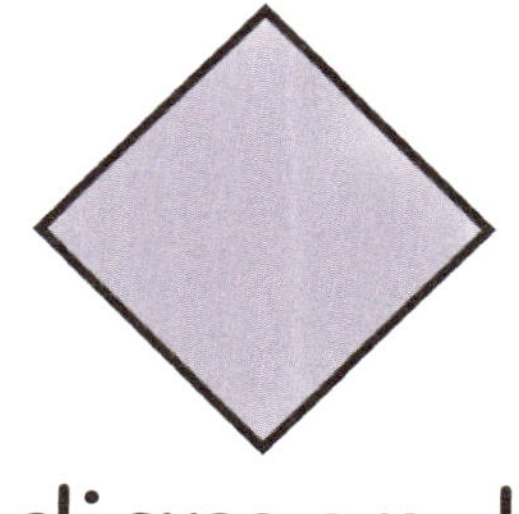

diamond

8

star

9

crayons

16

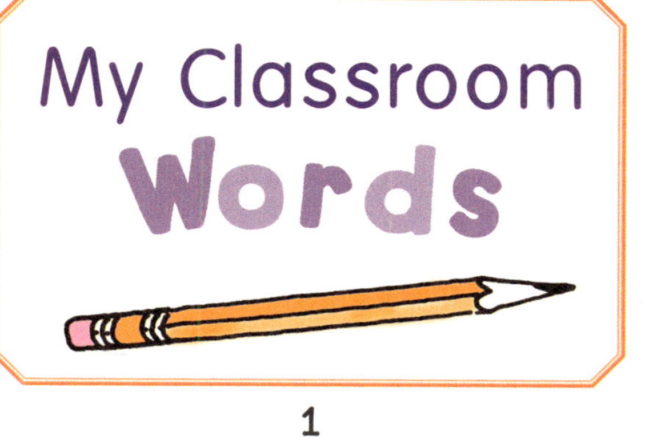

1

scissors

14

chair

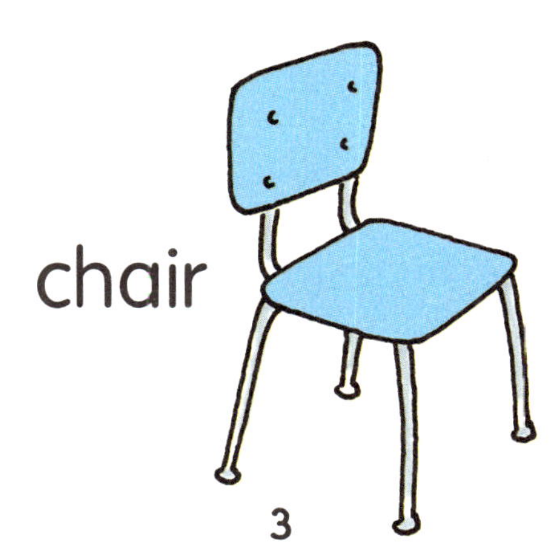

3

door

12

teacher

5

clock

10

book

7

desk

2

blocks

15

easel

4

map

13

student

6

glue

11

notebook

8

pencil

9

My favorite color is:

____

16

Rainbow in Your Pocket!

1

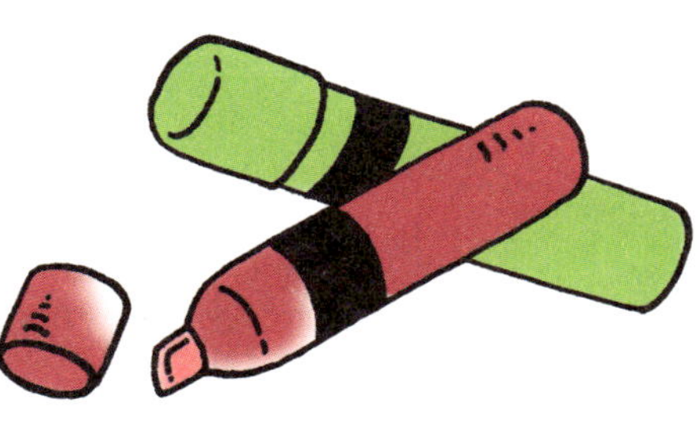

markers

14

green

3

paints

12

blue

5

10

brown

7

red

2

yellow

4

orange

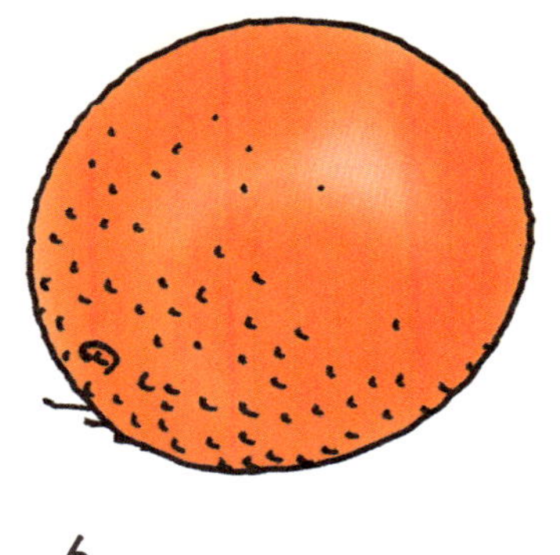

6

purple

8

pencils

15

crayons

13

rainbow

11

pink

9